BEFORE THE NEXT ATTACK

Bruce Ackerman

BEFORE
THE NEXT ATTACK

PRESERVING
CIVIL LIBERTIES
IN AN AGE
OF TERRORISM

Yale University Press

New Haven & London

Published with assistance from the foundation established in memory of Philip Hamilton McMillan of the Class of 1894, Yale College.

Set in Galliard by SPI Publisher Services.

Printed in the United States of America.

Library of Congress Cataloging-in-Publication Data

Ackerman, Bruce A.
  Before the next attack : preserving civil liberties in an age of terrorism / Bruce Ackerman.
     p.   cm.
  Includes bibliographical references and index.
  ISBN-13: 978-0-300-11289-4 (cloth : alk. paper)
  ISBN-10: 0-300-11289-0 (cloth : alk. paper)
  1. Terrorism—United States.   2. War and emergency legislation—United States.   3. War on Terrorism, 2001—Law and legislation—United States.   I. Title.
  KF9430.A932 2006
  342.73′062—dc22

                                                    2005028313

A catalogue record for this book is available from the British Library.

10 9 8 7 6 5 4 3 2 1

FOR JUDITH SHKLAR
WHO SHOWED ME THE WAY

CONTENTS

BEFORE THE NEXT ATTACK

INTRODUCTION: THE EMERGENCY CONSTITUTION

Imagine waking up the morning after the next terrorist attack. You may feel a range of emotions: grief, anger, fear. And you will be relieved when you turn on the television and hear the president promise decisive action. Spurred on by self-righteous indignation and anxious self-defense, the government will spend billions over the next few months to prevent the repetition of the disaster—and a good thing too.

Day after day, a predictable range of reactions will play themselves out on television: the emphatic gestures of solidarity with the thousands who have lost their loved ones in the senseless blast, and the red alerts, the subway searches, the countless shows of bureaucratic determination to stop the terrorists in their tracks and prevent a second strike. These visible demonstrations of fraternity and preparedness are a crucial part of any human response. And yet they serve only as prologue to a deeper struggle with a collective unease, verging on panic, that the shattering blast brings in its wake.

In speaking of panic, I don't wish to conjure images of frantic people pointlessly running about—although there will be some of that. I am gesturing toward a free-floating anxiety that insidiously increases our vigilance: we are hyperalert and hyperreactive. Even when we try to talk rationally about the attack and its aftermath, it won't be hard to miss the undertone of anxiety. And of course there will be politicians who seize on the incipient rage to thrust themselves into the center of political life. How, then, to deal with the political panic that will predictably ensue?

We panicked the last time terrorists struck, and the Patriot Act was the result. For all the hype, the statute contains a grab bag of provisions—some bad, some good, some trivial. For diagnostic purposes, it's more important to emphasize the panicky way Congress rushed the bill into law within thirty-three days of its proposal by then–Attorney General John Ashcroft.[1] Passed in response "to a largely undefined threat from a poorly understood source," Patriot was used as a symbol to reassure the country that Washington was grimly determined to step up the fight against terrorism.[2] It was the form, not the substance, of the law that really mattered: Patriot was a symbolic shake of the collective fist against the lurking terrorist menace.

And yet September 11 was merely a pinprick compared to the devastation of a suitcase A-bomb or an anthrax epidemic. The next major attack may kill and maim one hundred thousand innocents, dwarfing the personal anguish suffered by those who lost family and friends on 9/11. The resulting political panic threatens to leave behind a wave of repressive legislation far more drastic than anything imagined by the Patriot Act.

A downward cycle threatens: After each successful attack, politicians will come up with a new raft of repressive laws that ease our anxiety by promising greater security—only to find that a different terrorist band manages to strike a few years later. This new disaster, in turn, will create a demand for more repression, and on and on. Even if the next half-century sees only three or four attacks on a scale that dwarf September 11, the pathological political cycle will prove devastating to civil liberties by 2050.[3]

The root of the problem is democracy itself. A Stalinist regime might respond to an attack by a travel blockade and a media blackout, leaving most of the country in the dark, going on as if everything were normal.

This can't happen here. The shock waves will ripple through the populace with blinding speed. Competitive elections will tempt politicians to exploit the spreading panic to partisan advantage, challenging their rivals as insufficiently "tough on terrorism" and depicting civil libertarians as softies who are virtually laying out the welcome mat for our enemies. And so the cycle of repression moves relentlessly forward, with the blessing of our duly elected representatives.

Our traditional defense against such pathologies has been the courts. No matter how large the event, no matter how great the panic, they will protect our basic rights against our baser impulses.

Or so we tell ourselves—but it just isn't true. The courts haven't protected us in the past, and they will do worse in the future. We need a strong and independent judiciary, of course, but we need something more. We require an "emergency constitution" that allows for effective short-term measures that will do everything plausible to stop a second strike—but which firmly draws the line against permanent restrictions. Above all else, we must prevent politicians from exploiting momentary panic to impose long-lasting limitations on liberty. Given the clear and present danger, it makes sense to tie ourselves to the mast as a precaution against deadly enticements. This is the promise of the "emergency constitution," and this book explores how this promise might be realized in the real world.

Designing a limited state of emergency is a tricky business. Governments should not be permitted to run wild in the immediate aftermath of a terrorist attack—many extreme measures should remain off-limits. Even reasonable emergency measures can generate momentum that will be hard to stop when they are no longer necessary. It is no easy thing to design an emergency constitution that will control these pathological tendencies. Nevertheless, such a regime provides our best available defense against a panic-driven cycle and represents the most practical way to avoid the permanent destruction of our traditional freedoms.

Terrorism is a challenge facing all liberal democracies, and we have much to learn from the experience of other countries. Most of them haven't had the protection of two great oceans, or the luxury of looking upon grave threats as rare events. By the luck of the geographic draw, they have been forced to live with extreme danger for centuries. As a consequence, their constitutions often contain elaborate political safeguards on the use of emergency powers, providing ideas for the work before us.

But there is no constitution on earth that provides a perfect model—or even a half-decent one. They were all designed with problems of an earlier age in mind—the threat of an invasion of one state by another, or a violent coup by domestic extremists. The threat posed by twenty-first-century terrorism is different. In contrast to the Axis powers in World War II, Osama bin Laden does not have armies and navies that could physically occupy the United States. In contrast to the Communists, Al Qaeda does not aim for the violent takeover of Western governments by revolution. The risks it poses are grave but historically unique. Terrorist attacks may kill a hundred thousand at a single blow, generating overwhelming grief and rippling panic that may ultimately turn our government into an oppressive police state. But Osama and his successors won't ever occupy the country in the manner threatened by Hitler or Stalin. Territorial conquest is beyond their power. If anybody destroys our legacy of freedom, it will be us.

In speaking of an emergency constitution, I don't mean to be taken too literally. Almost nothing I propose will require formal constitutional amendment—the "emergency constitution" can be enacted by Congress as a framework statute governing responses to terrorist attack. But this won't happen unless we conduct a constitutional conversation in the spirit of our eighteenth-century Founders.

As James Madison cautioned, "enlightened statesmen will not always be at the helm."[4] To check the descent into despotism, the Framers created a system of checks and balances, and I continue this worthy tradition. My emergency constitution adapts our inherited system to meet the distinctive challenges of the twenty-first century.

First and foremost, it imposes strict limits on unilateral presidential power. Presidents will not be authorized to declare an emergency on their own authority, except for a week or two while Congress is considering the matter. Emergency powers should then lapse unless a majority of both houses votes to continue them—but even this vote has a temporal limit and is valid for only two months. The president must then return to Congress for reauthorization, and this time, a supermajority of 60 percent is required; after two months more, the majority will be set at 70 percent; and then 80 percent for every subsequent two-month extension. Except for the worst terrorist onslaughts, this "supermajoritarian escalator" will terminate the use of emergency powers within a relatively short period. It will also force the president to think twice before requesting additional extensions unless he can make a truly compelling case to the broader public.

Defining the scope of emergency power is a serious and sensitive business. But at its core, it involves the short-term detention of suspected terrorists to prevent a second strike. Nobody will be detained for more than forty-five days, and then only on reasonable suspicion. Once the forty-five days have lapsed, the government must satisfy the higher evidentiary standards that apply in ordinary criminal prosecutions. And even during the period of preventive detention, judges will be authorized to intervene to protect against torture and other abuses.

There is much to be said on these, and many other, matters. My particular answers to concrete questions—Why two-month extensions, not three? Why forty-five days of preventive detention, not sixty?—are unimportant, but it's always best to provide a concrete target for others to shoot at. In any event, we can't afford to lose ourselves in details. My aim is to provoke debate, not resolve it.

We are in a race against time. It takes time to confront the grim constitutional future that lies ahead; and more time to separate good proposals from bad ones; and more time to engage in a broad-based public discussion; and more time for farsighted politicians—if there are any—to enact a constitutional framework into law.

During all this time, terrorists will not be passive. Each major attack will breed further escalations of military force, police surveillance, and repressive legislation. The cycle of terror, fear, and repression may spin out of control long before a political consensus has formed behind a constitution for an emergency regime.

Then again, we may be lucky. Only one thing is clear: we won't get anywhere if we don't start a serious conversation. The stakes are high, because our current constitutional thinking and practice won't be good enough to contain the recurring political panics that will be one of the great facts of twenty-first-century life.

Words are the lifeblood of our constitutional life, and we are off to a bad start in describing our current dis-ease. The "war on terror" has paid enormous political dividends for President Bush, but it sends all the wrong signals for purposes of panic control. Calling the challenge a war tilts the constitutional scales in favor of unilateral executive action, and against our tradition of checks and balances.

There is something about the presidency that loves war talk. Almost two centuries ago Andrew Jackson was already declaring war on the Bank of the United States, indulging in legally problematic uses of executive power to withdraw federal deposits from The Enemy, headed by the evil one, Nicholas Biddle.[5] And more recent presidents have declared war on poverty, crime, and drugs. Even at its most metaphorical, martial rhetoric allows the president to invoke his special mystique as commander-in-chief, calling the public to sacrifice greatly for the good of the nation. The clarion call to pseudowar is just the thing to provide rhetorical cover for unilateral actions of questionable legality.

The war on terrorism isn't as obvious a rhetorical stretch as the war on poverty. Classical wars traditionally involve a battle against sovereign states, and it may seem a smallish matter to expand the paradigm to cover struggles with terrorist groups. But appearances are misleading.

Classic wars come to an end. Some decisive act of capitulation, armistice, or treaty signals the moment of termination, and in a way that all the world can see. This won't happen with the war on terror. If and when bin Laden is caught, tried, and convicted, it still won't be clear whether Al Qaeda has survived. At best, it will morph into other terrorist groups. Al Qaeda already is collaborating with Hezbollah, and how will anybody determine where one group ends and the other begins?[6]

There are more than six billion people in the world—more than enough to supply terrorist networks with haters, even if the West does nothing to stir the pot. So if we choose to call this a war, it will be endless.

Here is where the emergency constitution provides a crucial alternative. If left to their own devices, presidents will predictably exploit future terrorist attacks by calling on us to sacrifice more and more of our freedom if we ever hope to win this "war." But with an emergency constitution in place, collective anxiety can be channeled into more constructive forms. If I am successful, a shocked nation will no longer turn on the television to see the president pound the table and rededicate himself to "winning the war on terror." It will hear a different message:

> My fellow Americans, as we grieve together at our terrible loss, you should know that your government will not be intimidated by this terrorist outrage. This is no time for business as usual; it is a time for urgent action. I am asking Congress to declare a temporary state of emergency that will enable us to take aggressive measures to prevent a second strike and seek a speedy return to a normal life, with all our rights and freedoms intact.

I am under no illusions. It will take a lot of work before we can construct an emergency constitution that will induce the presidency to forgo the pleasures of war talk, especially given President Bush's initial success in persuading Americans to buy into his rhetoric. Thanks to the media's uncritical repetition of the president's mantra, everybody thinks it's obvious that we are in the middle of a "war on terrorism." Of course, many people disagree with the president's conduct of the "war," but no serious politician denies that we are fighting one—this certainly wasn't John Kerry's message in the last election. And it is unreasonable to ask serious politicians to move beyond misplaced war talk without providing them with an alternative framework for expressing a serious commitment to national security.

This is the point of my book. In offering up a constitutional alternative, I'm not building from the ground up. I'm seeking to develop ideas and practices that are already in common use. The newscasts constantly report declarations of emergency by governors and presidents responding to natural disasters—and though this is less familiar, American presidents regularly declare emergencies in response to foreign crises and terrorist threats. My aim is to develop these well-established practices into a credible bulwark against the presidentialist war dynamic. This is the best way of assuring that the morning after the next attack we will wake up free.

The success of this enterprise will depend in part on the Supreme Court. If it decisively rejects extraordinary presidential actions in the name of the "war on terror," it may help force the presidency to accept an emergency regime as its best available alternative. But the Court's first encounters with the subject leave a great deal open for the future, and the justices can't do the entire job in any event. Unless and until a larger public debate begins on the shape of an emergency constitution, there is no hope that our politicians will take the idea seriously.

We may be lucky: perhaps there will be no repetition of September 11 on an even greater scale. Or when the next strike occurs, perhaps the sitting president will be a heroic defender of civil liberties and refuse to succumb to the political dynamics of fear and repression. But things might turn out worse the next time round—perhaps the sitting president will combine the simplistic beliefs of George W. Bush, the rhetorical skills of Ronald Reagan, the political wiles of Lyndon Johnson, and the sheer ruthlessness of Richard Nixon into a single toxic bundle.

No constitutional design can guarantee against the very worst case, and no constitutional design is needed for the best of all possible worlds.

But there is plenty of room in the middle, and this is where human beings generally live out their lives. And this is where the emergency constitution can make a big difference—or so I hope to convince you.

I begin with a diagnosis of our present dis-ease: What is so dangerous about the notion that we are fighting a "war" on terror? Why do we need a new emergency constitution that is carefully crafted to recognize the distinctive character of the terrorist threat? Why isn't it good enough to use the tried and true system of our existing criminal law?

I then move from diagnosis to prescription: what principles should guide the construction of an emergency constitution?

I have already made my key point: we must control unilateral presidential power through the use of repeated Congressional reauthorizations, and encourage the rapid termination of the emergency by use of the "supermajoritarian escalator." But there are many other important issues that we need to explore.

Consider, for example, the fate of the principal victims of the state of emergency. Acting with extraordinary powers, the police and FBI may pick up thousands of terrorist suspects for preventive detention. Most of these people—probably the overwhelming majority—will turn out to be perfectly innocent. But under the emergency constitution, they must wait for forty-five days before they can gain their freedom through the standard mechanisms of the criminal law. Is this morally right?

I emphasize basic principles, suggesting how each part of the emergency constitution adds up to a larger whole. I then ask how the new emergency regime fits into the fabric of existing American law. Though nobody pays much attention to it, we already have a framework statute, the National Emergencies Act of 1976. Despite its many weaknesses, the statute's existence is important. It suggests that our challenge is to build on the efforts of the preceding generation, both by learning from its mistakes and by redeeming its effort to build a reliable system of checks and balances to control the potential abuses of emergency power.

I also consider how my proposal fits into our existing Constitution. Since it builds on the principle of checks and balances, there is no deep philosophical tension, and there is little doubt that the Supreme Court would uphold a thoughtful emergency powers statute if it ever cleared Congress. Nevertheless, the juxtaposition of the new and the old systems raises some fascinating questions about the capacity of our Constitution to endure.

I finally consider the worst possible case: a terrorist attack succeeds in decapitating the government, taking down the president and most of Congress and the Supreme Court in the blast. For obvious reasons, this isn't something that our eighteenth-century Founders worried much about, and our ramshackle system could easily generate a severe government crisis at a moment when strong leadership was imperative. Yet the problems with our current system are mostly products of inertia and inattention—here is an area where we can come up with a series of relatively uncontroversial solutions if Congress gives the problem serious attention.

This is a downer of a book, a study in lesser evils, to borrow the title of Michael Ignatieff's thoughtful essay.[7] But all my grim scenarios shouldn't entirely conceal rays of hope. Though our situation is grave, it is not as grim as the bad old days of the twentieth century, when Hitler and Stalin really did threaten us with physical occupation and political takeover. We managed to maintain our liberties during those perilous times, and with some institutional imagination, we can do it again.

Our great constitutional tradition of checks and balances provides the material we need to withstand the tragic attacks and predictable panics of the twenty-first century. The challenge is to think, and act, in a way that will sustain this tradition into a third century.

No small task, surely. But one that isn't obviously beyond us—or at least, this is the optimistic hope that informs the doomsday scenarios that follow.

PART

I

DIAGNOSIS

1

THIS IS NOT A WAR

"War on terror" is, on its face, a preposterous expression. Terrorism is simply the name of a technique: intentional attacks on innocent civilians.[1] But war isn't merely a technical matter: it is a life-and-death struggle against a particular enemy. We made war against Nazi Germany, not against the Blitzkrieg.[2]

Once we allow ourselves to declare war on a technique, we open up a dangerous rhetorical path. During times of panic, indiscriminate war talk will encourage a shocked public to lash out at amorphous threats without the need to define them clearly. Who knows who will be swept into the net?

There is a second big flaw. By calling it a war, we frame our problem as if it involved a struggle with a massively armed major power, capable of threatening our very existence as a free country. But terrorism isn't a product of overweening state power. It is a product of the free market in a world of high technology.

There have always been millions of haters in the world, but their destructive ambitions have been checked by the state's monopoly over truly overwhelming force. Terrorists might assassinate a nation's leader or blow up a building, but they could not devastate a great city or poison an entire region. These are things that only states could do. With the proliferation of destructive technologies, the state is losing this monopoly.

Here is where the logic of the free market enters. Once a technology has escaped a state monopoly, it's almost impossible for government to suppress the lucrative trade completely. Think of drugs and guns. Even the most puritanical regimes learn to live with vice on the fringe. But when a fringe group obtains a technology of mass destruction, it won't stay on the fringe for long.

The root of our problem is not Islam or any ideology, but a fundamental change in the relationship between the state, the market, and technologies of destruction. If the Middle East were magically transformed into a vast oasis of peace and democracy, fringe groups from other places would rise to fill the gap. We won't need to look far to find them. If a tiny band of extremists blasted the Federal Building in Oklahoma City, others will want to detonate suitcase A-bombs as they become available, giving their lives eagerly in the service of their self-destructive vision.

Preventive measures will sometimes fail. Once the state no longer monopolizes a technology of destruction, the laws of supply and demand will inexorably put weapons in the hands of the richest and best-organized terrorists in the marketplace, and government will be playing catch-up. The only question is how often the security services will drop the ball: once out of ten threats, once out of a hundred, once out of a thousand?

These basic points are obscured by the fog of war talk. Real wars don't come out of nowhere because the government has dropped the ball. They arise after years of highly visible tension between sovereign states, and after the failure of countless efforts at diplomacy. They occur only after the public has reluctantly recognized that the awesome powers of warmaking might be justified. Even sneak attacks, as at Pearl Harbor, are preceded by years of escalating tension that put the public on notice that a powerful nation-state, with an aggressive military force, threatens overwhelming harm to all we love.

But when terrorists strike, all we really know is that they managed to slip through a crack that the government failed to close. Given the free market in destructive technologies, we don't know whether we face a tiny group of fanatics, with a couple of million dollars, which happened to get lucky, or a more serious organization with real staying power. By lapsing into war talk we trigger a set of associations that are often false and frequently encourage the worst of panic reactions. We head down a misleading path suggesting that not only are "the terrorists" numerous and well organized, but they are somehow capable of wielding the earth-shattering forces mobilized by major nation-states. This is very unlikely: Osama in his cave doesn't remotely represent the totalizing threat of Hitler in his Chancellery. And yet in the aftermath of a sneak attack, our expansive war talk invites us to suppose that we should confide to government the awesome powers that might well be appropriate when fighting a Third World War.

The emergency constitution is predicated on a more accurate description of our situation: We are reeling in the wake of surprise attack, and we just don't know whether the terrorists were just plain lucky, whether they have the capacity to organize a rapid second strike, whether they are in it for the long haul. So let's do what's necessary in the short term, and buy some time to figure out what's appropriate in the longer run.

The short-term problem is the second strike. Though the government may be deeply embarrassed by the initial attack, it's the only government we have. The terrorist strike will predictably generate bureaucratic chaos, but we should grant the security services extraordinary powers needed to preempt the second strike that may (or may not) be coming. This is the real danger at the moment, and we should focus all our collective energies on preventing it from happening, rather than launching a never-ending war on terrorism.

I am getting ahead of myself. Before exploring the ways a state of emergency might help us restore constitutional sanity, it's best to trace the impact of the prevailing war talk on our existing practices. The "war on terror" not only invites an aroused public to lash out at an amorphous enemy. It also makes it easier for the president to fight real wars against real countries. And it encourages the public to grant powers that threaten grave and permanent damage to our civil liberties.

These disturbing tendencies are already in evidence in American constitutional development. Unless we make a determined effort to call a halt, the momentum will only accelerate over time.

The Two-Front War

The Constitution grants Congress the power to "declare war," creating an opening for the Supreme Court to tell the president what a "war" is and when the consent of Congress is required. But the justices have repeatedly declined this invitation. They refused to hear lawsuits challenging the Tonkin Gulf Resolution during the Vietnam era, and they won't be waking from their slumber any time soon.[3]

This means that a president pondering an old-fashioned war against a sovereign state has to prepare a political campaign on two domestic fronts as well. It isn't enough for him to convince ordinary Americans that it's right to fight one or another rogue state. He must also battle Congress for the right to make the final decision on whether to go to war. If it proves politically impossible for him to go to war without gaining the consent of Congress, he must try to squeeze the House and Senate into a political corner, giving them no choice but to rubber-stamp his decision. Transforming the problem of terrorism into a "war" helps the president on both fronts. Under the traditional understanding, each war against a sovereign state has to be justified on its own merits. The war against Afghanistan is distinct from the one against Iraq, and so forth. But once the public is convinced that a larger "war on terrorism" is going on, these old-fashioned wars can be repackaged as mere battles—as in President Bush's famous description of Iraq as "the central front" on the war on terrorism.[4] Rhetorical repackaging also makes it easier for the president to win on his second front, enabling him to take unilateral action without the consent of Congress. Everybody knows that the president, as commander in chief, has the constitutional authority to initiate "battles." It is only when he proposes an entirely new "war" that the consent of Congress comes into play. Even here, presidents often have committed forces without clear congressional consent—but especially in major initiatives, their authority to do so will encounter fierce, and often successful, political resistance.

As president and Congress square off against each other, the public understanding of the nature of war becomes an important factor in determining the outcome.[5] Once the president convinces the public that an invasion of a "rogue state" is merely a "battle" in the "war on terrorism," he is well on the way to winning his battle against Congress over final decision-making authority. To be sure, his opponents will predictably insist that the Constitution expressly grants Congress the power "to declare war." But the president can easily dismiss this point if the public is convinced that we are *already* fighting a war (on terror) and that the president is simply opening a new battlefront (against another sovereign state). Once the larger point is conceded, the president's powers as commander in chief will predictably carry the day in the court of public opinion.

And he will have sufficient support in the academic community to make his case seem legally respectable. Consider this particularly chilling statement from Professor John Yoo of the University of California Law School: "The world after September 11, 2001, . . . is very different. . . . It is no longer clear that the United States must seek to reduce the amount of warfare, and it certainly is no longer clear that the constitutional system ought to be fixed so as to make it difficult to use force. It is no longer clear that the default state for American national security is peace."[6] And it will never be clear until the public and the legal community repudiate the mindless war-talk which swirls around us.

From Rhetoric to Reality

A contrast between the first and second wars in Iraq suggests the corrosive influence of the "war on terror." These two military initiatives were the largest in recent decades. This did not stop either Bush I or Bush II from insisting on their inherent power as commanders in chief to commit the troops without the consent of Congress.[7] Despite their unilateralist pretensions, both presidents were obliged by political realities to go to Congress, but under revealingly different scenarios.

Before making his war in the Persian Gulf, Bush I first gained the consent of the United Nations Security Council and only then turned to Congress for authorization. This sequence established two major principles for the "new world order" then emerging from the Cold War.

The first principle was the double veto: the president would not launch a major war without the consent of both the U.N. Security Council and the U.S. Congress. Under the second principle, Congress would have the final say: only after the Security Council established that war was consistent with the U.N. Charter would Congress decide whether it was in the best interests of the United States.

The second time around, with the nation now embarked on a war against terror, Bush II dealt himself a stronger hand. He reversed his father's sequence and went to Congress first. A grant of plenary warmaking power, he explained, would give him a crucial bargaining chip in gaining the support of the Security Council for the Iraqi invasion: "If you want to keep the peace, you've got to have the authorization to use force," as he put it.[8]

Congress picked up where the president left off. A war resolution typically raises a profound but straightforward question: are you for it or against it? But suddenly lawmakers could vote for war and say they were for peace—they were merely providing the president with a much-needed bargaining chip.[9] George Orwell was the brooding presence in the hall: the vote had been transformed from a solemn act of accountability into a buck-passing operation.

It wasn't tough to see through this presidential power grab—it had all the delicacy of a sucker punch. But it floored Congress. Critics argued for a carefully limited Congressional resolution that required President Bush to return to Congress if he failed to convince the Security Council to authorize the use of force.[10] They campaigned for a vote in both houses to force Bush II to follow the path of Bush I. They got their vote but were overwhelmed by the public's support of "the war against terror," which blurred the distinction between the war in Iraq and the terrorist attack of September 11. The critics' carefully limited war resolution went down by substantial margins in both Houses, and the president gained his warmaking authority, with a gesture toward a peaceful resolution through the United Nations.[11]

With Congress out of the picture in the run-up to the invasion, public opinion polling took on a weight it should never assume. When the president finally threatened Iraq with war unless Saddam Hussein quit the country in forty-eight hours, the pollsters rushed to the phones to take the public pulse. By the next morning, they breathlessly reported that two-thirds of their 510 respondents supported the president.[12]

With the momentum provided by his leadership in the war on terror, Bush II had managed to push the warmaking system one large step toward presidential unilateralism. He had displaced Congress from its final say over matters of war and peace, substituting the fig leaf of pollster democracy.

I am not interested in refighting the war in Iraq.[13] My point is diagnostic. We should look upon Bush's success as an augury for the future. Suppose that the country is once again reeling from a devastating terrorist attack. And suppose that the sitting president is once again moving toward war against an enemy state that has no obvious relation to the terrorists who actually were responsible.

And yet, suppose further, he insists on lumping the two together as part of a vast and boundaryless "war on terror." He further insists that, as commander in chief, he has the constitutional authority to open up a new battlefront against the "rogue state" he is targeting for destruction. Who will stop him this time? Congress? If it was such a pushover the last time around, is it really likely to insist on making a sharp distinction between the terrorist attack on the one hand and the rogue state on the other?

Many factors will determine the answer, but certainly the "war on terror" doesn't invite Congress and the public to make the necessary discriminations.

It is a fair question whether an emergency constitution can encourage greater discernment, and I will return to this issue when we move from diagnosis to prescription. For now, it is enough to emphasize a first big problem with the now-dominant public rhetoric: The "war on terror" will make it easier for future presidents to react to the panic of a terrorist attack by launching an old-fashioned war against an unrelated rogue state, without submitting themselves to the narrowly focused congressional inquiry rightly demanded of such fateful decisions.

Shadow-Boxing

The law is a blunt instrument. It hacks the complexities of life into a few legal boxes, and obliterates the nuances. Thinking "inside the box" is especially dangerous where "war" is concerned. For example, the Spanish-American War was a war, and so was the Second World War, but the Spanish-American War did not involve a life-and-death struggle for political survival. This should make a big difference so far as civil liberties are concerned. Though many sacrifices were justified in the war against the Axis powers, it would have been absurd to make comparable demands in the war against Spain, an imperial power in terminal decline.

Yet once lawyers get trapped inside the box, such absurdities can readily seem to be the inexorable product of sound legal reasoning. War is war, and that is that: it is easy for lawyers to extend precedents upholding presidential power in big wars to cases involving minor skirmishes.

Terrorism raises problems that are distinct from both the Second World War and the Spanish-American. But once we call it a war on terror, we are in grave danger of treating these attacks as if they raised the constitutional stakes as did our life-and-death-struggle against Germany and Japan. As we shall see, the Supreme Court is already succumbing. In its initial foray into the subject, the Court has invoked repressive precedents from the gravest wars of the past as if they were applicable to our present predicament.

You can complain all you like about "thinking inside the box," but it has been a feature of the legal mind for centuries, nay, millennia. My solution, in any event, doesn't require some miraculous transformation. The point of this essay is to create a new legal box—the "state of emergency"—for lawyers and judges to use in dealing with the terrorist threats of the twenty-first century. Such an act of legal creation is always difficult, but there are too many inherent dangers in thinking within the "war" box.

During the worst of our wars, our political existence as a nation was at stake, and presidents acted unilaterally with devastating effect on civil liberties.[14] During the Civil War, President Lincoln asserted his power, without the consent of Congress, to jail American citizens on his own say-so, and to suspend their constitutional right to ask the courts for a writ of habeas corpus demanding their freedom. When challenged, Lincoln famously responded: "Are all the laws, but one, to go unexecuted, and the government itself go to pieces, lest that one be violated?"[15] During the Second World War, Franklin Roosevelt invoked extraordinary powers as commander in chief to order 120,000 Japanese—mostly citizens—into internment camps.

The most important thing to say about these precedents is that they are irrelevant. Only our habit of calling today's sporadic outbreaks of mass violence a "war on terror" makes them seem applicable. I do not minimize the terrorist threat. But we shouldn't lose all historical perspective: terrorism is a very serious problem, but it doesn't remotely suggest a return to the darkest times of the Civil War or World War II.

In confronting terrorism, we need to distinguish between two different dangers: the *physical* threat to the population and the *political* threat to our constitutional system. Future attacks undoubtedly pose a severe physical threat: terrorist strikes may kill tens of thousands at a single blow. But they won't pose a clear and present danger to our political system. Even if Washington or New York were decimated, Al Qaeda could not displace the surviving remnants of political authority with its own rival government and military force. The terrorists would remain underground, threatening a second strike, while the rest of us painfully recover and reconstruct our traditional scheme of government—providing emergency police and health services, filling vacancies in established institutions, and moving forward, however grimly, into the future.

Our most terrible wars not only involved mass slaughter but presented a genuine threat to the very existence of our government. Imagine that the Second World War had turned out differently: rather than suffering a defeat at Stalingrad, the Germans had conquered Moscow and invaded Britain, while the Japanese had won the Battle of Midway, and later landed on the West Coast. At that point, our future as an independent republic would have been at stake. Call this an *existential* threat to the nation. Before the Second World War, we faced it only once in history.

This was during the Civil War. And it was precisely the existential character of the threat that Lincoln emphasized when suspending fundamental rights against arbitrary arrest and detention. To repeat his famous line: "Are all the laws, but one, to go unexecuted, *and the government itself go to pieces*, lest that one be violated?" Lincoln was acting to sustain political survival, not to reduce the tragic loss of life. His efforts to save the Union almost certainly increased the carnage. If he had been interested in saving lives, he would have followed the advice of his predecessor, President Buchanan, and allowed the South to leave the Union in peace.[16] It was his insistence on saving the Union that led him to suspend constitutional rights against arbitrary arrest and detention.

This fundamental point is erased by an unthinking repetition of war talk. If the struggle with terrorism counts as a "war," it is all too easy for lawyers and judges to cite the wartime precedents of Lincoln and Roosevelt as if they were germane to our present predicament. After all, war is war, isn't it?

Lawyers may find this wordplay bewitching, but it represents the height of folly. We will pay a very high price for the legal mind's remorseless tendency to use a single label—war—to describe too many different things. Just as the Spanish American War did not pose an existential threat, neither does the struggle with terrorism. We will suffer grievous casualties in future attacks, but the only thing that genuinely threatens to jeopardize our polity is the war talk that we hear around us. It is precisely this rhetoric that will encourage courts to rubber-stamp presidential decisions to respond to terrorist attacks with escalating cycles of repression. If the courts don't challenge the language of war, they will ultimately acquiesce in the permanent destruction of our liberties.

Nazi Saboteurs

Judges are not immune from the swirl of melodramatic war talk, but the crucial issue will be fought out in terms of key legal precedents. A leading case comes from the darkest days of World War II. The year was 1942. The German army was slashing through the Soviet Union, and its air force was leveling London to prepare for a triumphant invasion. The Japanese had struck Pearl Harbor on December 7, 1941, and the United States was in a state of shock—no light on the horizon, no sign that we would be sweeping forward to victory in three difficult years. Our political independence was at stake.

In the middle of June two German U-boats landed on the East Coast under cover of darkness—one at Ammagansett Beach on Long Island, the other at Ponte Vedra Beach in Florida.[17] Each discharged four saboteurs, dressed in the full uniform of the German marine infantry, and armed with a supply of explosives. After burying their uniforms, they scattered in civilian garb for a covert campaign to blow up war industries and facilities.

They failed miserably. One of the saboteurs defected to the FBI, which swiftly rounded up the spies and trumpeted its success in the media, giving the country a much-needed boost in morale. Then President Roosevelt intervened to transform the publicity coup into a constitutional crisis. One of the saboteurs, Herbert Haupt, was a U.S. citizen, and all had committed crimes that were readily prosecutable in the federal courts.[18] But on July 2 Roosevelt created a military commission to try the eight men secretly. Acting as commander in chief, he told the federal courts to stay out of the affair.

With the military commission racing to judgment on the men, the saboteurs' lawyers rushed to the federal courts.[19] Sensing a direct threat to its authority, the Supreme Court hurriedly convened a special July session in Washington. But after hearing arguments, it immediately crumpled to presidential authority. On the following day, the Court orally upheld Roosevelt's decision in a case called Ex parte Quirin, deferring an opinion to the fall.

Chief Justice Harlan Fiske Stone assigned himself the job of writing the opinion, and he soon began to appreciate the legal difficulties of the Court's precipitous decision. He wrote to Justice Felix Frankfurter in September that he found it "very difficult to support the Government's construction of the articles [of war]."[20] But there was no turning back. A week after the Court announced its oral decision in late July, six of the eight Germans were executed—Haupt among them—making it impossible for the justices to change their mind without condemning themselves as well as the president.[21] As Stone put the point to Frankfurter in his September letter, it would "seem almost brutal to announce this ground of decision for the first time after six of the petitioners have been executed and it is too late for them to raise the question if in fact the articles [of war] . . . have been violated."[22]

Kill now, cover-up later: no believer in the rule of law can take pride in the *Quirin* decision. The justices' only excuse, if there was one, is that Congress had formally declared an all-out war against the Germans and that Roosevelt might not have obeyed a contrary order (or so his attorney general, Francis Biddle, suggested to the justices).[23]

Yet this disgraceful decision is now reemerging as the Bush administration's great legal precedent in the war on terror. *Quirin* provides the "slam-dunk" argument for apologists of presidential power. Recall that at least one of the eight Nazi saboteurs, Herbert Haupt, was a U.S. citizen: If the Court upheld President Roosevelt when he exercised his military jurisdiction over Haupt, why can't President Bush do the same when he suspects an American citizen is collaborating with the terrorist foe? War is war, isn't it? Bush and Roosevelt are both commanders in chief, aren't they? So if Roosevelt could seize Haupt in his war, Bush should also have the power to seize American citizens in the greatest war of our generation. Q.E.D.[24]

It's hard to find a more toxic example of thinking inside the box. Whatever the merits of Roosevelt's decision, and there are few, he was acting at a moment when Americans were fighting for their continued political independence. But this isn't remotely true of our current struggle. Though terrorism poses very real physical risks, it doesn't raise a comparable threat to our political integrity. To the contrary, the only way we can destroy our constitutional tradition is allowing the prevailing war talk to reinvigorate the *Quirin* precedent. And yet the Supreme Court is already showing disturbing signs of succumbing to the new war-equals-war logic.

Terror Warriors?

In June 2004 the Court considered the fate of two American citizens who had been thrown into military jail on the mere say-so of the president—though under vastly different conditions. Yaser Hamdi is a dual national—he is both a native-born citizen of the United States and a citizen of Saudi Arabia, where he moved as a child. American forces seized him on the battlefield in Afghanistan under disputed conditions. His lawyers said that he was an inexperienced aid worker caught in the wrong place at the wrong time, but the federal government filed an affidavit claiming, without proffering substantial evidence, that he was "closely associated" with Al Qaeda and "affiliated with a Taliban military unit."[25]

The government seized the second citizen, José Padilla, when he arrived at Chicago's O'Hare International Airport. In proudly announcing his detention as an "enemy combatant," Attorney General John Ashcroft did not claim that Padilla, like Hamdi, had fought on a traditional battlefield. He justified the seizure by claiming that it had "disrupt[ed] an unfolding terrorist plot to attack the United States by exploding a radioactive dirty bomb." Despite the gravity of this charge, Ashcroft refused to give Padilla a chance to defend himself before a jury of his peers, asserting that the commander in chief had the unilateral authority to detain anybody he designated as an "enemy combatant." Lest this claim of arbitrary power seem too raw for public consumption, he assured a national television audience that the administration had plenty of evidence to back up its decision: "We know from multiple, independent and corroborating sources that [Padilla] was closely associated with al Qaeda and that, as an al Qaeda operative, he was involved in planning future terrorist attacks on innocent American civilians in the United States."[26] Within days, alas, the administration was running away from its apocalyptic charges, and it was soon conceding serious problems with its evidence as well. As the months turned into years, the president's charges against Padilla would continue to shift, and in surprising ways.

Despite this slipping and sliding, President Bush would hold Padilla for three years before specifying criminal charges against him, denying him any chance to establish his innocence in the meantime. Even in Hamdi's case, the president's claims were remarkably extreme. He did not merely claim the right to detain Hamdi for the relatively brief time it took to remove him from the battlefield, and transfer him to a criminal court for trial. He asserted his power, as commander in chief, to throw Hamdi in jail on his sole authority until the war on terror came to an end.[27] As the Supreme Court was to emphasize, this meant that Hamdi faced "the substantial prospect of perpetual detention."[28]

To justify these extraordinary powers, the President's lawyers were not content to lift *Quirin* out of its historical context of total war. They argued that the war on terror authorized even more drastic steps than those contemplated by Franklin Delano Roosevelt. Whatever one might say of Roosevelt's conduct, his secret military commission held a formal hearing to ascertain the facts before Roosevelt himself decided on the punishment of the German saboteurs.[29] But President Bush did not make a similar gesture toward impartial justice—not even a pretense. His lawyers asserted that the Constitution didn't require the commander in chief to prove his case before a military tribunal, let alone establish its accuracy beyond a reasonable doubt before a jury of civilians. They claimed that Hamdi and Padilla could be held for the duration of an endless "war on terror" simply on the president's say-so—or more precisely, the say-so of some low-level official speaking in his name.[30]

These are staggering assertions in any context, but *Padilla* is the big case. All we really know about him is that he converted to Islam (as was his constitutional right) and that he later traveled to a variety of Islamic countries for extended periods (not a crime). Americans change their religions every day, and millions more fly back and forth from foreign lands. If this is enough to send Padilla into years of military imprisonment, no citizen is safe. Although the president claims to have more incriminating information on Padilla, we can only guess whether the government has a ghost of a chance of persuading a jury of his guilt—in a process in which his counsel could confront and cross-examine witnesses and require the prosecution to overcome the presumption of innocence.[31] We know only that the president thought that these are dispensable luxuries in the "war on terror." His lawyers are building the constitutional foundation for military despotism: although Padilla is the only American citizen locked up in a military brig on such slender evidence, this single case opens up the prospect of a legal order worthy of Stalinist Russia.

It can't happen here, we tell ourselves, and ordinarily we would be right. The writ of habeas corpus has for centuries been the great guarantee against arbitrary arrest and detention in the English-speaking world. Padilla's case is a legal no-brainer: his lawyer had every reason to expect any federal judge—conservative or liberal—to require the government either to charge Padilla with a crime or to release him immediately from military prison.

Yet a first-rate federal judge refused to order Padilla's release, succumbing to the misbegotten notion that he could be treated as a foot soldier in a "war on terror."[32] This man, a citizen of the United States of America, remained in solitary confinement for two years as his case proceeded up the judicial hierarchy to the Supreme Court.[33] When his moment of truth finally came, he failed to get relief. Instead of delivering a ringing reassertion of American freedom, the 5–4 majority decided that the issue was too hot to handle.[34] Seizing upon a jurisdictional pretext, it refused to reach any decision on the merits—sending Padilla's lawyers back to the lower federal courts for more litigation before they can return to hear the high court's judgment on the merits.[35]

This pause speaks volumes. It is a dark day in our history when an American citizen remains in solitary confinement for *three or four years* before the Court deigns to consider his plea for due process of law. To be sure, it is better for the Court to stage a strategic retreat than simply to capitulate to the war on terror. Nevertheless, its long pause suggests the disturbing possibility that a majority thinks that the president's sweeping claims to power over his fellow citizens represents a hard case, rather than a precedent-shattering assault on American freedom.

The Court's decision in the case involving Yaser Hamdi only serves to emphasize the justices' uncertainty over bedrock principles of due process.[36] Hamdi was a native-born citizen, but he was seized on the battlefield of Afghanistan, not the rampways of O'Hare.[37] There was a real war going on against the Taliban government, not a metaphorical one against an amorphous band of terrorists. Nevertheless, the administration's lawyers were not content to rest their claims on the traditional law of war. Once again, they asserted that the president could keep Hamdi in solitary confinement until that distant moment when the "war on terror" comes to an end.[38] And once again, they contended that the president could act unilaterally without according Hamdi anything resembling due process.[39]

With Hamdi cut off from his lawyers for almost two years, it was left to his father to claim that his son was an inexperienced aid worker—to which the government responded with a conclusory memorandum asserting his involvement with the Taliban, and the remarkable assertion that this memo sufficed to eliminate the need for any review by a civilian or military court.[40]

The Supreme Court responded with a cacophony of opinions, leaving it for future judges to speak more decisively. Nevertheless, it is a sign of the times that only two justices—Scalia and Stevens—insisted that the Constitution required the government to prove Hamdi's guilt, beyond a reasonable doubt, before a jury of his peers.[41] In their view, there was only one legitimate way to avoid this requirement: Congress must make use of its authority, granted by the Constitution, to suspend habeas corpus "when in Cases of Rebellion or Invasion the public Safety may require it."[42] Since nothing in Congress's authorization of the war in Afghanistan suggested a clear intention to suspend the Great Writ, this was an easy case for Scalia and Stevens—the government must either charge Hamdi with a crime or set him free.

Clarence Thomas found the case easy as well, but for very different reasons. On his view, the president's could detain Hamdi indefinitely *"even if he is mistaken"*—lest the point was missed, Thomas was good enough to put it in italics. If the president deemed it "necessary for the public safety" to detain enemy combatants, his factual findings were "virtually conclusive." And Thomas made it clear that he was prepared to extend this blank check far beyond cases involving battlefield detentions—indeed, far beyond the limits suggested by the Constitution's express limitation to cases of "rebellion" or "invasion." Thomas went out of his way to insist that there are "many other emergencies during which this detention authority might be necessary."[43]

This is one of the most ominous lines ever written in the history of the Supreme Court: Thomas is seeking to vindicate the president's authority *unilaterally* to declare an emergency in response to *any* perceived threat to the "public safety," and to throw his fellow citizens into *indefinite* detention *"even if he is mistaken."* This is an opinion that would seem extreme to jurists living in a Latin American "democracy" ruled by a caudillo, and it is a shocking intrusion onto the pages of the United States Reports.

To recapitulate: In its first serious confrontation with the problem, only two justices could be found who would stand up forthrightly for the Bill of Rights; and they were counterbalanced by one judicial supporter of presidential tyranny. It remained for Sandra Day O'Connor to play her accustomed role as swing justice, writing a decisive plurality opinion for herself and three colleagues.[44]

Her decision has important merits—especially its clear recognition that the "war on terror" raises different issues from a classical war against the government of Afghanistan. O'Connor cautioned that traditional understandings "may unravel" when applied to an "unconventional war" that might not be "won for two generations," leaving Hamdi open to a "substantial prospect of perpetual detention." But she didn't squarely declare perpetual imprisonment unconstitutional, limiting her ruling to the period during which "active combat" continued in Afghanistan.[45] While she left the big question unresolved, at least she didn't affirm the president's arbitrary power during a never-ending "war on terrorism."

So much for the good news, if it may be called that. The bad news is that O'Connor explicitly repudiated the Scalia-Stevens view. She did not merely authorize the commander in chief to detain American citizens for a relatively brief period on the battlefield. She refused to require the government to move Hamdi quickly out of the battle zone and into the courtroom to establish before a jury of his peers that he had committed a crime.[46] Speaking for four justices, she merely granted Hamdi the right to "a meaningful opportunity" to rebut his designation as an "enemy combatant" before a military tribunal—and her notion of "meaningful" falls far short, as we shall see, of civilian standards.[47] The bad news is this: the president, acting as commander in chief, can throw one of his fellow citizens in jail, without the elaborate guarantees provided by the Bill of Rights, for the many years that the American army will be fighting in Afghanistan.

Despite this grim prospect, it is worth emphasizing that Justice O'Connor (writing for a plurality of four) emphatically rejected Justice Thomas's indiscriminate embrace of military despotism. She recognized that Hamdi had a "liberty interest" in his freedom that deserved "weight" in the overall balance required by the Due Process Clause.[48] But she placed lots of counterweights on the other side of the scale, including makeweights like the inconvenience of requiring fighting men to return to testify—after all, they serve on the battlefield only for a limited time, and trials could be scheduled to meet their requirements. Worse yet, she suggests that detainees may be deprived of their constitutional rights to confront their accusers if the government declares that "sensitive secrets of national defense" are at stake.[49]

Hearings of this kind may easily degenerate into a parody of due process. Instead of respecting the traditional presumption of innocence, the O'Connor Four gave the government the benefit of the doubt; instead of insisting on the citizen's right to a trial by jury, it said that a military tribunal sufficed; instead of insisting on the right of cross-examination, it allowed the military to withhold critical witnesses. Although the popular press has haled *Hamdi* for reining in presidential power, I take a much dimmer view: a few more "victories" like this, and civil liberties will become an endangered species in the United States of America.

Hamdi is a special case. There is an obvious difference between seizing an American on the Afghan battlefield and seizing him at a Chicago airport. But will a majority have the courage to draw the line when cases like

Padilla return to the Court? Or will it allow the president to transform ordinary American citizens into foot soldiers in the war on terrorism? Will it allow the president to confirm his suspicions by bringing citizens before a military tribunal and requiring them to prove their innocence or face years of detention in a military prison?

Hamdi suggests disturbing judicial uncertainty on these basic questions. No less disturbing is the justices' treatment of *Quirin,* and particularly Herbert Haupt, the U.S. citizen who had been rushed off to the electric chair after receiving secret justice from an ad hoc military tribunal. Justices Scalia and Stevens urged reconsideration—"the case was not this Court's finest hour"—but the O'Connor Four emphatically refused: "*Quirin* was a unanimous opinion. It . . . provid[es] us with the most apposite precedent that we have on the question of whether citizens may be detained in such circumstances. Brushing aside such precedent—particularly when doing so gives rise to a host of new questions never dealt with by this Court—is unjustified and unwise."[50]

War equals war. This is just the legalistic slide that I have been warning against. Speaking broadly, the Afghan war is our generation's equivalent of the Spanish-American—a brief and easy victory on the borderlands of empire (with a cleanup operation lasting for years). And yet four justices of the Supreme Court find it "unwise" to ask "new questions" before applying a shameful precedent from World War II, rendered at one of the rare moments when the nation's political independence was genuinely under threat. It is a sad thing for the legal mind to slide so effortlessly from World War II to the war in Afghanistan; does it foretell a further slide from the conflict against the Taliban to the "war on terror"? Nothing is inevitable, but O'Connor's question-begging reliance on *Quirin* is not a ground for confidence.

The jurisprudential framework elaborated by Justice O'Connor will also make it easier for the Court to expand her doctrines to a wider field. She does not view *Hamdi* as a very narrow exception to a general rule guaranteeing jury trials. She analyzes her case through the lens provided by a much more general framework traditionally reserved for questions of public administration—involving the grant of licenses, welfare payments, and other matters of mass justice.[51] In defining due process in these areas, the Court has engaged in a freewheeling process of balancing public

against private interests—calibrating the degree of due process on a sliding scale, depending on a host of disparate factors. This is plausible when
it comes to deciding how much administrative process is required, say, to
revise the pollution permit granted a business operation, but it is chilling
to see the same approach applied in a case involving human freedom.
Only a modern-day Kafka could do justice to O'Connor's bland techno-
cratic finding that the military's "interest" in avoiding inconvenience tips
the scale against Hamdi's "liberty interest." In placing Hamdi in the
hands of military justice and requiring him to prove his innocence, the
Court not only endangered Hamdi's freedom for years to come. It gave
new life to the president's authority to make war against his fellow citizens, threatening the very foundations of a free society.

Cautionary Tales

There will be many more cases coming to the Court as a result of
the president's extreme claims in the war on terror; and each will provide
an opportunity to rethink and resolve some of the basic issues raised in
Hamdi—especially since it was impossible for five justices to agree on a
common approach on the first try. So it's especially important for the
Court to consider the impact of its initial decision on the lives of those it
has affected.

Hamdi's personal fate serves as a cautionary tale. Although the Supreme
Court handed the president a very substantial victory, it refused to follow
Thomas's suggestion that it simply rubber-stamp the commander in chief's
decision. The O'Connor Four, to its credit, did require significant evidence
of Hamdi's involvement with the Taliban—albeit evidence that fell far
short of normal constitutional standards. Nevertheless, despite the mod-
esty of the Court's demands, the administration declined to go forward
and establish that Hamdi was indeed an "enemy combatant." Instead, it
quickly offered Hamdi a deal: he would be released immediately if he
renounced his American citizenship and promised not to return to the
country for ten years. Hamdi quickly agreed. To the disgrace of American
jurisprudence, he has sacrificed his citizenship for his freedom.[52]

Hamdi's impact on Padilla's personal destiny has been no less profound. As we have seen, Attorney General Ashcroft initially charged that

Padilla was an "enemy combatant" intent on destroying an American city with a "radioactive dirty bomb." But once the Court decided *Hamdi* and returned Padilla's case to the lower courts for further proceedings, Ashcroft's grandiose assertions became dim memories. In their place, the government developed a new story. It had always claimed that Padilla was "closely associated with Al Qaeda" and had spent time in Afghanistan planning "acts of international terrorism," before success-fully escaping to Pakistan after September 11. But now the government added a new fact that it claimed was crucial: Padilla "was armed with an assault rifle" as he beat his retreat into Pakistan.[53] It did not allege, how-ever, that Padilla actually fought for the Taliban government in its war with the United States and its local allies. With its new allegations about the gun, the government could portray Padilla as bearing weapons in the "war on terror" even if he wasn't engaged in battlefield operations.

To be sure, Justice O'Connor's careful opinion in *Hamdi* had limited itself strictly to the case of battlefield seizures in a classic war against the Taliban government, and expressly refused to expand its ruling to include presidential detentions in an open-ended "war on terror." But the gov-ernment's discovery of Padilla's weapon provided it with the opening it needed to urge the courts to move beyond O'Connor's narrow decision. If Padilla was in Afghanistan, and possessed a weapon, why insist that he actually go onto the battlefield and fight for the Taliban in a classic war? Shouldn't it suffice to establish that he was an armed foot soldier in the "war on terror"? War equals war, doesn't it?

On its first trial run, this clever bit of lawyering went nowhere. The district judge who heard Padilla's case was far more impressed with the fact that Padilla arrived at O'Hare Airport in civilian clothes without any weapons, and that it was his ongoing threat to the United States, not his activities in Afghanistan, that made him a high-priority target for detention. He refused to expand *Hamdi* and vigorously protected Padilla's fundamental rights as a citizen—rejecting his designation as an "enemy combatant" and requiring the government to charge him with a crime and prove its charges, beyond a reasonable doubt, to a jury of Padilla's peers.[54]

But the president's lawyers were luckier when their case came before the court of appeals. This three-judge appellate panel glossed over the government's failure to allege that Padilla was actually fighting for the Taliban government on the battlefield. It was enough for them that the president claimed that he was "armed and present in a combat zone."[55] Rather than insisting on a trial by jury, the appeals panel simply asked the government to provide an adequate evidentiary basis for its charges before the military tribunal, or some other "neutral arbiter," envisioned by Justice O'Connor in her decision in *Hamdi*. But after winning this great victory, the administration refused to follow up by bringing Padilla before a military tribunal. Instead, it suddenly granted Padilla everything he had been requesting: it asked the court to release him from military custody and it charged him with a crime, thereby granting him all the protections of the Bill of Rights.

This sudden shift didn't reflect a change of heart. It was merely a clever effort to stifle Padilla's appeal to the Supreme Court. Once the appeals panel transferred Padilla to civilian control, the government could claim that his case was moot, and that the Supreme Court should no longer hear the case. But in a remarkable rebuke, the court of appeals rejected this maneuver. It kept Padilla in military custody, leaving it up to the Court to pass judgment on the president's extreme claims.

The government's new criminal indictment suggests the grave abuses involved. It has dropped any mention of a plot to blow up American cities, and has changed its story once again: Padilla is now alleged to be part of a small-time conspiracy assisting foreign terrorists to launch attacks overseas. Yet it was Ashcroft's sensational charges that led the president to throw Padilla into jail without a hearing for more than three years. "As the government must surely understand," the court of appeals added, this shift has "left the impression that Padilla may have been held for these years . . . by mistake."[56]

This ludicrous "bait and switch" should *never* happen in a free country, and now is the time to say so. America is slowly recovering from the panic of September 11, and it would accept a judicial decision repudiating extreme presidential power. But if the Court waits till the next attack, it will have trouble resisting a presidential power grab when a new wave of panic is sweeping the nation.

Whatever the Court does, the sequels to its initial decisions in *Hamdi* and *Padilla* teach two sobering lessons. The first is the ease with which presidential power overreaches the evidence as it sweeps its suspected adversaries into prison. In Hamdi's personal sequel, we saw the government refusing to undertake the (modest) task of establishing its charges before a military tribunal: the president's lawyers thought it better, apparently, to send the man to Saudi Arabia rather than risk the public embarrassment following upon a rejection of their evidence by a panel of military officers.

The present U-turn on Padilla suggests a similar act of overreaching. We take for granted the right of the accused, guaranteed by the Sixth Amendment, to learn "the nature and cause of the accusation against him." We should take it for granted no longer.

The second lesson suggests how quickly one bad decision leads to another. Justice O'Connor and her colleagues might have supposed that they had made only a small step in granting the president power to seize Hamdi on the battlefield and keep him in detention until military operations ended in Afghanistan; yet within a very short time, the court of appeals is using this limited precedent to enable the president to take another step in his campaign to strip American citizens of their constitutional rights. And if the Supreme Court allows the court of appeals' decision in *Padilla* to stand, it will then seem a small step to expand presidential power yet further. After the next attack, it may seem sensible to seize the next "enemy combatant" for transmitting information to terrorists who remain in a military zone, or sending money to support their operations. Only one thing is certain: the president's lawyers will portray these activities as far more threatening than the rifle that Padilla may (or may not) have carried in his flight from Afghanistan. Once the president establishes a legal beachhead in his campaign to seize Americans in the "war on terror," it will be tough to draw sharp lines distinguishing Padilla's case from many, many others. As the country moves, one step at a time, toward presidential tyranny, the military tribunals authorized by *Hamdi* will also generate a host of perplexing procedural questions: How little evidence suffices to justify how much detention? Can suspects ever get in touch with civilian lawyers? Can these lawyers ever scrutinize secret evidence? If so, on what terms? And on and on.

These are important issues, and hosts of legal articles will be written about them. But it is even more important to challenge the mindless talk of a "war on terror" that makes the entire militarized enterprise seem plausible. This is not a war, and the commander in chief should not be conceded the power to make war on his fellow citizens.

The Enemy Within

The war on terror has already swept thousands into detention, and worse. So why focus so much attention on only two victims—Yaser Hamdi and José Padilla?[57]

These cases present a unique threat to the survival of the republic. If the president can throw citizens into solitary confinement for years on end, our democracy is in very deep trouble. And it is not good enough to tell Americans that they can regain their freedom if they can convince a military tribunal of their innocence. The mere threat of arbitrary presidential action is sufficient to destroy normal democratic life.

Hamdi, if generalized, provides a legal formula for tyranny, nothing more and nothing less. Despite the troubling uncertainties on display in *Padilla,* the judiciary should struggle to regain equilibrium, and should narrowly limit *Hamdi* to the special case of battlefield seizures. A great tradition calls upon the courts to defend *all* American citizens who seek the protection of the Bill of Rights.

Compared with this, everything else is unimportant. But when judged by less apocalyptic standards, another problem is very serious. During real wars, America (like other nations) has taken draconian steps against enemy aliens within its midst—often forcibly removing them to detention centers for the duration—without bothering to prove their individual involvement in the enemy war effort. Authorization for this practice comes from the earliest days of the Republic. During the late 1790s, America was in the throes of its first great panic—the French were threatening an "invasion," at least according to the governing Federalist Party. Congress responded with the notorious Sedition Act, unleashing an extraordinary campaign of suppression, which led to the imprisonment of leading opposition publicists and newspaper editors. But this statute included one of my favorite devices—a sunset clause condemning the statute to lapse after two years unless it was expressly reauthorized.[58] By that point, Thomas Jefferson and his Democratic Republicans had ousted the Federalists from power, and they refused to consider renewal, burying the statute in historical ignominy.

Unfortunately, the Federalists did not tack a sunset clause onto another of their creations: their Alien Enemies Act authorized the president to detain enemy aliens for the duration of a declared war, or imminent "invasion," without bothering to prove their individual involvement in the enemy war effort.[59] The Jeffersonians didn't repeal this statute, and it remains on the books to this day.[60] And presidents have taken advantage of this authority, most infamously when President Roosevelt ordered tens of thousands of resident Japanese into detention centers after Pearl Harbor.

Once again, the most important thing to be said about this history is that it is irrelevant. The Alien Enemies Act is restricted to the real thing: cases of imminent "invasion" or a formal declaration of war by Congress. It would be a grave mistake to extend the practice of arbitrary detention of aliens to the "war on terrorism."

And yet this is what has happened since September 11. Although the administration has not explicitly invoked the Alien Enemies Act, it has used other statutes for the same end. It has transformed the immigration laws into a machine for the arbitrary detention of residents who come from the Islamic world—ordering secret hearings before immigration judges and using minor infractions to sweep thousands into detention centers to prepare the ground for their removal and deportation.[61] And it has manipulated other statutes to similar effect.[62]

These detentions raise grave constitutional questions. The Due Process Clauses apply to all "persons," not merely citizens. The Supreme Court has repeatedly insisted on this point, and it has also rigorously scrutinized efforts to discriminate against aliens under the Equal Protection Clause.[63] But will the Court buckle under the pressure of the war on terror and authorize a separate system of detention for resident aliens, allowing the president and Congress to sweep suspects away into detention on grounds, and with procedures, that would not be tolerated for citizens?

It's anybody's guess.[64] Only one thing is clear: a double standard would be a recipe for moral disaster. So long as aliens and citizens are treated alike, fear-mongering politicians will have to think twice before lashing out at the "enemy within." Any system that sweeps thousands of aliens into custody will also hit a large number of citizens—and once they start disappearing into detention centers, millions of voters will begin to worry whether they are next. These anxieties may serve as a political check against the worst abuses.

All bets are off once aliens can be swept away without exposing citizens to a similar risk. When voters are assured of better treatment, it will be easier for them to respond to repeated terrorist attacks by authorizing an escalating spiral of mass arrests and secret detentions that may degenerate into systematic torture.

Although American courts haven't (yet) taken a lead on the protection of resident aliens, the British judiciary has sounded the alarm. In December 2004 the House of Lords, in its judicial capacity, struck down antiterrorist legislation which authorized the government to detain aliens—but not citizens—for indefinite periods without trial. The Lords refused to allow the government to impose such a crushing burden only on aliens when there were citizens who posed a comparable terrorist threat. It ruled that all suspected terrorists must be treated equally—citizens and resident aliens alike—on pain of violating the European Convention on Human Rights.[65] Lord Hoffmann went further, unconditionally condemning indefinite detention without judicial process: "The real 'threat to the life of the nation' comes not from terrorism but from laws such as these."[66]

He is absolutely right, and the best way to arm ourselves against this danger is through an unremitting critique of mindless war talk. In an old-fashioned war between old-fashioned states, identifying "enemy nationals" was a relatively unproblematic business—just look at their passports. And if the enemy state was threatening our continuing existence, it might make sense to take desperate steps to restrict enemy nationals.

Terrorism raises different problems. We are dealing not with a well-organized and hostile state but with an unending series of fringe groups that may, or may not, have the capacity to launch second strikes. The attack on September 11 came from the Islamic world, but the next strike may come from some very different place—perhaps Mexico, perhaps Montana. War talk ignores this basic point, inviting us to target "suspicious alien terrorists" as if they were analogous to the "enemy aliens" traditionally detained during classical conflicts.

The point of the "state of emergency" is to break out of this box. Given our new problem, it is simply irrational to target aliens. We should be focusing on likely terrorists, whatever their citizenship status. Pretending otherwise leads us down an ugly path to moral disaster, encouraging us to lash out blindly at an enormous number of innocent people—there are twenty million alien residents in America—and to deal with those caught in the net with cruelty and disdain. Whatever else it may contain, the emergency constitution should apply to all residents equally, regardless of their citizenship.

My critique has its limits. I have been discussing the pathological potential of the "war on terror," not the problems involved in America's conduct of classical wars, like those in Iraq and Afghanistan. There have been plenty of pathologies here as well: not only the abuses at Abu Ghraib and Guantánamo but the astonishing success of the nation's leaders in avoiding accountability for these moral disasters.[67]

This remarkable whitewash desperately requires a host of institutional remedies, and a renewed commitment to the rule of law, both national and international. Perhaps this is an even more urgent priority, but it is not the problem I will be addressing in this book. My subject is not war but the perilous consequences of expanding war talk onto a new terrain. Thus far, nothing like Guantánamo has dramatized these dangers to the general public, but the Court's decisions in *Padilla* and *Hamdi* show that they are very real.[68]

Unless and until we supplant "war on terror" with a different constitutional rubric, presidents will use the slogan to win their ongoing struggle with Congress over the power to declare traditional wars against rogue states. And they will use it to batter down judicial resistance to their extreme efforts to strip suspects of their most fundamental rights. Each successful exercise in extended warmaking powers will create a precedent for the next president to build on.[69]

This is a serious enough problem for a single short book to focus on. Rather than ranging broadly into the international law of war, it will be enough to concentrate on a single question: how can an emergency constitution constrain the abuse of presidential power when the homeland is repeatedly shaken, at unpredictable moments, by the shock waves of terrorist assault?

2

THIS IS NOT A CRIME

The "war on terror" dominates political rhetoric, and so my first task has been to loosen its grip on the public mind. But "war" isn't the only big idea that recurrently emerges when we talk about our current predicament. "Crime" provides a second, and competing, paradigm: if politicians have been eagerly waging war, legal traditionalists have been insisting that the tried-and-true principles of the criminal law suffice to deal with our problem.

And to a large extent, they are right. The basic principles of criminal due process are the product of centuries of struggle against arbitrary power. They have proven their capacity to adapt to novel challenges before, and they should not be lightly sacrificed at any time, especially during moments of panic.

Nevertheless, the criminal law is fundamentally inadequate as a complete response to our present predicament. It requires supplementation by a carefully controlled framework for a state of emergency. My argument is based on principle, not expediency. I hope to show that the criminal law is itself based on premises that fundamentally limit its operation. The emergency constitution shouldn't be treated as an ad hoc exception. It proceeds from an appreciation of the principled limits on ordinary criminal law. It supplements, rather than distorts, the established legal tradition of criminal due process.

Nonsense, responds the traditionalist, and I will be presenting his critique before attempting a response. If I am successful, this will complete my ground-clearing operation. I will have shown that *neither* war *nor* crime provides an adequate framework for confronting the aftermath of a major terrorist attack, and that a carefully crafted emergency statute provides a principled response to the distinctive challenges before us.

The rest of the book then turns to questions of statecraft. The design of an institutionally credible emergency constitution is a tough job—maybe so tough that practical difficulties make the entire project a pipe dream. Surely this isn't the first time that a good idea is destroyed on the rock of institutional reality.

But let's put first things first: *is* the emergency constitution a good idea, one that targets a problem that will elude the criminal law? If the answer is yes, it will be time enough to confront the formidable difficulties involved in creating a credible "emergency constitution."

The Traditionalist Case

I have been urging you to view the "war on terror" as a misleading metaphor without decisive legal significance—more like the "war on drugs" or the "war on crime" than the war against Nazi Germany. On this large point, I don't anticipate much dissent from defenders of the criminal-law tradition. My problem, they would insist, is that I fail to carry my argument to its obvious conclusion: if the "war on terror" is merely smoke and mirrors, why not simply return to the tried-and-true principles of criminal due process and disdain the attractions of an emergency constitution?

Al Qaeda is not the only dangerous conspiracy prowling about in the world. Consider the Mafia, and how its ongoing operations kill thousands over time—with dramatic gangland killings punctuating the routine deaths of the drug trade. The Mafia has many of the hallmarks of terrorist groups: it is well organized, predatory, secretive, and disruptive of the social order. Despite the human devastation, nobody supposes that loose talk about a "war on crime" should deprive accused Mafiosi of their fundamental rights under the Constitution. Conspiracy is a serious crime, and crime fighters have special tools to deal with it.[1] But they don't respond with a state of emergency that suspends these guarantees. Why shouldn't similar adaptations of the criminal law suffice in the case of Al Qaeda?

Recall, too, the experience of the Cold War. There was pervasive talk of a Communist conspiracy—and in contrast to Al Qaeda, these shadowy cells of supposed plotters were supported by a great superpower commanding massive armies with nuclear weapons. American presidents had substantial evidence of links between domestic Communist cells and the Soviet GRU, which was a military organization.[2] For decades, we were only minutes away from an incident that could lead to nuclear holocaust. Domestic Communist cells were virtual front-line troops in something very close to a classic war between sovereign states.

Yet no president ever suspended the normal operation of the criminal law by calling domestic Communists "enemy combatants."[3] The Communist conspiracy was treated as a Communist *conspiracy,* as defined by the criminal law; the accused were provided all the traditional protections of criminal due process. To be sure, anti-Communist hysteria wrongfully destroyed countless reputations and careers, to our shame as a nation. But at no time did an American president attempt, in the manner of George W. Bush, to throw suspected Communist sympathizers into military prison without due process of law. If Cold War anxieties did not overwhelm us, why should war talk justify the use of emergency powers against small bands of terrorists who cannot rely on the massive assistance of an aggressive superpower?

The Question of Effective Sovereignty

These powerful questions provide a much-needed antidote to President Bush's expansive warmongering. Nevertheless, it is a mistake to ignore a distinctive feature of our present situation that makes the analogies to the Mafia and the Communists seem overly facile.

Let's begin with the Mafia. Even the most successful organized-crime operations lack the overweening pretensions of the most humble terrorist cell. Mafiosi are generally content to let government officials flaunt their symbols of legitimacy so long as gangsters control the underworld. They simply aim to control the "underworld" without making an open challenge to the surface legitimacy of the political order. Whatever else is happening in Palermo, the mayor's office is occupied by the legally authorized representative of the Italian Republic. But the point of a terrorist bomb is to launch a distinctly public and political challenge to the government. It aims to destabilize a foundational relationship between ordinary citizens and the modern state: the expectation of *effective sovereignty.*

Effective sovereigns don't promise their citizens a crime-free world. But they are expected to maintain control over the basic security situation—and it is precisely this expectation which is challenged by a terrorist attack. The tragic loss of three thousand lives in the September 11 attacks was traumatizing in itself. But it was Al Qaeda's success in shaking the public's confidence in the American government's effective sovereignty that gave the attack its overwhelming political resonance. For a while at least, it was perfectly reasonable for ordinary Americans to wonder whether the government really was in control of affairs within the nation's borders.

This public and political dimension of the terrorist threat makes the lessons from the McCarthy era more relevant, but once again there is an important difference. For all the McCarthyite talk of the Red Menace, the danger remained abstract to ordinary people, and the government's effective sovereignty was never seriously questioned. True, the Cuban missile crisis brought us to the brink of World War III, but it didn't conclude with an event, like the toppling of the twin towers of the World Trade Center, that publicly dramatized America's incapacity to defend its frontiers.[4]

The risk of nuclear devastation during the Cold War might well have been much larger than the terrorist danger today.[5] But we managed to avoid doomsday, and the threat of nuclear holocaust remained a threat. In contrast, the changing technological balance in favor of terrorists means that public affronts to effective sovereignty will almost certainly recur at unpredictable intervals, each shattering anew the ordinary citizen's confidence in the government's capacity to fend off catastrophic breaches of national security.[6]

Paradoxically, the relative weakness of terrorists compared with the Communist conspiracy only exacerbates the political problems involved in an effective response. If the Cold War had ever become a real battle, involving massive nuclear exchanges, Western civilization would have come to an end. The survivors would have been obliged to build a legitimate government from the ground up. This won't happen in the new age of terrorism. It may be only a matter of time before a suitcase A-bomb decimates a major American city, but there will be nothing like a Soviet-style rocket assault leading to the destruction of all major cities simultaneously. Despite the horror, the death, and the pain, American government will survive the tragedy. And it will be obliged to establish—and quickly—that it remains an effective sovereign, and has not been thoroughly demoralized by the lurking terrorist underground. To put my point in a single line: the normal operation of the criminal law *presupposes* the effective sovereignty of the state, but a major terrorist attack *challenges* it. Before it can operate a criminal justice system, the state must first assure its effective sovereignty.

This simple point helps explain something that is otherwise mysterious: how has President Bush's war talk managed to convince so many Americans that the criminal law isn't enough? He is, after all, one of the least eloquent presidents in recent memory, and he is assaulting some of the most hallowed aspects of our tradition. The sanctity of trial by jury is hammered home in countless television shows and civics classrooms. Everybody knows that the state must treat the accused as innocent until proven guilty before a jury of his peers. How, then, has the president managed to get away with his remarkable efforts to destroy these rights?

It is too easy to ascribe this rhetorical victory to the machinations of Madison Avenue when placed in command of the Oval Office. Presidents more persuasive than George W. Bush often have failed to convince their skeptical audience. Although the skillful exploitation of fear is part of the answer, there is another part as well: the partisans of the criminal law are tone-deaf when it comes to addressing the terrorist challenge to effective sovereignty. Whatever the many weaknesses of the language of war, it does permit the public to mark this crucial point. September 11 *is* like December 7, 1941—that other "day of infamy"—precisely because both the Japanese and Al Qaeda challenged the effective sovereignty of the United States, requiring the American government to reassert its control over the homeland in no uncertain terms.

Despite this key similarity, September 11 is different enough from December 7 to justify the creation of the "state of emergency" as an alternative to the state of war. But until we create this new framework, the public will predictably prefer war talk to crime talk—since only the former expresses the need to establish effective sovereignty as a precondition for civilized life. By calling it a "war," not a "crime," the government asserts, in no uncertain terms, that it will see to it that Al Qaeda's breach of our effective sovereignty was only a temporary lapse.

It is wrong, then, for legal traditionalists to treat the "war on terror" as if it were merely a symptom of collective paranoia, which Americans will come to regret as they recover their sobriety. War talk makes a fundamental point that the legal tradition fails squarely to confront: the criminal law treats individual cases *as if the larger question of effective sovereignty has already been resolved*. But terrorist attacks represent a public assault on this premise, and the visible affront to effective sovereignty will be exploited again and again by the terror warriors to aggrandize their power. If the tongue-tied Bush managed to win the struggle for public opinion over the legalists, future presidents will win the debate even more decisively, building on Bush's precedents in very damaging ways.

The Reassurance Principle

So neither "war" nor "crime" is really adequate. War does express the public affront to national sovereignty left in the aftermath of a successful terrorist attack. But war talk threatens all of us with arbitrary power exercised without the restraint of legal safeguards developed over centuries of painful struggle. "Crime" has proved itself adequate when dealing with dangerous conspiracies, but only within a social context that presupposes the government's effective sovereignty. What is required is a third framework which confronts the distinctive interest that comes into play in the aftermath of a terrorist attack.

Call it the *reassurance interest:* When terrorists strike at 9/11 scale, *nobody has the slightest idea of what may happen next.* The citizenry confronts the shock of the unknown, and the resulting anxiety is qualitatively different from many of the other uncertainties of life. We may not like to think about the risk of an early heart attack, or unemployment, or divorce, but we have a rough and ready sense of their probability, and try to manage them accordingly.

But the arts of risk management are radically inappropriate in the aftermath of a terrorist attack. To invoke a distinction first developed by Frank Knight, we are suddenly thrown into a world of unknowable uncertainty, not calculable risk.[7] To be sure, all of us occasionally encounter moments of radical uncertainty in our private lives, but our personal struggles with the unknown don't generally spread beyond family and friends. In contrast, a terrorist attack triggers pervasive uncertainty throughout the country about our collective capacity to maintain the fabric of public order.

The point of the emergency constitution is to confront this anxiety squarely, without doing permanent damage to our precious tradition of liberty. Reassurance takes two forms: symbolic and functional.

I have already been emphasizing the symbolic aspect: like a declaration of war, the proclamation of an emergency publicly recognizes that the terrorist assault on effective sovereignty strikes at a fundamental aspect of the social contract, and seeks to reassure the public that aggressive action will be taken to contain the crisis.

The functional aspect is directed at the pressing problem of the moment: the risk of a second strike. Here is where the big difference with the Japanese sneak attack becomes apparent. When the Japanese struck on December 7, their larger naval fleet lurked in the background—the risk of a second strike was very real, and unless and until something decisive was done to destroy the enemy fleet, the danger would remain.

Not necessarily so in the aftermath of a terrorist attack. Perhaps the terrorists were just lucky, and they have already shot their load. Perhaps they have prepared for one or two other sneak attacks. Or perhaps the country really is in for a long tough struggle against a deeply entrenched network. There is no way to know.

Functionally speaking, this means that the state should be granted extraordinary powers needed to prevent a devastating second strike, but only for a short period, with extensions granted reluctantly and in response to the evolving exigencies of the situation. Our reaction must be measured and situation based: that is precisely what the circumstances require, and what the emergency constitution authorizes.

However brief the period, extraordinary power raises extraordinary questions of moral principle. I will be focusing on the paradigm case, involving the power to seize suspects—perhaps thousands of them—and hold them for extended, but not unlimited, periods, before handing them over to the normal processes of the criminal law.

To keep the discussion concrete, it will help to anticipate a couple of central proposals. Under my emergency constitution, the security services have the power (1) to arrest on "reasonable suspicion," which is a standard that is substantially lower than the "probable cause" ordinarily required by the criminal law, and (2) to detain suspects for up to forty-five days before the prosecution is required to satisfy the traditional criminal law standards for arrest and conviction. The functional point of emergency detention is to prevent another terrorist attack, and thereby sustain the expectation of effective sovereignty which serves as the premise of social order.

This "second strike" rationale rests upon three functional premises. I assume, first, that a massive terrorist strike generates a great deal of bureaucratic confusion. The security services have been caught by surprise: they don't know what's going on, and their efforts to find out are deflected by recurring episodes of bureaucratic infighting, faultfinding, and blame evasion. And yet for all the backbiting, Homeland Security will be in a position to frame a short-term response. The bureaucracy has been busy preparing long lists of the "usual suspects" over the course of many years. This provides a basis for an emergency dragnet, but it will take more time to gain compelling evidence linking particular suspects to the particular conspiracy involved in the recent attack.

Nevertheless, and this is my second premise, time is of the essence, because the initial terrorist strike greatly increases the probability of a second major attack. Any well-organized conspiracy recognizes that, once the nation goes on red alert after the first assault, it will be much harder to plant new terrorist cells and materiel. If its attack isn't merely the result of a lucky break, the terrorists have probably prepared the way for a series of strikes before the first one occurs.

And if this turns out to be so—this is my third premise—the damages of a second strike will be very great indeed. Not only will it kill many people, but it will grievously demoralize the general public. When only a single attack has occurred, the citizenry can retain the hope that the disaster remains a rare and exceptional event. With repeated attacks on a massive scale, people face the open-ended prospect of great and unpredictable violence, leading to a quantum jump in general anxiety and signs of panic. This general unease, in turn, paves the way for a new cycle of political demagoguery.

Within this context, the instrumental case for an emergency regime is straightforward. Emergency detention will allow the security services to detain suspects on their "watch lists," without concretely linking them to the particular terrorist conspiracy that has demonstrated its potency. This dragnet will undoubtedly sweep many innocents into detention, but it may well catch a few key actors: disrupting the second strike, saving lots of lives, and deflecting a body blow to the body politic.[8]

This functional argument is entirely compatible with the symbolic aspect of the state of emergency. By declaring a state of emergency, the government is making it plain to its terrorized citizens that it is determined to restore the social contract between them, and by exercising emergency powers, it is taking effective steps to make this promise a reality.

Normalizing Emergency?

There are several ways that the legalist can defend himself against my critique. A first response is to co-opt my point by redesigning the criminal law to incorporate the reassurance rationale. If, as I have suggested, the criminal law is currently conceived in a way that presupposes the exercise of effective sovereignty, let's simply rewrite the criminal code to take into account the shattering need to reassure the public.

This may seem like an especially attractive option in English-speaking countries that are already adept in redefining the elastic crime of conspiracy. During the past generation, the United States redefined conspiracy law to make it a much more supple tool in the battle against organized crime.[9] Why not do the same thing again, and craft a special conspiracy statute that makes it easier to convict suspected terrorists? And while we're at it, why not change the rules for speedy trial and allow prosecutors discretion to keep suspected terrorists in jail for a longer time, on a less compelling evidentiary showing, before they must confront a jury?[10]

I confess that I am no great fan of conspiracy law—its distinctive doctrines already go too far in attenuating principles of individual responsibility that should remain at the core of criminal punishment. But even for those who disagree, the effort to co-opt the reassurance rationale has lots of problems. Most important, criminal law—however redefined—is keyed to the culpability of individual suspects at the time of their alleged offense. If somebody is somehow involved in a terrorist plot, he is guilty whether or not some unrelated group of terrorists has managed to set off a bomb the day before—or is plotting an attack the day after. Since criminality is independent of the decisions of unrelated actors, there is only one way to rewrite the criminal law to take account of the reassurance function: make it easier to prosecute terrorist conspiracies all the time, not only during moments of emergency, by further loosening the definition of conspiratorial involvement, and further weakening procedural safeguards surrounding these prosecutions.

I call this the normalization strategy, because it degrades the generally prevailing standards of criminal justice on the off-chance that terrorists will strike and the public will require extraordinary reassurance. But the moral dangers of this strategy should be obvious: Let us concede that, at times of emergency, it *would* be appropriate to subject people who do X to criminal sanctions. Why should *other* people be swept into the stigmatizing net of criminality during normal times when, by hypothesis, X is *so* removed from any real threat that it isn't appropriate to consider it criminal?

To avoid this repugnant result, it's possible to redefine the crime of conspiracy so as to make it time sensitive. The new statutory definition would make it a crime for anybody to involve himself in actions that have the slightest connection to terrorism, but only immediately after a massive blast. Such time-sensitive definitions don't really represent a radical alternative to my proposal for a state of emergency. They simply import the "state of emergency" into the fabric of the criminal law—but in an awkward way which makes this criminalization of emergency less effective and less just than the kind we will be considering.

There are two problems. Although the time-sensitive statute may cast an extremely broad net, it remains a *criminal* statute, and the Constitution would still require the authorities to come up with probable cause to believe that the suspect has committed the crime. But this places too heavy a burden on the overwhelmed security services immediately after a massive attack. At the same time, criminalization would justify detention for far longer than the forty-five days authorized by my proposal. Rather than giving the authorities simply a decent chance to meet normal legal standards, it would destroy the lives of people who would not ordinarily qualify as criminals at all.

The basic point is similar to my earlier critique of the language of war. If we use war to cover emergencies, we will allow our response to terrorist attacks to become too oppressive for too long. If we expand the definition of crime to cover emergencies, we will succeed in normalizing the oppressive use of the criminal law during periods of relative calm. And if we compensate by bringing in time-sensitive definitions into the criminal law, we will manage to be ineffective and draconian at the same time. We shouldn't be willing to pay this price, especially since an emergency constitution promises a more finely tuned response to the problem of public reassurance in the immediate aftermath of massive attacks.

But Is It Moral?

But all this talk of fine-tuning, I hear my critics reply, is merely a fig leaf concealing an ugly reality: the government, having failed to prevent the attack, is pandering to its terrorized constituents by unleashing the badly embarrassed security services for an indiscriminate dragnet that will predictably sweep thousands of innocents into detention. Even if released after forty-five days, these men and women have been done irreparable harm. Six weeks may seem a short time, but it is long enough to disrupt a life, and to create enormous anguish for friends and family. It is also long enough to stigmatize detainees in the larger community: when they return to work, they will have great trouble convincing fellow employees that the government has made a mistake and that they really aren't terrorists. And some won't be given the chance to explain: they will be fired straight-off by employers who are swept up in the superpatriotic fervor of the moment.

As to the "second strike" rationale, it is a fraud. Time and again, Americans have panicked and cheered their government as it swept thousands into jail during times of crisis, real or imagined. These dragnets have yielded precious little in the end. The story after September 11 is depressingly familiar. Attorney General Ashcroft swept thousands of Muslims into detention after 9/11 without establishing probable cause to believe they were connected with Al Qaeda—holding many incommunicado for months on end. Yet three years after the event, the Justice Department has managed to convict only Zacaraias Moussaoui in connection with September 11, and it has conspicuously failed to indict others on American soil who supported the conspiracy.[11] This dreary story is more or less a repeat of the lessons learned after the scandalous detention of Japanese Americans during the Second World War and of "anarchists" by Attorney General Alexander Palmer in a panic after the First World War.[12]

These emergency dragnets don't really work. They represent a primitive and paranoiac impulse to lash out at convenient scapegoats: nothing more, nothing less. It is just plain silly to disguise this point in the language of legal and moral principle. Let's just admit that sneak attacks bring out the beast in human beings. If there is a case to be made for an emergency statute, we should content ourselves with less pretentious justifications. Perhaps an emergency constitution might well serve as a pragmatic crisis-management device, channeling primitive energies into forms that prevent the slide to tyranny. If so, let's take it seriously; but please, please, no pontificating about the "social contract" and the moral imperative to respond "public affronts to effective sovereignty"!

Despite its hard-nosed appeal, this pragmatic approach is less realistic than it first appears. Most obviously, its casual dismissal of the second-strike rationale is a mistake. Nobody can pretend to certainty about the potential impact of a dragnet: while it may well fail to achieve its mission, it is *perfectly* possible that it will succeed in disrupting the terrorist network at a critical moment. To rule this possibility out of hand is itself a form of escapism that blinds itself to my basic point: a major terrorist attack throws us into a condition of *radical* uncertainty, in which *nobody* can responsibly claim to *know* the risk of a second-strike, much less that a dragnet is *certainly* inefficacious. The mere fact that dragnets have failed on one or another occasion does not imply they will always fail. This is just bad reasoning, unworthy of hardheads.

There are two reasons for thinking that a successful strike increases the risk of a second strike over the next few months. First, if the terrorists are well organized, they will have already prepared a second strike before the first took place, and the longer they wait, the better the chances that they will be discovered. Second, the security services will be thrown off balance by the first strike, but they will gradually regain bureaucratic equilibrium as time goes on. So it will make sense for well-organized terrorists to strike hard and quickly, while Homeland Security is struggling to locate the first set of perpetrators. To be sure, the sweeping detention of suspects on a short-term basis may fail to disrupt the terrorist effort. But it is simply dogmatic to assert that it can't possibly succeed.

I also reject the hardhead's grim view of the human condition. It's true, of course, that a sneak attack brings out the beast in humanity, but it is a half-truth. There is also something noble about the reassertion of effective sovereignty: its refusal to allow terrorism to defeat our hope for a normal life. The emergency constitution is not merely a form of enlightened panic management—though, of course, it is that. It is also an expression of the moral truth that an effective legal order is an essential precondition for civilized life.

We should reject, then, the moral and empirical premises informing the superrealist critique. Nevertheless, when stripped of its hard-boiled pretensions, it does raise a fundamental moral challenge. Quite simply, is it categorically wrong to throw so many innocent people into temporary detention on the mere off-chance that it will disrupt a second strike?

The Case for Compensation

This is hardly the only occasion upon which the state imposes heavy, and arbitrary, burdens. The military draft is an obvious example, especially one in which a lottery is used to select draftees from a larger pool. But given my distaste for war metaphors, I want to explore the moral problem by introducing a less question-begging thought experiment: the case of an emergency medical quarantine.

Suppose that a new killer virus quite possibly has escaped—nobody knows for sure—from a Defense Department laboratory in Fort Detrick, Maryland, and that if it is allowed to spread, the consequences could be a worldwide epidemic, killing millions. In response, public health authorities impose an immediate quarantine on everybody who happens to be within a five-mile radius of the lab at the time of the possible discharge. Motorists and visitors, as well as the men, women, and children unlucky enough to be at home or at work, are immediately denied exit from the quarantine zone and forced into shelters if they have no other place to go.

Given the novelty of the disease, there are no objective tests to determine whether anybody is infected, but the best guess is that the probability is very low. Unfortunately, the disease has a long incubation period—it takes forty-five days before its presence can be scientifically detected—and so tens of thousands of people are stuck in their tracks. Is it *immoral* to impose the quarantine on these unlucky people?

While pondering a reply, consider the obvious analogies to my emergency proposal (we will treat the dis-analogies later): like the quarantine authorities, the security services aren't authorized to act without any grounds for reasonable suspicion that the detainees may cause great harm; but if they are candid, they must acknowledge that the chance of any individual's infection is very low, and that the entire exercise may well turn to be a fool's errand—though for a noble cause. Now that you have made up your mind on the morality of the detention, here is my answer: it depends.

Begin with a quarantine scenario that I would condemn as immoral. There is a serum which, if administered, will greatly reduce the risk of infection. But the government refuses to administer it on the ground that it is "too expensive"—it costs $10,000 a person, the quarantine authority explains, and the extra money can't be found in the budget, especially given the enormous unanticipated costs of caring and feeding tens of thousands of people for forty-five days. The best that can be done, it says, is offer the serum to anybody willing to pay for it out of his own pocket.

This is wrong: once the government has singled out a presumptively innocent group to bear a crushing burden for the common good, it has a special obligation to do all it can to ease the burden, in compensation for the sacrifice.

To refine the point, I want to suggest that the obligation is special: In response to the possible threat coming out of Fort Detrick, the government may or may not choose to provide the serum to residents outside the quarantine area. After all, $10,000 a shot *is* an awful lot of money, and the risk, by hypothesis, is very low. When multiplied by the millions and millions of potentially affected people, it may well make sense to spend billions of dollars on other worthwhile projects. But cost-benefit analysis is categorically inappropriate when applied to the detainees: if they are asked to make a special sacrifice to reduce the risk to others, others have a special obligation to reduce the harm that the detainees will suffer. They must be made whole, to the fullest extent of our collective ability.

This point is increasingly recognized in existing practice. American policy takes special steps to assure that people in quarantine get all necessary services including "psychological support . . . and care for family members."[13] Some countries go further: During a recent outbreak of SARS, Canada and Taiwan provided financial compensation for the period of the quarantine.[14]

So long as the polity fulfils this obligation, it *is* legitimate for the state to disrupt the detainees' lives by placing them in quarantine.[15] Here is one of many places where the principles of modern liberalism sharply diverge from the doctrines of radical libertarianism that have seen a certain renaissance over the past generation. Liberals, no less than libertarians, place a strong emphasis on the right of each person to define his own path in life—but only as part of a larger vision of liberal community, not as an absolute prerogative of isolated individuals. When communal need is sufficiently compelling, everybody has a duty to do his part, even at great inconvenience.

All this may seem pretty obvious.[16] But it is worthwhile to belabor the point, since it may seem a good deal less obvious when the same principles are applied to our present problem. No less than medical quarantine, emergency detention will disrupt the lives of thousands to reduce the risk posed to millions. No less than during quarantine, the state must make the detainees whole as a condition for disrupting their lives. Public morality requires both a substantial money payment for each day spent in jail and an affirmative effort, upon release, to convince the skeptical public that it should not treat the detainees as presumptive pariahs—that, to the contrary, they are entitled to the presumption of innocence, just like the rest of us.

And yet, as the response to September 11 suggests, the public and politicians find it hard to live up to this elementary demand of justice. While Congress granted generous payments for the families of victims of the World Trade Center and the Pentagon (as it should), it has done nothing at all for those caught up in the Ashcroft dragnets.[17] To be sure, the families of terrorist victims suffer terrible permanent losses, while the detainees' lives are disrupted only temporarily. But a sudden seizure is a traumatic experience, especially when you know you have done nothing wrong. Nevertheless, Congress didn't even consider compensating the detainees caught up in the aftermath of the terrorist attack.

The Need for Reform

This moral blindness is typical. It took almost half a century before the Japanese Americans detained during World War II obtained financial compensation, and then only by a special act of Congress that awarded laughably tiny sums.[18]

Such callousness suggests a deeper distortion in our constitutional law. When a small piece of property is taken by the government to build a new highway, the owner is constitutionally guaranteed fair-market compensation, even if this is a trivial sum. The basic logic here is identical to the moral reasoning we have explored: when somebody is asked to bear an arbitrary burden for the public good, he has a special claim upon the rest of us.[19]

This moral point has been blocked by a narrow reading of the constitutional text: the Supreme Court has read the Fifth Amendment's compensation requirement for "private property" to include only the taking of physical objects, not the time and energy of human beings, let alone their basic claim to dignity. Yet "property" is a notoriously expansive term—John Locke believed that "property" embraced claims to life as well as to more conventional objects, and it wouldn't take a legal genius to make a similar move in the twenty-first century.[20] Curiously, the Supreme Court has never ruled squarely on this matter, which positively begs for test-case litigation.[21]

But our emergency constitution should explicitly require compensation, and not leave this matter of morality to the judges. It should guarantee each detainee a substantial payment for every day that his life has been disrupted for the greater good—say $500 a day. This demand is based on elementary principles of justice, but it will also have a desirable impact on the relevant bureaucracies. The emergency administration should be obliged to pay these costs out of its own budget, and this prospect will concentrate the bureaucratic mind on what is most vital in a democracy. The arbitrary stockpiling of suspects in prison will come with a price, and one that all of us will pay in taxes. The security forces will have new incentives to spend time and energy determining who has been snared by mistake.[22]

During the forty-five-day detention period, the emergency authority will have powerful incentives to search for further evidence of guilt. The strict deadline also fosters steadfast and diligent work toward a defined end state—forty-five days, and not a day longer, unless the authority comes up with evidence that satisfies the normal standards of the criminal law. When the government succeeds in sustaining this burden, the case for compensation becomes more complex. Once the detainees have been transferred to the criminal justice system, some will be convicted, but others will establish their innocence—and this, of course, should matter decisively on the compensation question.

The guilty should be denied all payments, but a tougher question is posed when, after a lengthy criminal trial, suspects are found innocent of terrorist complicity. These men and women can also make a strong moral case for compensation. As they spend months in prison awaiting trial, they suffer even greater losses than detainees discharged after forty-five days. But the criminal law has only slowly recognized the need for compensating the innocent, and then only in the most extreme cases. For example, convicted criminals can sometimes produce irrefutable evidence of their innocence after serving years in jail—in this era of DNA testing, this has become a distressingly frequent occurrence. In both Europe and the United States, there has been a broad recognition that such obvious miscarriages of justice require compensation.[23] For example, Congress has recently authorized payments of up to $100,000 a year to those falsely convicted of crime, encouraging the states to do likewise.[24] Yet there has been no equivalent appreciation of the need to compensate criminal suspects who aren't falsely convicted but simply spend months in jail before they are acquitted by a jury.

A serious discussion of an emergency constitution should encourage a vigorous debate on this larger subject. Surely it would be arbitrary for innocent people to get $22,500 for their first forty-five days in emergency detention and then get nothing extra if they are held in criminal custody for six months before a jury gets the chance to proclaim their innocence.[25] Congress should take the occasion to rethink its current compensation practices in regard to crime, and to make them much more generous.

Even without this broader reassessment, the special case raised by emergency detainees remains compelling. In contrast to the ordinary criminal defendant, these men and women have *never* been given the chance to contest their detention, let alone establish their innocence, under the traditional standards of due process—and when the state was put to the test after forty-five days, it wasn't equal to the task and was obliged to set them free for want of evidence. These people have been sacrificed for the common good in a special way. They should not be treated with the same callous indifference that America too often displays to those caught up in the criminal justice system.

Against Melodrama

Only one major thinker of the twentieth century treated emergencies as a central theme—and he, alas, turned out to be a Nazi. Carl Schmitt used the state of emergency as a battering ram against liberal democracy. On his melodramatic view, it represented the great moment of truth, in which the Supreme Leader suspended the law to reveal that the basis of authority was nothing other than His Overriding Will.[26] Though Nazism is dead as a political force, Schmitt's ideas cast a long shadow, making it seem almost obvious that the "state of emergency" is a lawless condition, in which ordinary political morality doesn't apply. At these moments of supreme peril in the life of the state, the law goes silent and the only serious question for serious people is: whose will to power shall triumph?

I do not doubt that there are such moments of supreme existential crisis. Just as the Axis powers threatened the political existence of the United States during World War II, so too the Civil War represented an internal threat—and we have seen both Roosevelt and Lincoln responding with truly extraordinary measures.

My point is that we are not living in one of those times. While terrorists *will* challenge the effective sovereignty of the state, they do *not* threaten to replace our political society with an alien power, which was precisely Hitler's aim; nor will they split it apart, as Jefferson Davis hoped. The threat posed by Osama and his successors is quite different— by assaulting our confident sense of sovereignty, they want us to destroy ourselves, throwing away our priceless heritage of liberal democracy in a panic cycle leading to authoritarianism.[27]

Within this context, the state of emergency isn't a way of suspending law and political morality. It is a way of expressing law and morality in a distinctive key, guided by special principles. The limits of these principles define the limits of the state of emergency. On the one hand, the reassurance function authorizes a short-term period of emergency detention— only long enough to allow the security services to regain equilibrium after a terrorist attack, so that they may gather sufficient evidence that will satisfy the criminal law of the merit of their reasonable suspicions. On the other hand, the principle of just compensation operates in a particularly compelling way to redress the inevitable injustices generated by the emergency response to the crisis.

We must build a new emergency constitution, but with modest expectations. If terrorist attacks become too frequent, no legal structure will save us from a civil liberties disaster. I do not suppose, for example, that clever constitutional design will suffice to constrain the repressive forces that may be unleashed by a Palestinian intifada that continues at its present intensity for years and years.[28] My proposals make the most sense for societies afflicted by episodic terrorism—where events like September 11 remain exceptional, and do not occur so often that the forces of unreason overwhelm even the best-laid plans to keep them in check.

Crystal balls are notoriously unreliable, but as I write these lines in the year 2006, episodic terrorism seems to be the most likely fate of the West in general, and America in particular, for a very long time to come. But thus far, our legal response to this prospect has been remarkably one-sided. We have spent enormous time and energy enacting bill after bill in an effort to reassure ourselves that we will prevent the next attack: the Patriot Act, the Homeland Security Act, the Intelligence Reform Act, and on and on.

But we have done nothing serious when it comes to confronting the inevitability of occasional failure and the episodic panics that are sure to come. It is here where constitutional structures can perform a crucial channeling function. Bad structures will channel temporary needs for reassurance into permanent restrictions on liberty; good structures will channel them into temporary states of emergency, without permanent damage to fundamental freedoms.

The trick is to tell the difference.

3

THIS IS AN EMERGENCY

I know that some people question if America is really in a war at all. They view terrorism more as a crime, a problem to be solved mainly with law enforcement and indictments. After the World Trade Center was first attacked in 1993, some of the guilty were indicted and tried and convicted, and sent to prison. But the matter was not settled. The terrorists were still training and plotting in other nations, and drawing up more ambitious plans. After the chaos and carnage of September the 11th, it is not enough to serve our enemies with legal papers. The terrorists and their supporters declared war on the United States, and war is what they got. [Applause.]

—President George W. Bush, State of the Union, January 20, 2004

No applause from me. I urge you to reject the president's false dichotomy and consider a different way of responding to the next terrorist strike: declare a temporary state of emergency, and wait for the smoke to clear before taking further action that may, or may not, include a decision to take the country to war against a rogue state.

But I have developed only the first stage of my thesis. Even if a state of emergency might, in principle, serve as a third way between "war" and "crime," a host of more practical objections loom. Legislative innovation is a tricky business. Although there is no denying the difficulties of our present legal situation, my shiny new solution might make matters worse. A statutory framework for emergency powers may contain serious blunders that will be difficult to change once solemnly enacted into law. The problem would be compounded if the framework were enshrined in the Constitution itself.

Putting aside the real danger of serious mistakes, an elaborate structure may increase the frequency with which the president makes use of extraordinary powers. The government now handles the overwhelming majority of disturbing events within the traditional framework of the criminal law. But the new machinery will normalize the rhetoric of emergency, making extraordinary powers part of ordinary politics. If you build it, they will come—once the emergency constitution is in place, the president may use it to handle middling crises, further extending his authoritarian reach. Worse yet, the new structure may not eliminate the president's propensity to abuse his war powers.

The result of all our labors may be the worst of all possible worlds: the president continues to indulge aggressive war talk against terrorists while exercising his new emergency powers against druglords and Mafiosi and other "forces of evil." At the end of the day, we may see a further dramatic erosion of the protections afforded by the traditional criminal law. All things considered, isn't it best to leave well enough alone?

Perhaps. But this chapter aims to shake up the complacencies that underwrite these predictable skepticisms. Our traditional ways of dealing with crises made sense when America was protected by two vast oceans. They are radically deficient in the high-tech twenty-first century. In this brave new world, our existing legal regime will respond to repeated terrorist attacks in predictably pathological ways, discriminating against the most vulnerable among us.

As we cast about for new solutions, another danger looms: the mindless imitation of one or another foreign model. It is only prudent to cast our eyes abroad in search of good ideas. The Atlantic and Pacific may have served this country as great safeguards over the past two centuries, but many leading nations have enjoyed no such luxury. Most states have been surrounded by potentially hostile powers, which have been eager to support domestic upheavals when it served their interest. As a consequence, they have had much painful experience with states of emergency. And as the world has made its great turn to liberal democracy over the past half-century, many modern constitutions have sought to distill their nation's sobering experiences in complex set of provisions that may provide us with ideas on the best way to handle emergencies. Shouldn't we learn from this experience?

Yes, but the collective fund of modern constitutional lore has surprisingly little to teach, and for a simple reason. Almost all of it deals with threats to the very existence of the state—yet this isn't the problem we confront today. Rather than responding to an existential threat, the challenge is to craft a distinctive framework that confronts the special problems of reassurance arising in the aftermath of a terrorist strike.

There is no country on earth that can afford to stick with its familiar ways. We need intercontinental dialogue, but by participants who recognize that minor variations on their traditional answers won't be enough. We must help each other confront the genuinely distinctive implications of the terrorist problem, which won't be going away any time soon. To start an international dialogue, I begin with the weaknesses of the American tradition, then turn to those characteristic of other Western constitutions.

Judicial Management?

The U.S. Constitution contains a rudimentary emergency provision, permitting the suspension of habeas corpus "when in Cases of Rebellion or Invasion the public Safety may require it."[1] But it leaves the rest to the judicial imagination, and over the years, the courts have responded with contradictory precedents that leave the extent of emergency powers in great uncertainty. Rather than yearning for greater clarity, should we, perhaps, learn to cherish the clouds of obscurity that presently obscure the legal horizon?

According to apologists, the present fog creates the perfect environment for the intelligent judicial management of crises—enabling the courts to deter too easy a recourse to emergency powers during normal times, while allowing politicians leeway when the going gets really tough. On this benign view, the ambiguous state of the precedents allows judges and other sages of the law to regale themselves with remarkably astringent commentaries on the use of extraordinary powers, cautioning all and sundry that they are unconstitutional except under the most dire circumstances. This creates a cloud of suspicion and restrains officials who might otherwise resort to emergency powers too readily.

Then, when a real crisis hits, judges can display remarkable flexibility for the interim, while covering their tracks with confusing dicta and occasional restrictive holdings. As the crisis abates, the legal community can inaugurate a period of agonizing reappraisal, casting doubt upon the constitutional propriety of the courts' momentary permissiveness. After a revisionist decade or three, the oracles of the law can return to their older habit of casting aspersions on the entire idea of emergency powers—leading to an atmosphere of genuine restraint, until the next real crisis comes around.[2]

So why not let this time-tested cycle of judicial management continue? If it was good enough for the twentieth century, why not the twenty-first? Because it presupposes a lucky society in which serious emergencies arise very infrequently—once or twice in a lifetime. This was more or less true in America in the past. Perhaps it was also true of the island polity of Great Britain from which our judicial tradition derives. But this premise is no longer valid. The realities of globalization, mass transportation, and miniaturization of weapons of destruction suggest that bombs will go off too frequently for the judicial cycle to manage crises effectively.

The Internment of Japanese Americans

The cycle of legal response to President Roosevelt's wartime decision to order the massive internment of 120,000 Japanese Americans provides a revealing example of both the strengths and limits of a judge-centered approach.[3]

Two months after Pearl Harbor, the nation was fighting for its very existence when the president, acting as commander in chief, issued an order authorizing military commanders to exclude residents of Japanese origin from their districts at their "discretion."[4] A month later, Congress confirmed Roosevelt's decision by enacting a statute making it a crime to disobey a commander's exclusion orders, setting the legal stage for a series of commands ordering all Japanese living on the West Coast to leave the potential invasion zone.[5]

Once they left their homes, where were they to go? Anti-Japanese sentiment was at fever pitch, and the governors of other states lobbied fiercely to prevent the refugees from entering their territory.[6] Their protests were effective, and the president created a War Relocation Authority to establish detention centers, where internees remained in the "constructive custody" of the relevant military commanders.[7] By October 1942 these camps already contained about one hundred thousand men, women, and children.[8] In contrast to the current war on terror, Roosevelt's War Relocation Authority quickly established procedures to separate loyal from disloyal citizens and to arrange for the release of the innocent.[9] But once again, intense wartime hostility slowed releases down. Once cleared of suspicion, detainees were not allowed to leave the camps until they satisfied the authority that they could find an appropriate place to live. And this proved difficult to do, though twenty thousand detainees were allowed to leave each year during 1943 and 1944.[10]

By this point, two legal challenges had reached the Supreme Court.[11] Fred Korematsu refused to obey the removal order, remaining on the West Coast until arrested and convicted at a criminal trial; Mitsuye Endo obeyed, but after establishing her loyalty to the authority's satisfaction, she went to court to protest its refusal to allow her to leave the detention camp until she could find some place willing to take her.

The Court decided the cases on the same day in 1944, and its treatment displayed a good deal of the subtlety prized by partisans of the model of judicial management. Speaking for a unanimous bench, Justice William O. Douglas granted Endo her immediate freedom, but he did not make large pronouncements on the constitutional issues. Instead, he (somewhat disingenuously) claimed that the president's orders themselves required Endo's release. On Douglas's view, Roosevelt was simply trying to protect the "war effort against espionage and sabotage," and once Endo had established her loyalty, the president's order provided no legal basis for further detention.[12] Like any other citizen, she had the legal right to move freely around the country, without the permission of Big Brother.

A clear decision, but a legally cautious one, since it didn't do anything more than interpret the president's text in a way that favored the cause of freedom. Nevertheless, *Endo* did serve to place a certain limit on the Court's emphatic support of presidential power in *Korematsu*. Speaking for a 6–3 majority, Justice Hugo Black rejected Korematsu's challenge to the military's sweeping exclusion orders. He conceded that "all legal restrictions which curtail the civil rights of a single racial group are imme-

THIS IS AN EMERGENCY   63

diately suspect." But he refused to question the military judgment that an invasion was possible:

> We cannot reject as unfounded the judgment of the military authorities and of Congress that there were disloyal members of that population, whose number and strength could not be precisely and quickly ascertained. We cannot say that the war-making branches of the Government did not have ground for believing that in a critical hour such persons could not readily be isolated and separately dealt with, and constituted a menace to the national defense and safety, which demanded that prompt and adequate measures be taken to guard against it.[13]

Korematsu serves as a paradigm case representing the "permissive" moment in the cycle of judicial management. It was followed by decades of revisionist activity that support the traditionalist's confidence in the recuperative powers of the legal order. By the 1980s it was hard to find a constitutional commentator with a good word to say about *Korematsu*.[14] Governmental institutions also responded to a broader change in public opinion. President Gerald Ford symbolically rescinded President Roosevelt's order authorizing the wartime detention in 1976, and Congress finally granted compensation to inmates of the camps in 1988.[15]

Nevertheless, the case was never formally overruled, a fact that has begun to matter after September 11.[16] Even today the case remains under a cloud. It is bad law, very bad law, *very, very* bad law: Roosevelt should never have allowed wartime hatreds to sweep an entire racial group into internment camps, without *any* individualized showing of collaboration with the enemy. But what will we say after another terrorist attack? More precisely, what will the Supreme Court say if Arab Americans are herded into internment camps? Are we absolutely certain that the wartime precedent of *Korematsu* will not be extended to the "war on terrorism"?[17]

Perhaps not, confesses the traditionalist, but isn't this precisely the genius of judicial management? The legal fog is sufficiently obscure so that the president knows that sweeping emergency actions are under a cloud: the courts may well strike down his actions, but then again, they may not if the situation appears really serious. Isn't this precisely the kind of flexibility that the commander in chief should have?

Penetrating the Fog

If we play out the judicial scenario further, we may become skeptical about placing all our bets on the courts. To give the traditionalists their due, I am happy to suppose that the Supreme Court uses *Padilla,* or some other case, to contain the corrosively permissive logic it developed for battlefield seizures in *Hamdi.*

But it does so in characteristically foggy fashion. Some justices denounce the president's assertion of power as flatly unconstitutional. Others write more cautiously: they avoid large constitutional pronunciamentos and state that the president's actions were not authorized under existing legislation. Maybe one or two dissent, denouncing their brethren for hobbling the president's capacity to wage the war on terror. Despite September 11, the Court does save us from our worst impulses, but the legal fog endures, leaving our constitutional future obscure.

But this time the recuperative phase of the judicial cycle is rudely interrupted by the terrorist attack of 2010, and then another in 2014. As the president makes new appointments to the Supreme Court, more and more justices become increasingly appreciative of the powers of the commander in chief. Slowly but surely, the legal fog lifts and the authoritarian powers of the president are revealed for all to see. Armed with these judicial opinions, almost any president will fiercely fight any effort by Congress to rein in his unilateral authority. We are well down the path to tyranny.

I may be too pessimistic: the courts may not falter, even after two or three or five terrorist strikes. Nevertheless, the risks are very real, and it is folly to suppose that *Korematsu*'s happy ending will repeat itself. Instead of trusting in the recuperative capacities of judge-made law, it seems wiser to consider a fundamental change in approach—one that adds a system of political checks and balances to the system of judicial constraints.

We may be reaching a propitious moment for reconsideration. Perhaps the Supreme Court will thwart the government's desperate efforts to avoid review in *Padilla* and use the case to announce strict limits on presidential power. Nothing could contribute more to national sobriety than a majority opinion that drew a clear constitutional line between the total wars of the past and the antiterrorist campaigns of the future. If the Court reined in the president, he would rapidly become a principal spokesman for a new statute creating a framework for emergency powers. With executive unilateralism closed off by the Court, Congressional authorization would suddenly provide the president with his only short-run hope of gaining extraordinary powers in the aftermath of a terrorist attack on American soil.

But even then, statecraft won't come easily. With the president on the legislative offensive, civil libertarians will predictably resist. If the justices reject presidential unilateralism in the Padilla case, civil libertarians will proceed to call for another round of heroic resistance to any congressional effort to create an emergency framework. To personalize their strategic point: "See Bruce, we told you so, Americans *can* count on the Court when the going gets rough. Now that the justices have held firm, it's silly to compromise our great victory by accepting the legitimacy of emergency powers. After all, what's wrong with the old-fashioned notion that everybody *always* has the right to demand *all* the hard-won constitutional protections proffered by the traditional criminal law? So let us fight onward in defense of the courts and liberty!"

I have already explained why an exclusive reliance on the criminal law is wrong in principle. But there is more than principle involved here: once the president and Congress make emergency legislation a high priority, they might well make a mess of it—rather than coming up with a carefully controlled framework, they might transform the measure into a sweeping authorization of all sorts of abominable practices. Perhaps my belief that American politicians can resist the politics of fear, even during relatively calm moments, is nothing more than ivory-tower fantasy.

We are dealing in imponderables, and thoughtful people will ponder the imponderable differently. Truth to tell, I don't even want to convince all my critics that they are wrong in fearing the worst, since a good statute will emerge only if civil libertarians fight hard against the predictable efforts by the White House to get Congress to write the president a blank check. Fierce resistance against an overly powerful presidency is an absolutely essential part of the play of political forces that may yield a satisfactory statute.

As will become clear, I have no intention of ousting the courts entirely from the management of emergencies or the guarantee of due process.

The question, instead, is whether we can design a structure that engages the courts, the president, and the Congress in a joint endeavor that—for all its predictable tensions—will generate a more resilient response to the episodic shocks that surely will shake us in the future.

Before confronting that problem head-on, let me pause to consider whether and how other constitutional traditions can contribute to its solution.

A Broader View

Americans have relied on the courts, which tend to deny that emergency powers exist—except, of course, when they change their minds. Many other Western constitutions do the opposite. They forthrightly proclaim the existence of emergency powers but then try to control the exercise of those powers through elaborate constitutional texts. They rely less on judicial creativity, more on the judgments of executives and legislatures, to keep extraordinary powers under control.

This orienting contrast is intriguing, and Americans should certainly consider whether their security situation has become more similar to that confronting most other nations—and consider what our friends have to say. While the Founders could count on a great ocean for protection, this no longer makes sense in a globalizing hi-tech world. It may no longer be sensible for a Constitution to make the briefest mention of emergency powers. Perhaps it is time for America to take a lead from the rising democracies throughout the world which treat the emergency constitution as a basic element in their overall design.

Yet it would be a mistake to go further and suppose that more modern constitutions have already answered the questions posed by modern terrorism. Their provisions for states of emergency have been shaped by their historical experience with very different sorts of crises. The twentieth century was an age of war and revolution, and understandably enough, these existential threats organized contemporary thinking about emergency. Rather than focusing on the need for reassurance in the aftermath of terrorist attacks, modern constitutions consider the very same sorts of problems that the United States confronted during the darkest hours of the Civil War and World War II.

Beyond the French Model

From this perspective, the French Constitution takes the same position that Lincoln and Roosevelt adopted during their moments of existential crisis. It grants the French president unilateral authority to declare an emergency, without conceding a supervisory role to the courts. Interestingly, though, it creates a more subtle dynamic that does involve the French Constitutional Court. Before declaring an emergency, the president must consult with the Court, which responds by issuing an advisory opinion that must be published to the general public. If the Court advises against the emergency declaration, the president can disregard its views—but a dissenting opinion will catalyze public opposition, serving as a (weak) check on an abusive use of power. Nevertheless, this interesting innovation should not divert us from the main point: not only is the French president free to declare an emergency, but he also is free to take "the measures required by these circumstances." The French Constitution refuses to declare anything off-limits during the struggle for survival.[18]

As in all such cases, these provisions are deeply rooted in national history—they express the theories and practice of Charles de Gaulle during the birth agony of the Fifth Republic. When considered on its merits, de Gaulle's approach is undoubtedly extreme. Nevertheless, it can't be categorically rejected when a nation is struggling for its very political existence. A constitution's framers simply cannot know the details of the particular scenarios that may threaten the life of the republic. Given their inevitable ignorance, it is hardly irrational to give broad discretion to the president. Any effort to impose legalistic restrictions might deprive the government of the very tools it needs to take effective action at its moment of truth.[19]

Nevertheless, French-style emergency regimes are *categorically* inappropriate for the terrorist threats of the twenty-first century. Government will not disintegrate in the face of a terrorist attack. There is a need to respond to the terrorists' breach of effective sovereignty, but not by giving the government carte blanche. To the contrary: the aim is to reassure the public by moving aggressively against a second strike *without* allowing the president to damage civil and political liberties on a permanent basis. Our constitutional problem is not that the government will be too weak in the short run but that it will be too strong in the long run.

This diagnosis sets a different challenge for constitutional design. If emergency powers are designed to assure the survival of the state, worrying too much about the long-run fate of civil and political liberties seems a great luxury: if the constitutional order disintegrates, it will be up to somebody else to worry about the long run. But if emergency powers are designed to reassure the public that a terrorist attack is only a temporary breach of effective sovereignty, we are operating on very different terrain. We can suppose that the regime is going to stagger onward, and the challenge is to provide the government with the tools for an effective short-run response without doing long-run damage. The last thing we want is to authorize the president to do whatever he considers necessary for as long as he thinks appropriate. This makes it far too easy for him to transform the panic following a horrific attack into an engine of sustained authoritarian rule and bureaucratic repression.

The French model is a nonstarter, but other the solutions designed by other leading countries can't be dismissed so easily. The modern German Constitution, for example, refuses to grant sweeping powers even under the most apocalyptic conditions—reflecting the catastrophic role that the Weimar Constitution's broad emergency provisions played in the Nazi ascent to power in the 1930s.[20] More recently, Poland and South Africa have reacted similarly to their disastrous experiences with long-term states of emergency under authoritarian regimes. Their new democratic constitutions retain a role for emergency power but explicitly enumerate a formidable set of fundamental rights that must be respected during crises.[21] They also experiment with innovative devices that speed the return to normalcy and restrict the emergency regime to its period of imperative necessity.

Some of these ideas will prove useful as we proceed, but they were not designed to confront the distinctive threats to effective sovereignty posed by terrorist attacks. They aim at very different targets: in Germany, the fear that the Soviet Union would invade western Europe and turn the country into a battle zone; in Poland and South Africa, the fear of the oppressive emergency regimes established by Polish Communists and South African Nationalists. These are variations on the theme of existential crisis. We can't assume that these provisions make sense when dealing with the episodic breaches of effective sovereignty threatened by modern terrorism. It is tempting, but wrong, mindlessly to carry forward any of these old solutions to the new problem. If older ideas apply, we can find out only after rethinking their relationship to the new challenge of reassuring the public that the government is acting decisively to prevent second strikes.

The British Tragedy

So muddling through isn't a sensible option on either side of the Atlantic. Americans should rethink their reliance on courts; other democratic countries should rethink their existing emergency constitutions. There is no better way to punctuate this conclusion by taking a glance at the United Kingdom, the world champion at muddling through. During the twentieth century, Britain's constitution has been noteworthy for its disdain for elaborate constitutional checks and balances. It has relied instead on the common sense and decency of statesmen and citizens to yield sound conclusions. The British have been happy to let others engage in fancy constitutional theorizing; practical statesmanship was more than good enough for them.

This no-nonsense approach has many attractions, but it has led to an unmitigated disaster when it comes to emergency powers. The British lapse can't be chalked up to a sudden decline in the quality of British leaders. To the contrary, Tony Blair has been the most substantial Western statesman of the past decade. And yet within three months of the terrorist attack on the United States, the Blair government enacted a statute that makes the Patriot Act seem mild by comparison.[22] Though parliamentary reconsideration has eliminated some of the worst abuses, the London bombings in July 2005 promise to unleash yet another cycle of repressive legislation.

Under current British law, there is no need to accuse a suspected terrorist of a crime to strip him of his liberty.[23] The Prevention of Terrorism Act dispenses with a traditional trial by jury, as well as with the need to prove guilt beyond "reasonable doubt."[24] The government must only convince a judge—not a jury—that the detainee is *probably* a terrorist.[25] Worse yet, the suspect can't learn all the evidence against him. The government can persuade the judge to hide key assertions in a confidential file, which is kept from both the suspect and his lawyer.[26] To safeguard the defendant's interests, the law creates a very small corps of special advocates, with security clearances, who can gain access to the file but can't tell the suspect what they have seen.[27] Little wonder that a couple of advocates have resigned in disgust, since it's awfully hard to defend your client when he can't help you pick holes in the state's evidence.[28]

As compensation for this utter failure in due process, the accused terrorist gains one advantage over the typical criminal defendant: he can't be thrown in jail. But he can be confined under house arrest, with his movements and access to the larger world kept under tight control; or, if the government is in a gentle mood, it may merely place him under curfew, or limit his access to means of communication, or deny him contact with other suspects, or subject him to electronic tagging, so that Big Brother can follow his every movement.[29]

This goes on for six months; but the six-month term can be extended again and again, so long as the same procedural charade is repeated. The image is reminiscent of a famous Kafka parable: the so-called "terrorist" may be confined at home indefinitely, as he shadow-boxes against evidence that he isn't allowed to see, all the while protesting his innocence but never getting a satisfactory answer as he waits and waits, until he dies, when the guard finally closes the door at which he was waiting, explaining that it had been kept open to maintain an illusion of freedom.[30]

And this is *England,* motherland of liberty; and this is England, a place that wasn't even attacked on September II. And when London was bombed in July 2005, the government responded with another cycle of repressive legislation. Its initiative criminalizes a broad class of "acts preparatory to terrorism"—an especially treacherous notion since the British definition of "terrorism" sweeps so broadly. Worse yet, the new legislation transforms a broad range of political activities into crimes against the state. Britain already criminalizes the "direct" incitement of terrorism, and this is perfectly appropriate: if somebody clearly encourages another to engage in a *particular* bomb plot, he certainly should be punished. But this is not enough for the Blair government. It has now made "indirect incitement" into a serious crime: Anybody who "glorifies, exalts, or celebrates" the commission of a terrorist act will face a five year prison term.[31]

This means that any spokesman for the Muslim community faces serious prison time if a jury finds that he has spoken out too emphatically on behalf of his constituents. The government has also struck a blow against the Muslim community's bookstores, threatening a seven-year sentence against anybody who distributes a "terrorist publication" that engages in "indirect incitement."[32] Blair overreached, however, in demanding authority to detain suspects for ninety days without producing *any* evidence of their guilt. When his own backbenchers rebelled, he was forced to cut back the ninety days to twenty-eight. This reduction should be applauded, but the fact remains that lengthy periods of arbitrary detention are now becoming a part of ordinary British life.[33]

All this, it should be emphasized, is occurring in response to a terrorist assault that pales in comparison with September 11, let alone the massive attacks of the future, where tens of thousands of innocents may be destroyed in a single blast. If this is the British response to bombs that killed fewer than one hundred Londoners, how will some future government respond to a truly devastating assault? After all, existing law *already* authorizes house arrest for anybody who is "probably" a terrorist. Why not lower the standard further to authorize indefinite detention on the basis of "reasonable suspicion"? And why stop at house arrest—why not throw these supposed terrorists into prison?

It won't be enough for the British to rely on their famed common sense and human decency to reject ever-harsher measures. The current laws already offend decency and violate the fundamental rights to fair process enshrined by the European Convention on Human Rights. But this didn't prevent their enactment. The British government simply invoked its prerogative, granted by the Convention, to enact measures that derogate from fundamental rights "in time of war or other public emergency threatening the life of the nation."[34]

The United Kingdom is thus far the only signatory to the European Convention that has publicly exempted itself from its fundamental guarantees in the war on terrorism. Given Britain's proud tradition, however, its actions threaten to set a precedent for others.[35] We should not allow Britain's former greatness to obscure the repressive character of its current response. This sad story should serve as a cautionary tale suggesting the remarkable power of the dynamics of fear and repression let loose by terrorist attacks.

It isn't obvious, of course, that a more elaborate set of constitutional arrangements could have prevented Britain's tragic slide toward a police state.[36] Perhaps an emergency constitution won't be enough to control the cycles of panic that haunt our future. But the British example should encourage us to take our project seriously, to consider how a credible emergency constitution might be constructed and what it might reasonably be expected to accomplish.

From Diagnosis to Prescription

The world is always changing faster than our ideas. When something new and disturbing happens, our first instinct is to rely on received wisdom, and see whether we can muddle our way through to a solution in a more or less satisfactory fashion. This is a healthy reaction—it takes lots of time and energy to come up with new frameworks of thought that will survive the test of collective reflection. And time waits for no man— we must act, and act decisively, to confront unfamiliar dangers with whatever tools we have at hand—"war," "crime," "emergency"—and hope for the best.

But this is only Stage One, and it is time to move on to Stage Two. Rather than throwing old ideas at newish problems, let's define the problem as clearly as we can and consider whether the old ideas are good enough. That's what I've been trying to do, and the results haven't been too consoling. Calling it a "war" on terrorism encourages presidential warmaking abroad and judicial abdication at home. Calling it a "crime" fails to acknowledge that the criminal law makes sense only if effective sovereignty has already been secured, and that government has a special interest in reassuring its citizens when terrorists succeed in calling this premise into serious question. Calling it an "emergency" gets closer to the point, but our traditions for handling emergencies have been shaped on old-fashioned premises that fail to correspond to terrorist realities: in the English-speaking world, that judges can handle the rare emergency that creates a genuine crisis; in other countries, that the only serious emergencies involve invasions or coups.

All this is distressing: after all, terrorism is a very serious problem, and we can't afford to roll with the punches. Nevertheless, a clear sense of the dangers of muddling through may provide the energy we need for a sustained ascent to Stage Three.

It's too simple to say that Stage Three involves the effort to solve the problem defined at Stage Two, if only because really intransigent problems don't lend themselves to neat and clean "solutions." But at least we can hope to develop better coping strategies once we have grasped more clearly the distinctive character of our problem.

Success here is to be judged in relative terms. Will we do better with a new framework for governing temporary states of emergency, or should we stumble forward with war, crime, and the misshapen notions of emergency already in our tool kit?

The only way to find out is to exercise our constitutional imagination, and see how far it will take us. Maybe not far enough—in which case, we will have no choice but to muddle our way through with the tool kit we have, and hope against hope that we may avoid the dangers that loom in the middle distance.

But perhaps we can take a step or two along the path marked by our Enlightenment Founders, and rework our great constitutional tradition to confront the challenges that lie ahead.

PART

PRESCRIPTION

4

THE POLITICAL CONSTITUTION

The problem is to prevent a second strike; the solution is to declare a temporary state of emergency. But between the problem and the solution lies the challenge: how to design an institutionally credible emergency constitution that will permit an effective short-term response without generating insuperable long-term pathologies?

My answer depends heavily on political checks and balances. This chapter elaborates the system, while the next considers the role of judges in assuring its integrity. I hope to provide operational principles, not blueprints. Particular details are merely illustrative and should not detract from the main point: to see how the emerging whole is larger than the sum of its parts. Though I write against the background of American institutions, the operational principles have a more general reach. They could apply, with appropriate adaptation, to any of the political systems—presidential, semipresidential, parliamentary—prevailing in the contemporary world of liberal democracy.

This isn't true of the concluding chapters, which consider the exceptional features of the American situation. Constitutional amendment is notoriously difficult in the United States, and there is no realistic chance that something as controversial as the emergency constitution would ever be enacted as a formal amendment. This constitutional roadblock does not prevent an effective response. Congress already has the constitutional authority to enact a framework statute that incorporates all the crucial elements of my proposal—or so I shall argue.

This conclusion shouldn't be surprising—the whole point of this essay is to adapt Founding principles of checks and balances to the exigencies of modern life, and it would be odd to learn that the Framers were the principal obstacle to my proposed reinvigoration of their principles. But stranger things have happened, and it is important to show how congressional authority to enact framework legislation is firmly supported both by the constitutional text and leading Supreme Court decisions.

I then devote a chapter to a final American particularity—our shocking failure to provide for the continuity of constitutional government in the event of a decapitating attack on Washington, D.C. Under existing law, a satisfactory Congress may be unable to assemble for months, and the future of the Supreme Court will be very uncertain. Presidential rule by emergency decree may become a necessity—and the acting president might turn out to be the secretary of agriculture. Unless we take corrective action, we will have lawless rule by untested and unknown leaders—just at moment when there is a pressing need for checks and balances to control emergency powers. Once again, it is possible to resolve the most serious problems through the enactment of a framework statute.

What is more, the need for action is so compelling that there is already an ongoing effort in Congress to solve pieces of the puzzle. This is not only good news in itself, but it may serve as an augury of progress on a broader front. Once Congress gets serious about assuring continuity for all four key agencies of the government—House, Senate, presidency, and Court—it may well come to understand that this is only one aspect of the larger problem raised by states of emergency.

Having set down some guideposts on the path from diagnosis to prescription, it's time to push forward with the case for checks and balances.

From Ancient to Modern

The Roman Republic attempted the first great experiment with states of emergency, and it serves as an inspiration for my heavy reliance on the political system for imposing the necessary constraints. At a moment of crisis, the Roman Senate could propose to its ordinary chief executives (the two consuls) that they appoint a dictator to exercise emergency powers. Sometimes the consuls acted jointly; sometimes one was chosen by lot to make the appointment. But in all cases, there was a rigid rule: the appointing official could not select himself. As a consequence, the consuls had every incentive to resist the call for a dictatorship unless it was really necessary. There was a second basic limitation: dictators were limited to six months in office. Their term was not renewable under any circumstances. About ninety dictators were named during the three-hundred-year history of the office, but none violated this rule. And no dictator used his extraordinary powers to name another dictator at the end of his term.[1]

During his six-month tenure, the dictator exercised vast military and police powers, but with a few significant limitations. Most notably, he remained dependent on the Senate for financial resources; he could not exercise civil jurisdiction as a judge (though he did have the power of life and death); and he was charged with suppressing domestic upheaval and protecting against foreign attack, but had no authority to launch offensive wars.[2]

The Roman model was very clever, but it is not practical under modern conditions. In contrast to the Romans, we do not depend on a rotating group of aristocrats exercising executive powers for very short terms. (The consuls rolled over every year.) We depend on a professional political class with a lifetime commitment to public office. We try to select the most seasoned statesman to serve as president or prime minister, and it would be odd to replace him with a temporary substitute just when the going got toughest. If we are lucky enough to have Winston Churchill when we need him, we should rejoice in our good fortune—not push him out for fear of his dictatorial ambitions.

Nevertheless, the Romans were right to search for clever institutional checks on the abusive potential of emergency power. Once we create an elaborate structure authorizing extraordinary action, there is a very real danger that ordinary officials will exploit the system to create too many "emergencies," and to extend them beyond the moment of their imperative necessity. If the Roman system of executive displacement is implausible, are there other checks and balances that will serve similar ends?

The Supermajoritarian Escalator

European nations have had a long and unhappy experience with emergency powers. Over the past two centuries, they have tended to give executives too much unfettered authority, both in declaring emergencies and in continuing them for lengthy periods.[3] As we have seen, this is categorically inappropriate when it comes to coping with terrorist attacks. The executive should be given power to act unilaterally only for the briefest period—long enough for the legislature to convene and consider the matter, but no longer. If the legislature is already in session, one week seems long enough; if not, two weeks is sufficient.[4]

The state of emergency then should expire unless it gains majority approval. But this is only the beginning. Majority support should serve to sustain the emergency for a short time—two or three months. Continuation should require an escalating cascade of supermajorities: 60 percent for the next two months, 70 for the next, and 80 for each subsequent period.

There are matters of principle here, but also issues of institutional design, involving the creation of appropriate political incentives. Principles first. The need for repeated renewal at short intervals serves as a first line of defense against a dangerous normalization of the state of emergency. Each vote publicly marks the regime as provisional, requiring self-conscious approval for limited continuation. Each ballot in the House and Senate requires a debate in which politicians, the press, and the rest of us, are obliged to ask once more: is this state of emergency really necessary?

The supermajoritarian escalator requires further principled commitments. Even if a bare legislative majority repeatedly votes to sustain an extension, this should not be enough to normalize emergency powers: we can never forget that hundreds or thousands are in detention without the evidence normally required, and that dragnets are continuing. The escalator expresses a principled presumption in favor of liberty and permits extensions only when there is growing consensus that they are required—most obviously, when a massive second-strike attack occurs, and the need to prevent another is imperative.

Despite repeated debates in the legislature, regular votes of approval threaten to erode the general sense that emergency powers should be reserved for truly extraordinary crises. By subjecting these decisions to increasing supermajorities, the constitutional order places the extraordinary regime on the path to extinction. As the escalator moves to the 80 percent level, everybody will recognize that the emergency can't last indefinitely. Modern pluralist societies are simply too fragmented to sustain such broad levels of support—unless, of course, the terrorists succeed in striking repeatedly with devastating effect.

The supermajoritarian case becomes even stronger once the dangers of political abuse are taken into account. A "state of emergency" provides a wonderful electioneering tool for the majority party: "All true patriots must rally around the government at the country's hour of need. We cannot give in to the terrorists by allowing them to force us to change our leaders when the going gets tough." This may be blather, but it will bring out the votes. Supermajoritarian escalators give smaller and smaller minority parties veto power over such manipulations. Even if the minority allows the emergency to continue during elections, the majority can no longer easily present itself as the country's savior, since the support of the minority is fundamental in sustaining the extraordinary regime.

The escalator also has a salutary effect on the executive. The president knows that he will have a tough time sustaining supermajorities in the future, and this will lead him to use his powers cautiously. The public will bridle if his underlings run amok, acting in arbitrary ways that go beyond the needs of the situation. So the political check of supermajorities not only makes the emergency regime temporary but makes it milder while it lasts.

It also forces the executive to recognize the injustices imposed by emergency rule. Each terrorist wave will generate a distinctive demonology. Right now, the demons come largely from the Arab world, but twenty years onward, they may emerge from Latin America or China. Or some shadowy band of home-grown terrorists may have adopted a creed, secular or religious, that pushes them down the path of destruction.

Each demonology will mark out segments of the domestic population as the "obvious" target for emergency measures, but the supermajoritarian escalator will give the targeted group some political power to check obvious abuses. This may not operate too forcefully during the present wave, since Arab Americans are a relatively small voting bloc, but it will serve as a more potent check in Europe, given the larger size of its Arab and Islamic minorities. The next terrorist wave may well shift the ethnic distribution of political interests in very surprising directions—forcing the executive to be mindful of unnecessarily alienating substantial segments of society during moments of crisis.

Even when the prevailing demonology casts a relatively small shadow on domestic politics, the supermajority escalator will provide political cover for civil libertarians who are looking for an excuse to call an end to the emergency regime. Immediately after the terrorist strike, they can polish their antiterrorism credentials by voting for the state of emergency when only a simple majority is required. This is the moment for maximum reassurance, and it is overwhelmingly likely that most legislators will support the measure regardless of protests from their libertarian colleagues. So there is no real harm done if the vote is 99–1 rather than 75–25.

As time marches on, contrarian legislators will be accumulating political capital that makes defection easier as the need for reassurance declines: "I have now voted twice to continue the emergency, but enough is enough. I want to commend the president for keeping the situation under control, but now that the situation is stabilizing, we should return to the protection of our normal liberties. If we allow the continued erosion of our freedoms, the terrorists really will have triumphed."[5]

The political dynamic also will shift. As dragnets and curfews begin, some constituents will be bitterly aggrieved by their operation—and after forty-five days, detainees will start emerging to denounce their incarceration. No politician likes to deal with this kind of anger, especially since they won't get rid of it after a single vote to renew. If a second strike does occur, Congress may well take the heat and continue the emergency to reassure the rest of the terrorized population. But the presumption for liberty built into the supermajoritarian escalator will gradually erode support in the absence of clear and present danger. As the escalator rises to 80 percent, and surface calm returns to ordinary life, it is only a matter of time before the next extension fails, and the emergency comes to an end, at least for now.[6]

But won't the escalator give the terrorists a new strategic advantage? They will know when the emergency is scheduled to expire, and this will help them plan their next assault to coincide with the return to normalcy. Won't the escalator only make things worse, not better?

This is a fair question, but I'm unconvinced. First, the counterscenario presupposes a strategic capacity that the terrorists may or may not possess: most fanatics aren't in the habit of inspecting their enemy's statute books. Second, even if they do appreciate the significance of the escalator, it won't tell them what they really want to know: the actual termination of the emergency depends on the president's capacity to build a broad political coalition in Congress, and this often won't be clear until the final votes are taken. And third, even if the terrorists are brilliant political analysts, it still won't be clear that the best move is to strike quickly after the emergency terminates—this will virtually guarantee that a new emergency will gain the support of the requisite supermajority. And then it will be very tough to convince Congress to permit expiration for a long time to come. So it's not very likely that clever terrorists would use the escalator as a trigger for immediate attack; and less savvy ones won't be in a position to strategize at this level of sophistication.

What *is* clear, however, is that it will always be scary to bring the state of emergency to an end. We will never know for sure that the terrorists won't strike. But that's precisely why the escalator is important—there will always be sensible people urging us to wait a little while longer. And if we take their advice, the emergency will go on and on—until the very notion of a free society becomes a distant memory. At some point—and some rather early point—we just have to take our chances and preserve our legacy of freedom.

Minority Control of Information

The supermajoritarian escalator will shorten the state of emergency and soften its administration, but it will not work miracles. After all, the emergency begins with a terrorist attack that deeply embarrasses the nation's military, police, and intelligence services. The political recriminations will be intense: whatever the FBI and CIA did was not enough, or so the critics will claim, and with 20-20 hindsight, it will be easy to find clues that might have alerted hypervigilant guardians of order. The bureaucratic reaction will be swift and predictable: on the one hand, high-ranking actors will try to displace responsibility for past mistakes; on the other, they will strike out aggressively against the forces of evil.

But especially in the beginning, the security services will be thrashing about a good deal. If they had been on top of the conspiracy, they would have intervened beforehand. So they are almost certain to be in the dark during the early days after a terrorist attack. Nevertheless, early dragnets may well be functional, and not only because they provide appropriate television footage for calming public anxieties. While many perfectly innocent people will be swept into the net, the "usual suspects" identified by counterintelligence agencies may contain a few genuine conspirators. If we are lucky, the detention of a few key operators can disrupt existing terrorist networks, reducing the probability of a quick second strike and its spiral of fear.

But a huge number of mistaken detentions is inevitable. The executive will have an enormous political incentive to keep this information secret. Worse yet, the supermajoritarian escalator will only heighten this perverse incentive. Perhaps the president or prime minister can convince his party loyalists to remain faithful when the opposition press generates a public uproar by headlining the worst abuses wreaked upon the most sympathetic victims. But if the emergency regime requires the increasing support of the legislative minority, party loyalty is a nonstarter when it comes to building a broad coalition in support of the emergency. The president's only hope of satisfying the supermajority requirement may lie in treating as top secret all potentially embarrassing facts surrounding the dragnets.

Despite the grave risk of partisan abuse, a simple rule requiring total openness is simpleminded. It is perfectly reasonable to keep some secrets away from the public eye. Terrorists are newspaper readers and Internet surfers like the rest of us, and they can learn a lot about the government's surveillance activities that might allow them to escape detection. Much of this information becomes unreliable rather quickly. News of particular dragnets may pinpoint geographical areas that terrorists should avoid. But investigators change focus frequently, and news no longer has much value a week later. Other information, however, will have more enduring significance. What to report and what to keep secret?

A political system of checks and balances provides distinctive tools for a constructive response. While the executive is in charge of day-to-day affairs, the emergency regime returns to Congress every two months. The legislature cannot act effectively if it is at the mercy of the executive for information. What is more, the state of emergency can survive only with the support of an increasingly large legislative coalition. It follows that the majority party should not be allowed to use its normal control over the legislature to deny information to the minority. To the contrary, our emergency constitution should contain special safeguards to assure that the minority is well informed when it is asked to join in authorizing the next extension of the emergency regime.

I would go further: Members of opposition political parties should be guaranteed the majority of seats on the oversight committees. The chairpersons of these committees should also come from the opposition, though it should not be allowed to select any candidate it likes. Instead, it should be required to offer a slate of three nominees to the majority and allow majority members to pick the chairperson they find least offensive.

Such practices may seem alien to Americans, who take it for granted that the legislative majority should control all committees.[7] But this isn't true in other leading democracies. In Germany, for example, Chancellor Gerhard Schroeder's Social Democratic Party controls a minority of Bundestag committee chairs.[8] Minority control means that the oversight committees will be not lapdogs for the executive but watchdogs for society.[9] They will have a real political interest in aggressive and ongoing investigations into the emergency regime.

The emergency constitution should require the executive to provide the committees with complete and immediate access to all documents. This puts the president and his advisers on notice that they can't keep secrets from key members of the opposition, and it serves as an additional check on the abuse of power. The committee majority, dominated by the political opposition, should also decide how much information should be shared more broadly. This means that information won't be suppressed merely because the government finds it embarrassing. At the same time, the oversight committees won't make everything public—this would open them up to the charge of giving aid and comfort to the terrorists. The point is to provide the minority party with a platform that permits it to display itself as a loyal opposition—keeping the executive honest, putting a floodlight on egregious abuses, but at the same time demonstrating a bipartisan determination to maintain the emergency regime as long as conditions warrant—and foremost, to be a good steward for the nation.

Members of the oversight committee of each house should be explicitly required to give a report to their colleagues, in secret session if necessary, as part of the debate on each two-month extension. Even here, they can hold back particularly sensitive details to reduce the risks of damaging leaks. Nevertheless, they will have every incentive to apprise the majority and minority of the main costs and benefits of continuing the emergency. Legislators, in turn, will have the fundamental right to pass on the main points to the public as they debate and defend their votes.

We have designed a permeable sieve, not an impenetrable wall of secrecy. But that is just the point. In the immediate aftermath of a massive attack, the need for emergency measures may seem self-evident, but their necessity must be continually reassessed as time marches on. An extraordinary regime cannot be allowed to continue for four or six months, or longer, without the *informed* consent of the broader public. Leading members of the opposition are in the best position to appreciate this value. We should leave it to them to play a central gatekeeping role.

This will also allow them to play an increasingly important role in determining the future direction of the emergency effort, and not only whether it should continue. While operational decisions should be left squarely in the hands of the executive, leading cabinet members should be regularly required to justify their priorities before congressional committees. In the aftermath of a major attack, countless risks will loom on the horizon—far too many to handle with the scarce bureaucratic resources at the government's disposal. It will be tempting for the executive to respond by focusing on a few worst-case scenarios without seriously considering whether other greater dangers exist. Hard choices are inevitable, but they should not depend on the accidental order by which one or another bureaucracy comes up with an action plan focusing on one or another catastrophic possibility.

Authoritarians suppose that these tough strategic decisions are best made in secret by a small cadre of like-minded presidential appointees. They are mistaken: this is precisely the setting in which groupthink can lead to a disastrous focus on a few options determined more by personal dynamics and bureaucratic power plays than by reality-based cost-benefit analysis. Executive decision makers, if they are forced to justify their strategic choices to a skeptical and well-informed group of politically savvy outsiders in the House and Senate, will be obliged to anticipate a much broader range of options. And they will have to take the priorities of these outsiders seriously, since they hold the key to a continuation of the emergency.

This doesn't imply that the president will ultimately defer very much to Congress when establishing the operational agenda: he will have lots of cards to play in the ongoing political game. But it does suggest that tough strategic choices will be made against a much broader agenda of possibilities than might have otherwise come to the surface in a small-group setting of like-minded executive officials.

Finally, when the emergency comes to an end, the constitution should require a wide-ranging legislative review, chaired once again by an opposition member with an opposition majority, critiquing the administration of the entire operation. A public report, containing formal recommendations, would be due within a year.

If it is successful, the supermajoritarian escalator will do much more than assure against the indefinite extension of the emergency beyond the period of compelling necessity. It will also encourage greater responsibility by the political opposition in criticizing emergency administration, and greater intelligence by the executive in wielding the extraordinary tools placed at its temporary disposal. But even if the president and the congressional opposition don't rise to the occasion, the escalator's guarantee against a never-ending state of emergency is a good enough reason to make it a key element of any future constitutional framework.

The South African Breakthrough

I have begun with the problem of legislative control because it exposes the most important constitutional weakness of existing practices throughout the world. We have already seen Lincoln justifying his unilateral suspension of habeas corpus at the beginning of the Civil War. The French Constitution is equally explicit, but misguided, in authorizing the president to declare and maintain an emergency unilaterally.

The Germans do better, insisting that a state of emergency gain the support of a simple majority of the Bundestag.[10] However, they don't have any requirement for regular renewal: their Basic Law allows the emergency to continue indefinitely until majorities of both houses of Parliament vote to eliminate it.[11] Broadly speaking this is also true in the new constitutions of central and eastern Europe. Only Russia gives its president unilateral emergency authority.[12] The rest generally require parliamentary consent, and Hungary requires a two-thirds majority before an emergency goes into effect.[13] Countries like Chile, Portugal, and Turkey go further, requiring a regular reauthorization of emergency powers, as proposed in this essay. But these countries don't adopt a supermajoritarian escalator, and so fail to create adequate safeguards against the normalization of emergency conditions.[14]

In contrast, Poland and South Africa deserve special attention, since they confront this problem head-on. Here is Poland's scheme: On recommendation of the Council of Ministers, the president can declare an emergency for a period no longer than ninety days. If he wants a one-time extension, he can obtain sixty more days with the express approval of a majority of the Sejm (the more powerful chamber in Poland's bicameral system).[15] But then the state of emergency *must* come to an end.

This absolute ban on further extensions is rooted in the country's terrible experience of the 1980s.[16] The Communist government responded to the rise of Solidarity with a continuing state of emergency, giving the citizenry a bitter appreciation of the perils of normalizing an extraordinary regime. It only makes sense that their new constitution tries to make a repetition impossible.

But it is never wise to create an absolute barrier between law and life. The current constitution is an invitation to lawlessness. Real-world conditions might create a compelling case for continuing the state of emergency beyond five months. Constitution or no constitution, the president will predictably respond to the commonsense demands of the situation, override the written restriction, and continue the emergency. Is this what we really want?

Yes, say some very distinguished legal scholars. In recent work, Professors Oren Gross and Mark Tushnet recognize that this public break with the rule of law is a desperate expedient.[17] But they argue that it is superior to the normalization of emergency powers once their ongoing use is tolerated by the Constitution. If a president acts lawlessly from time to time, his conduct doesn't corrupt the legal system by creating precedents that endure indefinitely. And when the emergency comes to an end, the lawless officials may find themselves subject to legal liability unless their fellow citizens choose to ratify their actions retroactively.[18]

But, of course, there is a downside. Lawlessness, once publicly embraced, may escalate uncontrollably. By hypothesis, we are dealing with a terrorist strike that has generated mass panic. Once officials make a virtue out of lawlessness, why won't they seek to whip up mass hysteria further and create a permanent regime of arbitrary rule?[19]

Gross and Tushnet offer us a grim choice: legally normalized oppression or a lawless police state. Before placing our bets, it seems wise to reconsider this high-stakes gamble. Undoubtedly, there are times when a political society is struggling for its very survival. But my central thesis is that we are not living in one of these times. Terrorism—as exemplified by the attack on the World Trade Center—does *not* raise an existential threat, at least in the consolidated democracies of the West. If Professors Gross and Tushnet are suggesting otherwise, they are unwitting examples of the imperative need to rethink the prevailing rationale for emergency powers. We must rescue the concept from Nazi thinkers like Carl Schmitt, who used it as a battering ram against liberal democracy. Rather than indulge in melodramatic invocations of existential threats, liberal constitutionalists should view the state of emergency as a crucial tool enabling public reassurance in the short run without creating long-run damage to foundational commitments to freedom and the rule of law.[20]

From this vantage, recent developments in South Africa represent a genuine breakthrough. South Africa during the apartheid era parallels Poland's under Communist rule: each nation suffered bitterly from an ongoing state of emergency.[21] But this experience led to some fresh thinking in South Africa, which has produced the first supermajoritarian escalator in the constitutional world.[22] Under its Constitution, a state of emergency can be introduced with the support of a simple majority of the national assembly, but it must be renewed at three-month intervals by "a supporting vote of at least 60 per cent of the members of the Assembly."[23] To be sure, the escalator takes a simple two-step form—first a simple majority, then 60 percent, without any further upward adjustment. This creates a problem in a country like South Africa, where a single political party regularly wins very large parliamentary majorities: it might be possible to obtain virtually indefinite extensions on party-line votes.[24] Only a more elaborate multistage mechanism can reliably steer the system toward the eventual dissolution of emergency conditions. Nevertheless, I am greatly encouraged by South Africa's example: it is one thing for a theorist, sitting in New Haven, to commend the idea of a supermajoritarian escalator; it is quite another for a constitutional convention, reflecting on its historical experience, to enact the principle into its higher law.

The challenge is to develop the South African idea to its fullest potential and to move onward to elaborate other structural mechanisms for disciplining emergency powers. For example, no established democracy has yet taken a serious step to control the abuse of information by the executive branch during emergency periods. But as we have seen, the supermajoritarian escalator may make it even more tempting for the executive to conceal embarrassing facts. Both in theory and in practice, we are only at the beginning of the process of taming the use of emergency powers by the creative development of checks and balances.

Restricting Emergency Power

Without checks and balances, other forms of restraint aren't worth the paper they are written on. Although the Constitution may contain an impressive set of legalisms limiting emergency power, they won't mean much so long as the president has the sole power to say what they mean. Lawyers are cheap, and the president can always call upon the best and brightest to stretch the legalisms to cover his case. Though opponents may energetically protest, the resulting fog will only serve to perplex the general public—who will be far more impressed by the president's demand for decisive action.

Legal restraints begin to bite only when the Constitution clearly requires the executive to share decision making with others. Perhaps the president can exploit a political panic to gain a single act of legislative consent even when real-world conditions don't qualify under constitutionally applicable standards for an emergency. But this gap between law and the real world will prove to be a serious obstacle if he must repeatedly return to the legislature for increasing shows of supermajority support. Within a short time, the gap between legal requirements and common-sense realities will tend to legitimate legislative resistance and push fence-sitters into the "no" column at voting time. To put the point in a single line: legal restrictions on emergency power can serve only as a comple-ment to, not a substitute for, checks and balances.

Defining the Threshold

So long as this key point is recognized, we can take the next step and ponder the sorts of legalistic limitations that make sense. Begin at the threshold: I have been speaking broadly of "major terrorist attacks," but what precisely does that mean? Should the emergency constitution allow the president and Congress to trigger a state of emergency only if a massive attack has actually occurred? Or should it permit the government to preempt an imminent attack on a finding of "clear and present danger"?

I would insist on an actual attack. A "clear and present danger" test generates unacceptable risks of political manipulation. Presidents and prime ministers receive daily reports from their security services on ter-rorist threats. These risks ebb and flow, but they are always portrayed as serious: How many times has our Department of Homeland Security issued "orange" alerts? Security services have no incentive to play the role of Pangloss. Politicians will never lack bureaucratic reports detecting a "clear and present danger" on the horizon.

These internal security reports will always carry a "top secret" label. The executive will—understandably—be reluctant to share them since they will inevitably reveal the extent to which our spies have penetrated the terrorist network. So how are the rest of us to assess whether there really is a grave danger?

It is fatuous to require the president to go to court and persuade judges that he isn't crying wolf yet again. By the time due process has been observed, the situation will have changed once more, for better or for worse. In contrast, a major terrorist attack is an indisputable reality, beyond the capacity of politicians to manipulate. That's what makes it so scary. And that's why it serves as the best trigger for an emergency regime.

The argument for insisting on an actual attack seems compelling. We come to a tougher question: Attacks come in different sizes—from a single suicide bomber to the nuclear desolation of an entire city. How big an attack should be required? Consider, for example, the terrorist attack on London mass transit in July 7, 2005—more than fifty dead, hundreds injured. The attack generated great anxiety, exacerbated by further incidents in the following weeks. Nevertheless, we all will have to learn to live with attacks on this scale. We cannot let ourselves be hardened by repeated scenes of pointless carnage and grief. We must reach out and respond to the victims of these tragedies—but *not* by rushing to impose the crushing burdens of a state of emergency. These should be reserved for shattering events on a much vaster scale. After all is said and done, London life returned to normal, more or less, within a week or two, of the bombings—with few of the signs of public hysteria characteristic of great panics. This relatively cool response undoubtedly does great credit to British national character, but it is also a function of the scale of the blast: Would Londoners have responded with the same sangfroid if the Houses of Parliament had been destroyed, or twenty-five thousand of their fellows had been killed?

September 11, to my mind, represents the low end for the legitimate imposition of a state of emergency. Small-scale bombings, with traditional technologies, simply don't generate the searing breach of effective sovereignty that makes emergency power seem an appropriate response. If car bombings and the like were the only disturbing events in our future, I would not be writing this book. But the remorseless proliferation of technologies of mass destruction suggests, alas, a grimmer prospect—sometime over the next half-century, some tragedy will occur that makes September 11 into a mere prologue to a new age of terrorist mass destruction. The challenge is to get legally prepared before the next great disaster, without allowing the state of emergency to be trivialized in responding to the low-level bombings that will sadly become part of the background conditions of ordinary life.

Unfortunately, it isn't easy to devise a compelling legal formula that will identify the appropriate triggering event. Some of my friends have suggested that the provision specify a quantitative bright line: "A state of emergency may be proclaimed by the executive in response to a terrorist attack that kills two thousand innocent civilians in a way that threatens the recurrence of more large-scale attacks. The declaration lapses within seven days unless approved by a majority of the legislature." This is the best way, they suggest, to avoid a slippery slope into the normalization of extraordinary powers. They have a point, but I would prefer a legal provision that would explicitly make room for self-consciously political judgment, authorizing an emergency declaration for "terrorist attacks on the scale of those which occurred on September 11, 2001." A president who compared an isolated subway bombing to September 11 would obviously be exaggerating and face a tough time in the legislature if he sought to declare an emergency. The prospect of embarrassing legislative failure should help deter trigger-happy behavior.

The effort to define a legally compelling threshold leads to a larger point. Generally speaking, the world's constitutions deal with all emergencies as if they were essentially alike. The Constitution of South Africa is typical in authorizing a state of emergency when "the life of the nation is threatened by war, invasion, general insurrection, disorder, natural disaster or other public emergency."[25] But this "one size fits all" approach is a mistake. Standards and procedures that may be appropriate when the very existence of the republic is at stake will be too permissive when dealing with terrorist attacks. Emergency constitutions should be multitrack affairs that differentiate among types of threat.

Canada can serve as a good model. Its Emergencies Act distinguishes between four types of condition—natural disasters, threats to public order, international emergencies, and states of war—and treats each separately. For example, terrorist threats to public order require renewal by Parliament every 30 days, while war emergencies require a revote every 120 days—a sensible differentiation, though it would have been even better if Canada also had adopted a supermajoritarian escalator in the terrorist case.[26]

Good ideas come from many places, but no country has yet devised a fully adequate model. The best thing to do is engage in a scavenging operation, searching for gold nuggets wherever we can find them.

Protecting Political Freedom

Another danger of an all-purpose framework is its tendency to conflate crises of political authority with the very different emergencies generated by devastating natural disasters—floods, epidemics, tsunamis, and the like. The recently enacted British Civil Contingencies Act makes this mistake (among many others), defining an emergency to include "an event or situation which threatens serious damage to human welfare . . . to the environment . . . or to the security in the United Kingdom or a Part or region."[27] When the focus is on environment and welfare, it seems reasonable for the British statute to grant emergency powers to "prohibit . . . assemblies of specified kinds, at specified places or at specified times"—such restrictions may well be imperative in halting the spread of epidemics and the like.[28]

But it is quite another matter when it comes to terrorist attacks. As we have seen, the distinctive feature of terrorism is, above all, its *political* challenge: its public affront to the capacity of the state to sustain effective sovereignty over public order. Unless special steps are taken, this political affront is likely to generate an effort at the suppression of the political freedoms of any group that remotely can be viewed as "giving aid and comfort" to the terrorist cause. This destruction of democratic rights is not only wrong in itself; it is fatal to an emergency constitution that crucially depends on a system of political checks and balances. Within this context, a successful effort to repress freedom of debate and assembly strikes at the heart of the central political mechanism for controlling the abuse of emergency power.

Moreover, the case for restricting political freedom is problematic at best. Serious terrorists aren't in the habit of circulating concrete plans in public. So the argument for suppression of political speech is much more indirect. By clamping down on public professions of extremism, the government may prevent the recruitment of impressionable youths into the terrorist cause. And the silencing of the extremists may also provide an opening for more moderate voices in the communities most prone to violence.

These claims are implausible. In the Internet age, radicals have an enormous capacity to reach their audiences—the government censors will be playing a hopeless game of catch-up, as Web sites morph from one day to the next. Ineffective efforts at suppression will serve only to gain attention for the fringe groups, as rebellious youngsters try to find out what all the fuss is about. This perverse dynamic gains further energy when terrorism has roots in religious conviction. Nobody gives up his religious beliefs without a struggle—government censorship only drives extremist groups underground and makes them more attractive to personality types prone to martyrdom.

It is only a matter of time, moreover, before heavy-handed efforts at censorship will strike at entirely legitimate political organizations, generating angry protests from the moderate community—forcing the government either to back down in the face of protest or to muscle its way forward. The second response is sure to alienate many moderate voices that the government was hoping to reinforce. Those supporters who remain loyal to the government will find their position undermined by the radicals who will seek to discredit them as collaborators with a repressive regime.

Terrorist ideology is, of course, the ultimate source of terrorist actions. But full and free debate is a liberal society's best hope against extremism in all its forms. The emergency constitution should hold firm to fundamental legal doctrines forbidding prosecution for advocacy of obnoxious ideas, while authorizing the punishment of speech that plays an instrumental role in concrete criminal conspiracies.[29]

It should also provide relief against more insidious dangers to freedom of political expression. The government will have a great temptation to abuse its emergency powers by restricting the capacity of its political opposition to engage in a wide range of standard activities—especially those involving assemblies of hundreds or thousands, or even tens of thousands. Feigning deep regret, the authorities will assert that the risk of a terrorist bomb is simply too great to allow the demonstration to occur at all—or, more insidiously still, they may seduce the opposition into enjoying a simulacrum of political life in exchange for crippling restrictions on the right to assemble.

These limitations on popular protest not only damage the system of democratic checks and balances on which the emergency constitution relies. They also undermine the larger project of returning to normalcy with all deliberate speed. It should be up to citizens, not the authorities, to decide whether they will risk their lives in defense of political freedom. The fact that tens of thousands demonstrate publicly not only shows that the terrorists have failed to break our political will—it also encourages the millions of bystanders to stand firm. Rather than repressing political expression, the emergency authorities should be affirmatively charged to give such demonstrations special security priority.

The priority of political liberty is firmly rooted in basic principles and culture, and reinforced by strategic considerations: if the government can impose special restrictions on our freedom of action, opposition parties will have a new incentive to vote for the premature termination of the state of emergency—this will be the only way to regain their full powers to organize for victory at the next election. By expressly insulating political expression and association from the emergency power, the Constitution not only underwrites the checks-and-balances system that makes emergency power tolerable; it also encourages the minority to contribute constructively to the legislative decision on its termination.

The Question of Scope

I have been focusing on the paradigmatic use of emergency power—the power to seize human beings and dramatically limit their freedom without satisfying the normal standards of due process. But emergency powers will extend much more broadly. Here is a short list: curfews, evacuations, compulsory medical treatment, border controls; authority to search and seize suspicious materials and to engage in intensive surveillance and data compilation; freezing financial assets and closing otherwise lawful businesses; increasing federal control over state governments, expanding the domestic role of the military, and imposing special limitations on the right to bear arms—to name only some of the hot-button items.[30]

Political compromises will be necessary, and cleverness too, when it comes to defining the metes and bounds. Since my point is to begin a serious conversation, not to produce a definitive blueprint, I am content to offer a few orienting observations on a very complex subject.

Redefining Normality

Begin with the obvious: the emergency constitution won't do much good if other laws already grant the president more-sweeping powers. So long as this is true, the president will simply refuse to ask Congress to declare a short-term emergency. He will rely instead on his preexisting sources of authority, and our labors will have been in vain. This means that the emergency framework should explicitly repeal preexisting statutes incompatible with the new regime and authorize strict judicial scrutiny of similar laws in the future.

Two basic principles should guide reappraisal and repeal. The first is minimalist, and I will call it the requirement of operational primacy. This involves an aggregate assessment of the overall legal authority granted to the president under existing law. The minimalist seeks to prune these authorities so that, overall, they grant the executive substantially less power than that generated by the new regime. Without fulfilling this test, the emergency constitution will be a dead letter.

Operational primacy requires the critical scrutiny of a wide range of statutes—dealing with resident aliens, immigrants, "material witnesses," and many other matters. These statutes should be cut back very significantly to make room for the operational primacy of the emergency system—and once this happens, the courts should be explicitly empowered to make sure that primacy isn't eroded by piecemeal legislation over time. Only in this way can the continuing practical importance of the emergency regime be sustained. This seems a minimalist point, but there is a larger implication worth emphasizing: Operational primacy will almost invariably require the redefinition of normality, *and in a way that increases freedom.*

A similar redefinition of normality will also occur if Congress takes a more ambitious approach. Many statutes have been enacted in recent years in response to terrorist incidents. If an emergency constitution became a serious project, it should catalyze a comprehensive reappraisal of all of this ad hoc legislation. At present, civil libertarian critics have only one option for criticizing these measures—they must urge their straightforward repeal. But the rise of emergency constitutionalism gives them a second option—these provisions are now applicable on a permanent basis, but why not make some or all of them applicable only during temporary emergencies?

With this new question in the mix, many previously permanent provisions might well be demoted to emergency operation, if not repealed entirely. Call this the demotion strategy, and it provides one more reason for civil libertarians to temper their opposition to the very idea of an emergency constitution. If this strategy is deployed with skill, fewer provisions of the Patriot Act and other legislation might remain valid on an everyday basis.

The availability of the new option does not, of course, guarantee wise decisions.[31] In any event, the task of defining the scope of power is virtually endless, and endlessly contestable. Aside from matters of substance, there will be continuing disagreement on the wisdom of leaving broad discretion to the emergency authority, and the extent to which Congress should try to tie the bureaucracy's hands with incisive statutory commands. It will be easy to get sidetracked in this forest and lose a sense of perspective.

Two Dangers

Even at this distance, I can see two dangers. As legislators concentrate on particular emergency powers, they might try to exempt the operation of one or another authority from the regular two-month extension periods. For example, it might be quite expensive to set up a complex control system around the nation's reservoirs, and a good deal of this investment might be "wasted" if Congress voted to terminate the emergency after only two months. So why not, in this particular case, allow six months of operation before emergency powers can be terminated? If this move were allowed, it is easy to foresee a proliferation of different time periods for different functions—all justified in the name of efficient emergency operations and bureaucratic expediency. As long as we look at each function separately, the cost savings might well be considerable.

Nevertheless, economic considerations don't remotely justify a deviation from the requirement that Congress vote to reauthorize the entire package every two months. The point of packaging is political, not economic: to concentrate public attention and political responsibility on a single up-or-down vote. If the president and Congress can obfuscate their accountability by a host of votes—extending some powers, ending others—the broader public will no longer be in a position to penetrate the haze, and one or another powerful special bureaucratic interest will be able to gain low-visibility authority to retain particular emergency powers for excessive periods of time.

The second danger is far more serious. Instead of engaging in a wide-ranging debate, our leading politicians continue to ignore the task of defining the scope of emergency power until the next major attack. At that point, the president preempts the entire issue by imposing martial law. The ground for this sweeping assumption of power has already been prepared. Although the contents are secret, the American military has "devised its first-ever war plans for guarding against and responding to terrorist attacks in the United States, envisioning 15 potential crisis scenarios and anticipating several simultaneous strikes around the country." Governing law places stringent restrictions on the use of troops domestically, but "Pentagon authorities have told Congress they see no need to change the law. According to military lawyers here, the dispatch of ground troops would most likely be justified on the basis of the president's authority under Article 2 of the Constitution to serve as commander in chief and protect the nation. 'That would be the place we would start from' in making the legal case, said Col. John Gereski, a senior [military] lawyer. But Gereski also said he knew of no court test of this legal argument."[32]

If Congress doesn't take up the task of defining the scope of emergency powers now, the president will resolve the issue later in his capacity as commander in chief. After months or years of presidential martial law, perhaps the courts will intervene to rein in excesses, perhaps not. But the great questions involved in defining the scope of emergency power will never be resolved through broad-ranging debate and democratic decision.

This is simply unacceptable.

The emergency constitution should be focused specially on terrorist attacks, and should not be concerned with other crises. It should authorize a declaration of emergency only when a truly devastating attack has occurred, and it should permit the continuation of the emergency for short intervals only if increasing legislative supermajorities give their consent. Minority political parties must be given special powers to investigate the real-world operation of the emergency regime and to publicize the facts as they see fit.

Whatever other restrictions on liberty are authorized, the emergency constitution should explicitly protect the full political freedom of all residents. It should not allow particular grants of power to endure once the general emergency has been terminated under the supermajoritarian escalator.

One final piece of the puzzle demands extended attention. We can't gain a glimpse of the emerging whole without bringing the courts back into the picture.

5

THE ROLE OF JUDGES

We have been constructing a political machine to restrain the use of extraordinary power, but can it operate reliably on its own? Or does it require the judiciary to play a series of backup functions? If so, are judges up to the job? These questions explore the capacity of courts to superintend the institutional dynamics of the new system—intervening at strategic moments to sustain its operation at times of stress.

I will call this the problem of macromanagement, and it will generate lots of hard questions. Whatever the right answers, the issues are very different from those arising from a more traditional judicial task: deciding the fate of particular detainees in individual cases. Call this the challenge of microadjudication, and we will be treating it separately before considering the ways in which macromanagement and microadjudication shape each other dynamically over the course of time.

Macromanagement

Should judges be asked to second-guess the initial decision by the president and Congress to declare a state of emergency?

There is only one case in which early intervention is plausible. If, as I suppose, the emergency constitution insists on an actual attack, the president should not be allowed to declare an emergency merely to preempt a terrorist attack that he claims to be very likely. Even if Congress gave its support to such a maneuver, the judiciary would be on firm ground in invalidating it. As we have seen, there are powerful reasons to reject emergencies based on presidential perceptions of "clear and present danger." And it's a straightforward matter for judges to police this boundary: it doesn't take a lot of evidence to determine that there hasn't been any attack and that the president is simply acting on the speculations of the CIA and FBI. What is more, the president and his party in Congress may well have powerful political reasons to abuse emergency declarations: it may, depending on the circumstances, place the opposition on the defensive. Given the obvious risks of political abuse and the ease of determining whether a significant attack has occurred, there is room here for a decisive judicial response.

But judges should act with great restraint once an attack occurs, even if there is fair dispute whether the attack is so large as to justify an emergency response. With the country reeling, it simply cannot afford the time needed for serious judicial review. If the president can convince a majority of Congress of the need for emergency authority, this should suffice. At this early stage, we should rely on the legislature, not the judiciary, to restrain arbitrary power. We should leave it to elected politicians, not judges, to estimate the chances of a second strike and the likelihood that a dragnet will reduce the risk. Any effort at second-guessing will inevitably parody the judicial ideal. There simply won't be enough time for the dispassionate consideration of evidence and the reasoned elaboration of judgment.

But perhaps there is room for a weakened form of judicial review. I have already noted an ingenious French provision that requires the president to consult with the constitutional court but gives him unilateral power to ignore its advisory opinion, should the Court condemn his action. This is an interesting idea, but I don't think it should be adopted. Since a Court won't have time to reflect fully on the matter, it will almost always rubber-stamp the president's decision; and even if the court protests, the president has the perfect right to ignore the admonition and proceed anyway. This precedent will damage judicial authority when it comes to later, and more appropriate, interventions by the judges. I strongly support checks on presidential power, but the French are wrong in looking to the courts rather than the legislature as a first line of defense. All things considered, the judges should sit on the sidelines while the political branches, aided by the supermajoritarian escalator, determine whether the threat of a second strike is serious enough to merit a continuing state of emergency.[1]

Courts have a more important role to play on more-procedural matters. For example, the emergency constitution places the legislative oversight committees in the hands of the minority party and virtually guarantees an ongoing struggle between Congress and the president over control of information. These unending tensions are entirely healthy, and judges should be reluctant to intervene. It is much better if the political protagonists work out reasonable accommodations on their own.

Nevertheless, the executive has most of the chips in this game, and if it abuses its bargaining power, judicial intervention sometimes may be necessary. This will call for a great deal of judicial tact and discretion in sifting the facts of particular cases—a matter that can be discussed intelligently only at retail, not wholesale.

Courts and Crisis

Other procedural questions raise larger issues of principle. The great danger is this: The supermajoritarian escalator will eventually require the termination of the emergency regime, but the president may simply refuse to give up his emergency powers. Rather than meekly bowing before the law, he uses his popular support to launch an all-out assault on the emergency constitution: "As President, I cannot allow this puny minority of naysayers in Congress to sabotage the national interest. Although they have managed to gain twenty-five votes in the Senate to defeat a further two-month extension, I choose to stand with the seventy-five senators who wanted the emergency to continue. At this moment of supreme crisis, I call upon the American people to support the security services, which will continue exercising their powers until I tell them to stop."

Here is where the judges must step in and insist on the rule of law. Their opposition will transform the nature of the political battle. The president can no longer pretend that he is merely fighting a small band of pig-headed politicians in Congress. He must take on the courts as well, casting himself as an enemy of the entire constitutional order. These are high stakes indeed, and should deter much reckless presidential behavior.

But not all. Demagogues may call the courts' bluff, and then it will be up to the country to decide. At least the courts will go into the struggle on relatively advantageous ground. The president's breach of the rule of law will be plain for all to see: the vote was 75–25 when the supermajoritarian escalator required 80–20. The court will not be obliged to justify its intervention with hair-splitting legalisms and complex argument. The issue will be clean and clear: is the country prepared to destroy the rule of law and embark on a disastrous adventure that may end with dictatorship?

To increase the pressure on the president further, the emergency constitution should explicitly command the courts to begin habeas corpus hearings immediately upon the legal termination of the emergency. This will require countless officials throughout the country to ask where their ultimate loyalties lie—to the usurper or to the Constitution. At least some will uphold the law and hand their prisoners over to the judges, putting the burden on the usurper to take further extraordinary actions. All this may help provoke a popular movement in support of the Constitution—or it may not. Resolution of the struggle ultimately will depend on the character and will of the people.

Courts as Guardians

So much for apocalypse. Perhaps more troubling, the emergency constitution may also come to an end with a whimper, not a bang— through a gradual process of subtle legislative erosion, rather than melodramatic confrontation. In this scenario, the president doesn't blatantly flout the law. Instead, he tries to persuade Congress itself to undermine the supermajoritarian escalator.

To define this gambit, consider that even under emergency conditions, the legislature will be passing lots of statutes on humdrum matters. Call this "ordinary legislation," and on these issues, the rule of simple majority voting will continue to apply. This point will provide the president with a strategic opening. After he loses the supermajoritarian vote on emergency power by, say, a margin of 75–25, he may simply ask Congress to grant him broad new powers by enacting new "ordinary legislation" through a simple majority vote. If this gambit succeeds a few times, the new statutes will have given the president all the emergency powers he wants—and the supermajoritarian escalator will have been rendered pointless. The emergency constitution may remain on the books, but presidential end runs will have made its limitations irrelevant to the real world of power.

Here is where active judicial review is crucial. The courts should strictly scrutinize any new grants of extraordinary power that make it unnecessary for the president to invoke the emergency constitution. They should not simply test this new legislation against standard constitutional principles. Since the panic-driven enactment of a series of statutes will undermine the president's incentives to use the emergency constitution, courts should go further and strike down any legislation which significantly erodes the need to obtain supermajoritarian approval for extraordinary powers.[2]

The courts, in short, should understand themselves as the *guardians of the emergency constitution*. Judges can take on this task with relative confidence, since they won't be rendering the government powerless by rejecting panic-driven legislation. Active judicial review will simply push the government into the channels established by the emergency constitution. Rather than rejecting the new legislation on its merits, the courts should simply tell the president to make his case to Congress under the terms specified by the supermajoritarian escalator. If he can convince a supermajority to go along, more power to him (literally); if not, he shouldn't be able to undermine the emergency constitution through panic-driven legislative exceptions. Except in the most compelling cases, it is far more important for the courts to safeguard the fundamental principle that emergencies aren't forever, and that panic-driven evasions of this principle are intolerable.

To be sure, the ongoing response to a terrorist attack may well reveal weaknesses in the original grants of power provided by the emergency constitution—perhaps it was too generous in some respects, too niggardly in others. But it will be time enough to consider serious revisions once the sense of crisis begins to lift and the public has had a chance to reflect on its collective experience.

Microadjudication

Serious constitutional thought focuses on pathological cases, and for good reason: by preparing for the worst, we make it less likely to happen. But the pathological perspective generates distortions of its own, overemphasizing the fragility of the institutional structures we have been building. The enactment of an emergency constitution will occur only after lots of political debate, and against the background of a broad consensus. This political conversation and commitment will yield a moral environment that makes it more difficult for presidents and legislators to abuse the new framework at moments of crisis. If we are lucky in our leaders, they will look upon the emergency constitution in a favorable light: rather than seeing it as an obstacle, blocking their reach for arbitrary power, they will appreciate how it enhances their legitimate authority to act decisively at times of crisis. Within a relatively favorable environment, judicial interventions should be few. Although the judges should be prepared to serve as guardians of the emergency constitution, the scheme will operate best when they hold this power in reserve.

In contrast, the courts will always be active on a second front, involving the microadjudication of cases raised by particular detainees. Before confronting the problem directly, consider how three key aspects of the emergency framework already shape the environment surrounding detention. One basic safeguard is provided by the political element of the emergency constitution—the supermajoritarian escalator puts prosecutors on notice that the emergency will not go on and on. We also have imposed two fundamental limits on the abuse of power. The emergency authorities can't detain any individual suspect for more than forty-five days—at which point the prosecution must make its case under the ordinary standards of the criminal law. And the government must also compensate detainees $500 for every day they are deprived of freedom.

These three elements in concert ensure that the "emergency" will denote not a period of sheer lawlessness but a time for prosecutors to undertake serious investigations of each individual case. Forty-five days isn't a very long time to get enough evidence to satisfy the traditional test of probable cause: consider the chaotic bureaucratic conditions in the aftermath of a major attack and its monumental stockpile of extra work. And the supermajoritarian escalator adds extra pressure. Prosecutors won't know precisely when the emergency will end—perhaps in two months, perhaps in six. But they will know that, once termination occurs, they will then have to move forward promptly on *all* those in custody. This will push them to begin serious work at once: with hundreds or thousands in custody, they will try to clear out those who have been arrested by mistake. Otherwise, they can't focus their energies on suspects who are worth really serious investigation.

The requirement of just compensation will have a similar impact. Up to this point, I have built my argument for payment on basic principles of justice: just as we don't expect property owners to sacrifice for the public good without just compensation, we shouldn't ask detainees to make an even more crushing sacrifice without paying them for their time and the assault on their dignity. Yet this principle of justice will also encourage expeditious fact-finding. The security services will save $500 for every day of needless detention avoided. Especially if the bureaucrats see this item appear on their budget, this incentive should help overwhelm the inertia that might otherwise lead them to prolong detention to the bitter end of the forty-five-day period.

It is a mistake, then, to conceive of emergency detention as a period of utter lawlessness: the prosecutor's need to prepare for a legal day of reckoning and the bureaucratic response to the budgetary pressures for compensation create their own incentives for the speedy discharge of the innocent. Within this context, I do not favor immediate judicial hearings that weigh the evidentiary basis for detention in individual cases. Nevertheless, suspects should be taken expeditiously before a judge even if they aren't given a chance to rebut the charges against them, and prosecutors should place the grounds for their suspicion on the record.

This preliminary hearing operates as a first line of defense against arbitrary conduct. At the very least, the preliminary hearing will force the prosecutor to obtain a statement from the security services, explaining why it believes that its suspicions are "reasonable"—the operational standard under the emergency constitution.[3] If the statement turns out to be a sheer fabrication, it will later serve as a basis for a lawsuit for punitive damages, once the emergency has been terminated.

The initial hearing will also provide the detainee a bureaucratic identity: a face that the authorities must register and recognize. It is incredibly easy for people to get entirely lost in a system reeling in response to the unexpected attack. While an innocent person will not take great solace in learning that he is "Suspect 1072," whose detention certificate has been submitted to "Judge X" on "Day Y," these formalities will serve to start the clock running and alert all concerned that there *will* be a day of legal reckoning forty-five days hence.

Such a lengthy period is regrettable, but by hypothesis, the security services will be scrambling to create a coherent response to the larger threat. They will be stretched too thin to devote large resources to evidentiary hearings in the immediate aftermath of the attack, and if they skimp on legal preparation, they may fail to make a compelling presentation. They may even fail to provide judges with all of the evidence that actually exists in the agencies' computer banks, leading to the judicial discharge of detainees who have genuine links to terrorist organizations. Given this risk, most judges will bend over backward to give the government the benefit of the doubt, leading to lots of hearings without much effective relief. A bit of legal realism suggests, then, that the bad consequences of the forty-five-day delay can be readily exaggerated—not because there won't be countless cases of unjust detention, imposing harsh burdens on detainees and their families, but because judges will, in any event, be very cautious in freeing suspects in the immediate aftermath. It is even possible—though this is entirely speculative—that the interests of some detainees might actually be served by the forty-five-day delay: After six weeks have passed, a judge might well be tougher on the prosecutor's case now that he has been given a real chance to search the files and find out what's really there. If the answer is very little, the judge might well discharge a detainee who would have been kept in confinement at an earlier moment.

Torture

I would set a different goal for the courts when dealing with cases arising during the forty-five-day period. Decency, not innocence, should be their overriding concern. *Do not torture the detainees.* That should be an absolute, and judges should enforce it rigorously. The fact that many of the detainees are almost certainly innocent makes this ban more exigent.

Professor Alan Dershowitz has recently urged us to rethink this absolute prohibition. If we were confronted with a terrorist who could tell us where Al Qaeda would strike next, wouldn't it be right to torture him to save the lives of thousands?[4]

I am entirely unimpressed with the relevance of these musings to real-world emergency settings. Security services can panic in the face of horrific tragedy. With officials in disarray, with rumors of impending attacks flying about, and with an outraged public demanding instant results, there will be overwhelming temptations to use indecent forms of interrogation. This is the last place to expect carefully nuanced responses.

Dershowitz recognizes the problem and proposes to solve it by inviting judges to serve as our collective superego, issuing "torture warrants" only in the most compelling cases.[5] But judges are no more immune from panic than the rest of us. To offset the rush toward torture in an emergency, they would be obliged to make their hearings especially deliberate and thoughtful. But if they slow the judicial proceedings down to deliberate speed for diligent review, the terrorists' second strike will occur before the torture warrant can issue. Serious deliberation is simply incompatible with the speedy response required in the aftermath of an attack. Once the ban on torture is lifted, judges can't be depended on to stand up to the enormous pressure for instant results. Some—if not all—will become rubber stamps, processing mounds of paper to cover up the remorseless operation of the torture machine. And once these judicial collaborators have been identified, the torturers will steer their warrant requests toward their allies on the bench and away from judges with the strength to withstand bureaucratic pressure and the integrity to seek out the truth.

Even a few judicial lapses will have a devastating impact on the general public. The "torture warrants" will carry a message that transcends the cruelties and indecencies involved in particular cases: "Beware all ye who enter here: Abandon all hope of constitutional protection. No one swept into the emergency dragnet can be sure of returning with his body and soul intact. The state is hurtling down the path of uncontrolled violence." Once word gets around that judges cannot be trusted to guard against abusive torture, ordinary people will wonder whom they *can* trust.

Dershowitz fails to confront these problems. He recognizes that torture may have long-run legitimacy consequences but fails to consider its devastating short-run impact.[6] Our overriding constitutional aim is to create an emergency regime that remains subordinated—both in symbol and in actual fact—to the principles of liberal democracy. Without the effective constraint of the rule of law, it is far too easy for the emergency regime to degenerate into a full-blown police state.

But it is one thing to keep torture a taboo, another to define it. If judges are to intervene effectively to assure humane treatment, they should candidly recognize that "torture" doesn't define itself, and confront some tough line-drawing exercises. It is easy to condemn the extremely narrow definition of torture propounded by the Bush administration in its "war on terror," but any plausible definition will place some hard-driving interrogation tactics on the legal side of the line.[7] As the Bush fiasco suggests, there is a crucial relationship between process and substance here.[8]

The Justice Department did not expect its notorious "torture memos" ever to see the light of day: they were prepared in secret to provide confidential guidance to the security apparatus. This is a recipe for legalistic inhumanity. The pervasive secrecy suggested to the president's lawyers that they wouldn't have to pay a price to their reputation if they interpreted the law to permit abusive conduct—no hostile newspaper attacks, no scholarly critiques, only applause from the security services. But if they resisted the intense pressure to help fight the "war on terror," they would be rewarded with a reputation for legalistic obstructionism that would hurt their future careers within the executive branch.

To be sure, they still had to struggle with their moral and legal consciences, and I don't doubt that the Bush Justice Department *did* confront the issues with real seriousness. But the results only show that conscience alone is not enough to overcome the overwhelmingly unfavorable bureaucratic dynamic. The key, for me, is not merely the secret memoranda's extremely permissive interpretation of the applicable law on torture, authorizing many inhumane practices that the Bush administration had no trouble calling "torture" when undertaken by Saddam Hussein.[9] Even worse, the Justice Department memoranda assured members of the security services that they could violate these permissive definitions and escape criminal prosecution as torturers, and that it was even unconstitutional for Congress to override the president's authorization of torture.[10] This sort of legal extremism would never survive a second reading if its authors believed that their memoranda would ever see the light of day.

As events proved. Once the memos were leaked to the public, administration officials immediately began to distance themselves from them.[11]

This is an administration famed for its grim determination to "stay the course," regardless of public opposition. The same top officials remained in charge, and they had not visibly changed their hearts and minds on the matter. Nevertheless, they began beating a retreat before a firestorm of public criticism, downplaying the role of the memos in the past and finally renouncing their future use after six months of bobbing and weaving.[12] But the underlying problem remains: the executive continues to claim the authority to define guidelines for interrogation in secret—and so the same perverse incentives apply.[13]

To put the structural point in human terms, consider the case of Jay Bybee, the assistant attorney general in charge of the office that prepared the torture memos during 2002. By the time he signed the memo insulating torturers from prosecution, Bybee had already been nominated for a prestigious appellate judgeship by President Bush.[14] The memos, however, were still executive secrets when he appeared before the Senate Judiciary Committee for confirmation. When senators repeatedly asked him about his role in defining the legal parameters for the war on terror, Bybee simply stonewalled: "As an attorney at the Department of Justice, I am obliged to keep confidential the legal advice that I provide to others in the executive branch. I cannot comment on whether or not I have provided any such advice and, if so, the substance of that advice." Or so he told Senator John Edwards, and many other senators who raised similar questions. Nevertheless, the judiciary committee gave him a pass, and the Senate confirmed his nomination, despite the efforts by Senator Richard Durbin and others to put their colleagues on notice: "Mr. Bybee is the most recent example of an appellate court nominee who has stonewalled the Senate Judiciary Committee. I do not believe that such conduct should be rewarded." But it *was* rewarded, by a vote of 74–19, on March 13, 2003.[15] After that more than a year passed before the *Washington Post* broke the news about Bybee's torture memo on the front page of its issue of June 8, 2004.[16] Although leading members of the administration now condemn his conclusions in the memo as "sophomoric," Bybee continues to enjoy his lifetime appointment to this day—apparently, the Senate is perfectly satisfied with his "good behavior."[17]

The moral of this story couldn't be clearer. Executive secrecy rewards the team player, who gives the security services what they want, over the legalistic "obstructionist," who tells them what they don't want to hear. And make no mistake. There are many, many ambitious lawyers who are quick to draw the obvious lesson from the Bybee story: play with the team and become a leading judge.

The emergency constitution must break with this logic and create a very different institutional setting for the tough decisions required in creating operational rules dividing torture from decent treatment. It should require that the nature of the decency guidelines be debated and decided in public. And the ultimate decisions shouldn't be made by the president's top lawyers and national security advisers. Independent judges should play a dominant role.

A good model is the special commission which establishes guidelines for criminal sentencing in the American system. The Sentencing Commission has seven members, three of whom are federal judges. The president gets to pick these judges from a panel of six submitted by the Judicial Conference of the United States. All of the president's nominees must be confirmed by the Senate.[18] In the analogous case of the Decency Commission, a majority of the panel should be drawn from the judiciary, permitting the judges to constrain the more operational concerns of other members, whose backgrounds could properly reflect more practical security experience. It should be up to the commission, not to the president's lawyers or the emergency authority, to establish interrogation guidelines in advance.

Emergency Due Process

With the standards in place, the judiciary will be in a better position to respond quickly once an emergency occurs and the inevitable allegations of abusive tactics arise. This is not a moment to engage in lengthy deliberation and litigation on the definition of torture. It should be a time when the judges are prepared to intervene decisively to enforce well-established decency guidelines. But how are the detainees to get these complaints to the courts in a speedy fashion?[19]

Here is where the right to counsel enters—a right that has proved remarkably vulnerable in America in the aftermath of September 11.[20] Regular visits by counsel are the crucial mechanism for policing against torture. Once security services know that detainees have direct access to the legal system for their complaints, torture will no longer be a thinkable option.[21] It's true that contact with counsel may make detainees more resistant to some forms of legitimate questioning. They may feel less isolated and vulnerable, and so may prove less cooperative. Interrogators can, of course, compensate by changing the carrot-stick ratio, emphasizing the rewards that will come with collaboration. But this may not always work, and the emergency authorities may sometimes lose valuable evidence. But the ban on torture should be nonnegotiable: it is simply the price that any decent society must be willing to pay, and its violation in times of emergency is, as we have seen, especially perilous for the project of liberal democracy.[22]

Counsel will play other important roles. Lawyers must have the ability to collect exculpatory evidence rapidly before memories fade or physical materials disappear. Otherwise, the suspect's hearing on the merits will turn out to be a farce. Lawyers also play a crucial intermediary role between detainees and their families, friends, and employers in the outside world. These people must be in a position to hear, and quickly, that the detainee has not disappeared into a police-state hellhole. Friends and family should also be permitted to monitor the attorney's performance to ensure that their loved one is treated with respect, and to replace him with another provided at state expense, if they so choose.

Special limitations on these rights may be tolerable—so long as they do not undermine the fundamentals. For example, the detainee's intimates must have access to his counsel, but they may be forbidden to publicize further any information they receive. Some restrictions on the right to choose particular lawyers may well be tolerable. But we are reaching the realm of reasonable disagreement, and I am restricting myself only to the basics.

To secure fundamental rights, we should take steps to anticipate a final abuse: Suppose that, after forty-five days of detention, the government cannot produce the evidence required to justify further incarceration. The judicial hearing concludes with the release of the detainee, but the security services respond by seizing him at the courthouse door and arresting him for another forty-five-day emergency detention. We require an adaptation of the "double jeopardy" principle to block this tactic. While the security services have the power to detain new suspects so long as the state of emergency continues, they can't engage in revolving door maneuvers. The state has already had its chance and has failed to find substantial evidence of his complicity with the ongoing terrorist conspiracy. If further investigations uncover new evidence, the police should arrest the suspect once again—but this time, the prosecution must make its case for detention under the standard ground rules established by the criminal law.

Emergency's End

I have been trying to define the juridical floor, not the ceiling, which any civilized society should construct before accepting an emergency constitution. Despite this minimalist aspiration, we have already derived a formidable series of judicially enforceable rights—the right to decent treatment, to a lawyer, to a strictly limited period of detention, and to fair compensation while in custody—and, doubtless, more should be added to this list. These substantial safeguards should not blind us to an obvious point: by depriving suspects of immediate hearings on the merits, the emergency regime *does* deprive them of fundamental rights. This is a very real loss, but the emergency constitution offers some consolation in the middle run, encouraging judges to protect rights more aggressively than they might otherwise.

My middle-run argument requires us to return, once again, to the supermajoritarian escalator and its likely impact upon judicial behavior. To make my case, allow me a relatively uncontroversial assumption: Judges tend to be rather conservative folk who are likely to interpret their legal remit very cautiously during the immediate aftermath of a massive terrorist strike. Even if we insisted that they operate under "normal" standards of criminal due process, most would give great leeway to the authorities during the period of acute crisis. The law doesn't interpret itself: criminal codes are full of ambiguities which judges can exploit, if they choose, to justify a great deal of deference. Since this is very likely in the aftermath of an attack, it is an open question how much the emergency constitution sacrifices in terms of *effective* judicial supervision.

In contrast, the supermajoritarian escalator will encourage more-aggressive judicial protection over the middle run. As the months pass, the escalator allows termination of the emergency by a vote of 21 percent to 79 percent. And once the legislature has taken the lead, the judiciary will be far more comfortable in resuming its normal role as a strong protector of individual rights. The key point for judges is that the legislature has taken public responsibility for terminating the emergency in a highly visible fashion. Even if only 21 percent of the House or Senate voted to terminate the emergency, the judges are now off the hook, and if public opinion reacts with alarm to their reassertion of judicial authority, they can respond by pointing to their recent legislative mandate: if the emergency is over, the judges are only doing their jobs in insisting on ordinary standards of due process. And they will reassert their authority even though a majority of the legislature, and the general population, may not yet have fully recovered from the anxieties generated by the terrorist attack. So the emergency constitution offers a trade-off of sorts—a reduction of due process in the short run, followed by its enhancement over the middle run.

Once this point is appreciated, some readers may condemn my proposal for scheduling such a rapid return to judicial normalcy—after all, it will only take six months for the full 80 percent supermajority requirement to kick in. Isn't this too quick?

Reasonable people can disagree—and the emergency constitution can be redesigned easily to accommodate these disagreements. Simply recalibrate the speed of the supermajoritarian escalator—changing the extension periods from two to three months, say, thereby slowing the rate of ascent to the supermajoritarian heights. But as you tinker with the terms, remember this: No matter how you redesign the escalator, the return to judicial normalcy will always inspire lots of anxiety in the hearts of lots of people. The "war on terror" will never end. There always will be disaffected groups scurrying about seeking terrible weapons from unscrupulous arms dealers and rogue states. There always will be fear-mongering politicians pointing with alarm to the storm clouds on the horizon. And there always will be many people who, understandably enough, have not recovered fully from the trauma of the last repugnant attack. Even committed civil libertarians will find it hard to suppress residual doubt: is it really safe to lift the state of emergency?

I do not wish to deny the reality of these anxieties. To the contrary, they motivate my call for a constitutional approach to the problem. We should take advantage of periods of relative calm to anticipate the political difficulties involved in returning to juridical normalcy and take steps now to channel the predictable political resistances of the future. We should not allow reasonable disagreements to generate constitutional paralysis. Every terrorist attack will make it more difficult to frame a response that prevents the permanent erosion of civil liberties. Almost any supermajoritarian escalator is better than the status quo.

A More Dynamic View

I have been distinguishing between macro- and microjudicial interventions—the former dealing with the integrity of the system as a whole, the latter with individual cases. But this neat distinction will blur over time. Individual detainees, once released, will file legal complaints alleging abusive treatment. These lawsuits will accumulate into larger patterns as they slowly reach appellate tribunals. With any luck at all, the state of emergency will have ended before the highest court begins to consider a series of typical grievances stemming from the recent crisis.

Microadjudication will merge into macromanagement. The high court should do justice in particular cases, but in ways that will shape future patterns of emergency administration. How might the structure of the emergency constitution guide the path of this ongoing judicial dialectic?

Consider how judicial perceptions will be shaped by the requirement of just compensation to detainees. Since everybody will be receiving a substantial payment for their time in jail, only lawsuits alleging truly outrageous conduct will seem plausible. This is just as it should be. Even in retrospect, the courts should give a wide discretion to the judgments of the emergency authorities.

Nonetheless, there will be abuses. Even if the system steers clear of torture, the emergency will predictably tempt some members of the security services to use their extraordinary powers in the service of personal vendettas: Inspector Smith has always hated his next-door neighbor, Jones, and seizes the chance to throw him behind bars for forty-five days by calling him a terrorist.

Proving animus is always difficult, but the procedural framework will make it possible. Although an evidentiary hearing may be deferred for

forty-five days, the emergency constitution requires an immediate preliminary hearing, at which the prosecution must state the grounds of suspicion that support the detention. If it later develops that these charges
are bogus, the question naturally arises whether the officials making them
were acting in good faith. The entry of a few awards for punitive damages
will also have a structural consequence—both the bad publicity and the
budgetary hits will induce agencies to get rid of their "bad apples" and
institutionalize more rigorous controls.

A more systemic problem may arise if criminal prosecutors use emergency powers as a shortcut for ordinary procedures. Even though the
prosecutor may not have enough evidence to move against a suspected
car thief, why not call him a terrorist and subject him to immediate
detention and interrogation?

In these cases, structural remedies are even more important than damages. The judges should take steps to assure that charges of prosecutorial
abuse are thoroughly investigated, and that wrongdoers face the prospect
of serious discipline, including disbarment. If particular government
offices are generating patterns of pervasive abuse, the judges should be
prepared to appoint special masters charged with the task of reforming
pathological organizational structures that lie at the root of the disorder.

And then there will be problems of ethnic, religious, and racial profiling. Some terrorist episodes will not invite this practice since the perpetrators are drawn primarily from the dominant groups—consider the
Oklahoma City bombing. But the current war on terrorism is fraught
with anti-Islamic and anti-Arab prejudices that could turn very ugly
under emergency conditions.

The International Covenant on Civil and Political Rights sets the right
standard. Article 4 applies even during states of emergency and bars
states from discriminating "*solely* on the ground of race, colour, sex, language, religion or social origin."[23] In signing the Convention, the
United States accepted this provision without reservation but filed an
"understanding" that it did not "bar distinctions that may have a disproportionate effect upon persons of a particular status" during a "time of
public emergency."[24]

During the early period of panic, it will be tough for courts to determine how well the security services are complying with these principles.

While a dragnet may well sweep certain groups into detention dispropor-tionately, this may be entirely due to the group's disproportionate con-nection to a particular terrorist conspiracy. But as the smoke clears and the emergency lifts, patterns of gross discrimination may well emerge. Once again, the challenge for courts is not only to provide punitive dam-ages for abusive conduct but to consider how they might encourage the bureaucracy to take structural measures to reduce similar discriminatory impulses when future emergencies strike.

One key pressure point involves the bureaucratic identification of potential suspects. On September 11 the American government's "no-fly list," banning suspected terrorists from commercial aviation, contained precisely sixteen names. By late 2004 there were more than twenty thou-sand, and similar lists are proliferating to bar suspects from sensitive occupations and the like.[25] Due process is minimal—when a person arrives at the airport, he is simply told that he can't fly and is given pre-cious little means to contest his designation: even Senator Ted Kennedy had trouble getting his name off the list. This is wrong in itself, but it becomes utterly unacceptable if these lists become the foundation for emergency dragnets.

The answer is straightforward in principle, if complex in practice: give suspects ample due process rights to challenge their designation and thereby remove their names from the list of suspects before the next attack occurs. The chance that genuine terrorists will avail themselves of these rights is minimal—by showing up at a hearing to challenge their designation as prime suspects, they place themselves in the hands of the government and confront immediate detention if the security services turn out to have substantial evidence of their terrorist involvement. In contrast, hearings will offer innocents the chance to clear their names and evade future dragnets.

There will be lots of problems of institutional design involved in assuring a fair hearing while preventing leaks of classified information. But there are sensible ways to manage this problem—for example, the government could create a panel of lawyers with security clearance, provide their services to complainants free of charge, and give them incentives to interrogate the bureaucratic authorities aggressively.[26] Due process may come at a high price. Since the lists already contain tens of thousands of names, it will require thousands of hearings and hundreds of thousands of lawyer-hours devoted to fair and accurate determinations.

Nevertheless, there is a morally compelling case for accepting these costs, given the obvious threat to the liberty of innocent people. Individualized hearings also provide a crucial safeguard against the evident dangers of racial and ethnic profiling in targeting prime candidates for emergency detention. Since the judiciary won't be in a good position to control covert discrimination in the immediate aftermath of a terrorist strike, it should at least guarantee that people can challenge their terrorist designations beforehand, and refute casual suspicions based on guilt by association.

As experience accumulates over time, other patterns of individual complaints undoubtedly will accumulate. The challenge for both courts and agencies is to learn from these complaints and take ongoing measures that will make emergency administration tolerable, if never satisfactory.

Let's move back a step and take the measure of the overall proposal. Simplifying drastically, I will sum up with three principles drawn from each of three domains: political, economic, and juridical. Politically, the emergency constitution requires increasingly larger majorities to continue the extraordinary regime over extended periods of time. Economically, it requires compensation for the many innocent people caught in the dragnet. Legally, it requires a rigorous respect for decency as long as the traditional protections of the criminal law have been suspended.

Supermajorities, compensation, decency. These three principles, and their corollaries, do more than provide substantial protection to the unlucky individuals caught in the net of suspicion. They combine to present a picture of the "state of emergency" as a carefully limited regime, tolerated only as a regrettable necessity, and always on the path toward termination.

The emergency constitution rejects the allure of authoritarian solutions. An emergency does not require the services of a single great leader who will save us all if we only give him supreme power as commander in chief. To the contrary, this top-down vision virtually guarantees failure, even if the supreme leader is supremely suited for the job.

The greatest man at the top remains deeply dependent on the bureaucracies below for his sense of evolving realities on the ground. Yet in a strictly hierarchical setting, these bureaucratic underlings will predictably tell the Great Leader what they think he wants to hear, suppressing their inevitable blunders while trumpeting their triumphs. And unless he is very wise, the Great Leader will surround himself with yes men who refuse to challenge his premises and applaud while he transforms his personal hunches into massive initiatives. Within this setting, the man at the top can blunder onward down his initial path long after most sober observers recognize the need for a midcourse correction or an agonizing reappraisal.

The emergency constitution creates a very different environment. While granting operational authority to the executive, it gives Congress and the judiciary key roles in an ongoing debate over the uses and abuses of emergency power, and the need for its continuation. By separating out the ultimate power to control the emergency from the operational power to administer it, checks and balances permits the man at the top, no less than the general public, a much richer understanding of the evolving situation. His underlings will no longer find it in their interest to hide inconvenient truths if these will be exposed by the oversight committees of Congress or judicial hearings into detainee abuse. And the president himself will want to be the first to know the bad news, so that he can preempt the storm of criticism that will surely follow when it is exposed to public view. Over time, the system of checks and balances will permit the great leader, the bureaucracy, and the rest of us a precious opportunity: we may actually learn from our mistakes, and manage more intelligent responses to the ongoing terrorist threat.

This vision of the state of emergency is at war with the authoritarian impulse to shut down the noisy argument of a democratic society and crush the terrorist menace under the iron discipline of the commander in chief. The longing for clean lines of authority should not be confused with the constructive use of political intelligence in planning, executing, and terminating a period of extraordinary action. A clear and clean organizational chart is no substitute for an ongoing and multifaceted debate on what is really going on in the world, whether existing policies are failing a reality test, and which priorities make the most sense.

To be sure, the rise of an emergency constitution marks a turning point in our history. We must soberly recognize that the moment of triumphalism after 1989 has come to an end, and that liberal ideals may sometimes require extraordinary actions in their defense. But nothing that has happened in recent years requires us to throw overboard everything we know about power—most notably, that absolute power corrupts absolutely.

6

AMERICAN EXCEPTIONALISM

Terrorism isn't a uniquely American anxiety. The next massive strike may occur in Paris or Berlin, New Delhi or Tokyo. Since this is a worldwide problem, I have been sketching the outlines of a general solution. But each country has a different constitutional tradition, and no single proposal will fit all institutional setups.

As we take the next step toward implementation, one point is key: some constitutions are much harder to change than others. Generally speaking, constitutions written in the twentieth century have done a pretty good job of avoiding the dangers of extreme rigidity—making amendment difficult, but not too difficult. In contrast, the United States' eighteenth-century constitution has, in modern times, become almost unamendable on matters that stir even modest controversy. As a consequence, my talk about an "emergency constitution" has different legal valences in America and elsewhere. If this book succeeds, it will contribute to a serious dialogue in many countries about the wisdom of constitutional revision. But in the United States, it is entirely unrealistic to agitate for formal amendments—the task, instead, is to persuade Congress to build upon existing emergency legislation and create a "framework statute" that controls presidential power and protects fundamental rights.

Looking first to the conversation beyond America, it is especially important to provoke discussion in countries like France and Germany, whose constitutions already contain elaborate emergency provisions. These texts were not framed with the distinctive problem of terrorism in mind. They focus on external attacks and internal coups that threaten to destroy the regime. Unless these constitutions are modified, they will predictably misfire, authorizing disproportionate measures that may not even significantly respond to the need for reassurance provoked by the attack.

In the United States, constitutional debate must proceed on different lines. As recent experience has proved, the existing system for constitutional amendment contains so many veto points that it will even defeat proposals that have gained a broad national consensus. No controversial change has won enactment for seventy-five years.[1] There is no realistic chance that a comprehensive emergency provision will survive the obstacle course marked out in the Constitution, requiring three-fourths of the states to join with two-thirds of Congress in the approval of a proposal.

Friends of an emergency constitution should take an alternative path that has been smoothed by many previous efforts during the course of the twentieth century. When faced with new and unruly realities, Congress has regularly enacted "framework statutes," which seek to impose constitutional order on problems that were unforeseen by the Founders. Some thirty years ago, Congress took this path in passing the National Emergencies Act of 1976. Experience under the act shows that it can't deal with terrorism without fundamental revision, but the statute's very existence is important. It tells us that we aren't building something out of nothing. Congress has already gone on record affirming the need to control the pathologies of emergency power. The challenge is to create a much more effective structure, carefully adapted to the distinctive challenges of terrorism.

This chapter considers the special problems raised by the enactment of a framework statute, rather than a formal amendment, under the U.S. Constitution. I suggest that this difference in legal form won't require significant deviations from the basic principles set out in the preceding discussion. Our constitutional tradition provides us with all the tools we need for a compelling response to the problem of terrorism. Perhaps this conclusion is unsurprising, given the central role played by checks and balances both in my proposal and in the Founders' Constitution, but it is important to make the legal case if a serious and sustained conversation is to begin.

Lessons of Experience

The most notable framework statute of the twentieth century was the Administrative Procedure Act that imposed the rule of law upon the regulatory state.[2] The Founders did not foresee the rise of bureaucracy, and for a long time, Congress endowed each new regulatory agency with its own statutory relationships to the presidency, legislature, and the courts. As legal idiosyncrasies multiplied, the bewildering complexity endangered the very notion of the rule of law—and in the aftermath of the New Deal, Congress established a more general framework that gave public administration a new sense of legitimacy. Though it was packaged as a statute, the Administrative Procedure Act was the product of constitutional thought, and over the past sixty years, the courts have given quasi-constitutional status to its principles. It's easy to quibble endlessly over the act's particular provisions, but the overall result has been a triumph of constitutional adaptation. The framework provided by the statute has successfully imposed fundamental constraints on bureaucratic government in the name of democracy and legality.[3]

We have been less successful when it comes to states of emergency, but it has not been for want of trying. From the Great Depression through the Cold War, Congress passed some 470 statutes granting the president authority to exercise one or another power during a declared state of "national emergency," and presidents made abundant use of these proliferating authorities.[4] But in response to executive abuses, culminating in the Watergate scandal, Congress inaugurated a new approach based on a framework statute. The National Emergencies Act of 1976 terminated all existing emergencies and established a uniform procedural framework for the future exercise of emergency powers.[5] Unfortunately, it didn't go further to revise the disorganized, but massive, grants of substantive authority to declare emergencies that the presidency had accumulated over the decades.[6]

The act has been frequently tested over the past thirty years, most notably in foreign affairs.[7] Although presidents never used it to detain suspects before September 11, they regularly invoked it to block foreign assets and restrict foreign travel.[8] A generation's experience has only dramatized the weaknesses of the existing framework.[9]

Not only does the president retain the power to declare an emergency unilaterally, but the statute's weak consultation and reporting procedures have been diluted or ignored. The statute provides that "each House of Congress shall meet" every six months to consider a vote on terminating the emergency.[10] Yet neither chamber has ever met to take this action, ignoring the many presidential declarations that have continued for more than six months. Despite the mandatory force of the word *shall*, courts have found "no legal remedy for a congressional failure to comply with the statute."[11] Although the statute requires emergency declarations to lapse automatically after one year, there is nothing to stop the president from renewing them immediately, and he has often done so—annually extending a state of emergency with Iran, for example, for a quarter of a century.[12]

Even if Congress took its oversight responsibilities more seriously, the statute doesn't provide it with an effective mechanism to control an over-reaching president. When it was originally passed, the statute authorized Congress to terminate an emergency, despite the president's objection, by means of a concurrent resolution passed by a majority in both houses.[13] But once the Supreme Court held legislative vetoes unconstitutional, Congress amended the act to require a joint, instead of a concurrent, resolution.[14] Since these are subject to presidential veto, it now requires a two-thirds majority to override the inevitable opposition of the White House—something that will never happen during periods of crisis. Even if such a miracle occurred, the president could use his unilateral authority to proclaim a new emergency under the same (or different) statutory authority.

All of this is disheartening, suggesting to some that it is hopeless to call on Congress to exercise oversight.[15] But it is poor institutional design that lies at the bottom of the current troubles. Under current law, the president is perfectly happy when Congress fails to discharge its functions of oversight and control, since it leaves his emergency declarations intact. Yet this won't be true under my proposed alternative. To the contrary, the president's declaration will lapse after a week or two unless he gets Congress to give its affirmative approval, and escalating supermajorities must keep approving his initiative every two months or so.

This single change makes all the difference: it suddenly becomes imperative for the president to keep on pushing for up-or-down votes in Congress if he hopes to continue the emergency in force. Congressional passivity isn't an immutable fact of nature; the present structure invites the president to prevent congressional action; the alternative transforms him into its preeminent advocate.

The only question is whether, when put to the test, Congress will turn out to be a rubber stamp, routinely approving presidential power, even when the escalator moves into the stratosphere. In the end, this depends on whether there are enough people in this country who are willing to mobilize in defense of our heritage of freedom. But I see no reason for despair, so long as senators and representatives are no longer in a position to evade responsibility on the issue. There may well be times when a series of major attacks will lead thoughtful citizens to temper their libertarian zeal for a time, but this is, I suggest, as it should be. Once a semblance of sustained calm has been restored, Congress won't remain passive for long.

To test political intuitions on the matter, return to the case of José Padilla—the American whom the government has imprisoned for more than three years without proving its case in any court. But this time indulge me with a thought experiment. Suppose that, sometime in the 1990s, Congress had glimpsed the tragic possibility of September 11, and had possessed the wisdom and will to prepare the legal terrain in advance. Reflecting on the obvious inadequacies of the National Emergencies Act, it adopted a framework statute that required escalating supermajoritarian approval for emergency detentions. Can there be any doubt that, three years after September 11, the required supermajority would long ago have evaporated into thin air?[16]

Even if Congress had rejected my proposal to limit individual detentions to forty-five days, the termination of the emergency would have put the government to the test—either convict Padilla of a crime before a jury of his peers or set him free. Under the system of political checks and balances, Padilla would have received due process long ago—and yet, under the present system, which depends principally on the judiciary, it took three and a half years for the government to charge Padilla with a crime. Worse yet, it is anybody's guess when and whether the Supreme Court will redeem the proud tradition of the Bill of Rights.

But Is It Constitutional?

My proposal has three basic aspects—political, juridical, and economic—and I shall make life easy for myself by beginning with the last: there is absolutely no constitutional problem in granting emergency detainees significant payments for the time they spend in confinement. To the contrary, well-established constitutional principles of just compensation give abundant support to this decision.

The constitutional arguments in support of the political and juridical planks of my framework are a good deal more complicated, but in the end, equally compelling. I focus on the two most problematic elements of the scheme.[17] The first involves personal liberty—the authorization of emergency detention for forty-five days without anything resembling normal due process. The second involves the ground rules of the legislative game—the effort to move beyond majority rule and require the president to obtain increasing levels of supermajoritarian support to continue the state of emergency.

On first glance, these issues may seem entirely unrelated, but appearances are deceiving. Distinctive strands of the American constitutional tradition will allow us to tie them together into a compelling whole. Before elaborating the linkages, it is best to consider our problems one at a time.

Suspension of Habeas Corpus

Preventive detention—of anybody, for any length of time—is a very serious matter. Anglo-American law has set its face against it for centuries. In a free state, nobody should be subject to arbitrary detention, and the writ of habeas corpus is there to protect that right—requiring the government to establish the legality of any act of incarceration under the prevailing standards of constitutional due process. My proposal's suspension of this requirement for forty-five days amounts to a partial suspension of the Great Writ—a grave matter, surely, but is it unconstitutional?

The Constitution explicitly authorizes suspension of habeas corpus in "cases of rebellion or invasion [when] the public safety may require it."[18] But unfortunately, the history behind these phrases is not very revealing. At the Constitutional Convention, Charles Coatesworth Pinckney initially proposed that the writ "should not be suspended but on the most urgent occasions, & then only for a limited time not exceeding twelve months."[19] This provoked Gouverneur Morris to suggest the formulation that ultimately prevailed. Morris's language narrowed Pinckney's notion of "urgent occasions" to "rebellion or invasion," but neglected to include his twelve-month sunset provision.[20] In his notes recording the Convention's proceedings, James Madison doesn't explain why Morris excluded the sunset clause—it isn't even clear whether the members actually debated the issue. The entire matter arose at a late stage and did not receive the serious treatment it deserved.[21]

This deficiency was not cured in the course of the ratification debates. Speaking broadly, the clause only provoked a serious debate about federalism: given the powers of the individual states to suspend habeas corpus, was it really necessary to grant a similar power to the federal government?[22] This issue pushed the problem of criteria to the periphery. If there was a serious debate about the meaning of *rebellion* or *invasion,* it has been lost to history. The record does contain a fascinating tidbit: the New York State Convention, as one of its proposals for additional amendments, did suggest a six-month termination clause.[23] This gesture gives a bit of historical lineage to my own efforts to impose strict temporal limits on both individual detentions and the general state of emergency. Beyond this, the historical fragments simply don't support confident statements about Founding intentions.

The language of the actual text is more instructive. Begin with the idea of an "invasion." The text does not speak in terms of a legal category like "war" but addresses a very concrete and practical problem: If invaders challenge the very capacity of government to maintain order, a suspension of the writ is justified when "the public safety may require it." It is this challenge to effective sovereignty that makes the constitutional situation exceptional.

This is also the space that my proposal seeks to occupy. Events like September 11 are distinctive in destabilizing the citizenry's confidence in the sovereign's capacity to defend the frontiers, and my proposal is tailored to respond to the anxious sense of uncertainty that will predictably ensue. On an instrumental level, my proposal authorizes emergency dragnets that seek to remove key operators from the scene and thereby eliminate further "invasions." On a symbolic level, it reassures the citizenry that effective steps to counter the "invasion" are under way.

But this rationale covers only terrorist attacks, like those of September 11, involving invaders from abroad. Future cases may well require further reflection on the concept of *rebellion,* and how it differs from riots and mass disturbances. The crucial dimension is political self-consciousness. When a mob runs amok, looting and destroying, it may cause great damage and anxiety, but this doesn't amount to a "rebellion" unless mob leaders challenge the political legitimacy of the existing system. This is precisely the mark of the a typical terrorist attack: the group does not merely blast innocent civilians, but "claims credit" for the attack and seeks to justify it by denouncing the government in power.

This distinguishes terrorism from mob violence, but perhaps *rebellion* requires something more elaborate? Perhaps it requires the group to form an alternative government and proclaim its legitimate authority?

The history of the Suspension Clause allows, though it certainly doesn't require, an expansive interpretation. The key precedent involves the suspension of habeas corpus by President Ulysses S. Grant in his effort to suppress the Ku Klux Klan in the South after the Civil War. Congress authorized the president to suspend the writ, but it did not require him to assert that the Klan was trying to overthrow the government, much less form an alternative one. Under statutory definition, it was enough to qualify as a "rebellion" if the Klan was "organized and armed, and so numerous and powerful as to be able, by violence, to either overthrow or *set at defiance* the constituted authorities of such State."[24] This formula from the Reconstruction era states the aims of modern terrorism with preternatural precision: defiance of the authorities is the essence.

Though history gives some support to a broad view of the suspension clause, I don't wish to deny the obvious: When one ordinarily speaks of an "invasion" or "rebellion," the paradigm case involves far more than a single terrorist attack, however large it may be.[25] It conjures up an ongoing series of violent actions—and, as we have seen, one of the distinctive features of our problem is that a single terrorist attack does *not* necessarily imply that there will be many more to come. While future attacks may well be in the offing, the terrorists may have gained an isolated victory over the security services, and no further acts of "invasion" or "rebellion" are in prospect. If Congress ever authorizes the suspension of the writ in response to an event like September 11, it will be occupying the border-lands of its constitutional authority.

Not, mind you, that such a decision would go beyond the constitu-tional line—to the contrary, it is entirely reasonable for Congress to fear the worst and take energetic action to cut off a second strike. Nevertheless, the Constitution does not speak of "reasonable" suspen-sion of habeas corpus; nor does it even embrace suspension on "urgent occasions," as Pinckney proposed. If time passes without further major incidents, it becomes increasingly implausible to speak of a single attack—or even two—as amounting to an *ongoing* "rebellion" or "inva-sion." These concepts themselves already require Congress to impose time limits on the exercise of its suspension powers.

The Supreme Court suggested as much in *Duncan v. Kahanamoku*, arising in the aftermath of the Japanese attack on Pearl Harbor.[26] The governor of Hawaii had immediately suspended the operation of the ordinary courts, requiring civilians to defend themselves against criminal charges before military tribunals. When the military convicted a couple of civilians later in the war, they challenged this suspension in carefully modulated terms. They conceded that the governor's action was legiti-mate in the immediate aftermath of Pearl Harbor but convinced the trial court that there was no imminent threat of an invasion at the time they were tried.[27] The Court took careful note of this point in holding that Duncan could not be deprived of his rights to trial by jury. Writing for the majority, Justice Black recognized that the larger war against Japan was still continuing, but with Japan on the road to defeat, the risk of invasion was no longer sufficiently imminent to justify the imposition of martial law.[28]

Strictly speaking, the Court's decision involved an interpretation of the Organic Act that served as Hawaii's territorial constitution, not the concept of *invasion* that justifies suspension under the federal Constitution. Nonetheless, Black went out of his way to emphasize that "whatever power the Organic Act gave the Hawaiian military authorities, such power must therefore be construed in the same way as a grant of power to troops stationed in any one of the states."[29] As Justice Frankfurter suggested in his dissent, *Duncan* stands for a remarkably stringent temporal limitation on the sort of "invasion" that justifies suspension of habeas corpus. The case arose a mere eight months after an invasion undeniably occurred at Pearl Harbor. The attacker was still in the field, albeit with a declining capacity to strike at Hawaii. If suspension of ordinary criminal procedures wasn't justified in this case, Congress seems to be under an imperative obligation to make sure that its response to a major terrorist attack doesn't continue indefinitely without a compelling showing that a second strike poses an imminent danger.

Here is where the supermajoritarian escalator plays a key role. In the immediate aftermath of a major attack, it permits a simple legislative majority to authorize the partial suspension of the Great Writ and enter the constitutional borderland. But as time passes, it requires Congress to take the Constitution seriously by recognizing that an "invasion" or "rebellion" is an ongoing affair—and that if the suspension of habeas corpus is to endure, it should be based on a broadening consensus that the first strike is indeed catapulting us into a continuing crisis comparable to the classical paradigm cases contemplated by the text.

To put the point in terms developed by James Madison long ago, realistic constitutionalists should not place too much confidence on the power of words like *rebellion* or *invasion* to check the abuse of power. "Experience assures us," Madison told us in the *Federalist Papers,* that textual formulae are "greatly over-rated" as a check on predictable abuses. Rather than relying on "parchment barriers" to check predictable abuses, institutional remedies are "indispensably necessary."[30] The supermajoritarian escalator is precisely the remedy required in the present case.

We have arrived, then, at the promised link between two key features of my proposal—the suspension of habeas corpus and the supermajoritarian escalator. The second guarantees that the first will be kept within constitutional bounds. But before we can make this linkage secure, we must consider the escalator from a second vantage point.

The Analytics of the Escalator

To make further progress, deconstruct the supermajoritarian escalator into its two conceptual building blocks. The first is the sunset idea: emergencies terminate after a brief period unless Congress expressly extends them. The second is the supermajoritarian idea: simple majorities aren't enough to defer the sunset for two more months—only an escalating supermajority will suffice.

Taking the building blocks in turn, sunsetting raises no significant constitutional problem. Congress does it all the time: for example, Congress placed a four-year sunset on key portions of the USA Patriot Act, requiring express reauthorization by the end of 2005.[31] If this is okay—and nobody doubts that it is—Congress also could require emergency reauthorizations every two months. The only serious question is raised by the supermajoritarian feature: is it constitutional to depart from simple majority rule and impose an escalating requirement of 60, 70, or 80 percent?

We can't reach a final conclusion without confronting one of the text's great silences. Both British and colonial legislatures used simple majority rule when enacting statutes, and the Framers certainly supposed that this rule would continue to operate as a baseline. But nothing in their text expressly requires this, and the Constitution contains a number of supermajoritarian provisions designed for special circumstances, like the Senate ratification of treaties or a congressional override of a presidential veto.[32] The dispositive question is whether this list is exhaustive, or whether Congress can add more supermajoritarian rules by enacting new framework statutes.

Over the past generation, the Court has looked skeptically upon congressional efforts to change the foundational rules for legislative enactment.[33] As a general matter, I think such skepticism is appropriate. When one Congress imposes a supermajoritarian rule, it makes it harder for future Congresses—with very different political majorities—to enact their will into law. Any effort by a momentary majority to shackle a later one raises serious legitimacy questions, and ones that have preoccupied me for a long time.[34]

But happily, there is something special about this case that permits us to avoid a large detour into grand theoretical matters. Though the Constitution does grant Congress the power to suspend habeas corpus, the text makes it clear that this power should be used only under very exceptional conditions—as it says, in cases of "rebellion" and "invasion"—and not otherwise. This contrasts sharply with standard grants of legislative authority. For example, when the Constitution gives Congress the power of taxation, it contemplates its constant exercise, and it is textually neutral concerning the propriety of a very broad range of taxes.[35]

Given the exceptional character of habeas suspension, Congress's decision to restrain itself through a supermajority rule should be viewed much more sympathetically. If a new framework statute ever emerges, it should not be disparaged as a narrowly partisan effort by a momentary majority to make it harder for political opponents when they come into power. It should be viewed as a bipartisan effort to breathe new life into the constitutional meaning of the Suspension Clause. As we have seen, the Founders did not make a serious effort to define the precise limits of "invasion" and "rebellion." And even if they had, they were in no position to refine their thoughts in a way that could adequately confront the distinctive features of twenty-first-century terrorism. By adopting the super-majoritarian escalator in advance of future attacks, Congress is taking the precise step that will discourage predictable manipulations of the guiding constitutional concepts during moments of panic—without, however, making it impossible for suspension to occur when there is a broadening constitutional consensus that the country faces a challenge comparable to the classic "invasion" or "rebellion." If there ever was a time to respect Congress's role as an interpreter of the Constitution, this is it.[36]

In short, the distinctive framework of American constitutionalism permits us to solve two key problems at once through a process of reflective equilibrium. On the one hand, the restrictive language of the Suspension Clause provides a specially powerful reason to uphold Congress's decision to restrain the abuse of its emergency powers by imposing a super-majoritarian escalator on itself. On the other hand, the supermajoritarian provision makes it more constitutionally acceptable for Congress to find that a single terrorist attack is tantamount to the kind of "rebellion" or "invasion" that authorizes suspension of habeas corpus in the first place.

Can American Courts Do the Job?

When working smoothly, the framework statute shouldn't require aggressive management by the courts—but, as we have seen, there may well be moments when the judges must act aggressively to assure the integrity of the system. Yet once again, American exceptionalism raises distinctive constitutional problems. In countries that enact the emergency framework as a formal constitutional amendment, the courts can exercise their normal powers of judicial review to strike down statutes which undermine the emergency constitution. But since the American framework will be enacted as a statute, not an amendment, it requires further argument to establish that the Supreme Court can play a similar supervisory role during moments of crisis.

To set the stage, suppose that the coming years bring a serious effort by Congress and the president to collaborate on a new emergency statute. After lots of pulling and hauling, a broad bipartisan coalition comes together in support of the Emergencies Act of 2009, incorporating the basic elements of my framework.

Then, happily, nothing happens. The terrorist threat is somehow deflected from the homeland for years and years—until some unspeakable disaster strikes in 2015, and the framework confronts its first real test. As the supermajoritarian escalator increases to 80 percent, the effort to extend the emergency fails in the Senate by a vote of 75–25. But the majority does not take its defeat lightly. In a fury, it urges the immediate repeal of the framework statute, and by a simple majority vote. Does the Supreme Court have the power to intervene at this point and strike down the repeal, restoring the escalator in full force? If not, doesn't the possibility of repeal by a simple majority make the supermajoritarian escalator into a bad joke?

Before exploring the role of the Court at such moments, I want to emphasize the political checks that will operate to resist repeal. For starters, the framework statute would never have been enacted without lots of hard work from lots of senators and representatives. Many of these people will still be on Capitol Hill, and their seniority will put them in key positions. Congress is full of devices through which senior leaders can postpone a vote on the floor until passions cool down a bit. They will have taken pride in their earlier achievements and they will try to prevent repeal from reaching the floor, saving their politically vulnerable colleagues the need to pander to the fears of the general public. Even if the matter does get to the floor, the great debates that surrounded the earlier enactment of the Emergencies Act won't have been forgotten. They will enable defenders of the act to invite the voters to see the repeal campaign as a symptom of a panic reaction that threatens the survival of liberal democracy.

There can be no guarantees. But it is too quick to predict confidently that the majoritarian repeal of the escalator will be an easy political matter. Even though a two-month extension fails in the Senate by a margin of 75–25, this hardly implies that fifty-one of the seventy-five senators who voted yes will be prepared to destroy the entire framework. And if the statute manages to survive one or two political ordeals, it will become much more difficult for later majorities to engage in a wrecking operation. By a curious paradox, the failed efforts to repeal the framework will lead to its symbolic reaffirmation and consolidation as a time-tested mechanism for regaining political equilibrium during periods of great stress—or so one may hope.[37]

But enough happy talk. When push comes to shove, Congress and the president may well pander to the public by repealing the framework, and it will remain for the Supreme Court to show its hand. To define its proper role, we must reflect further on the constitutional implications of the framework statute's intimate relationship to the Suspension Clause.

As we have seen, *any* restriction of habeas corpus in response to terrorism requires Congress to explore the twilight zone of its constitutional authority: It is a stretch to say that one or two attacks—even very serious ones—amount to an "invasion" or "rebellion," especially if they aren't followed up by an ongoing series of major assaults. Not an indefensible stretch, but a stretch nevertheless. This was my key point in defending the constitutionality of the supermajoritarian escalator in the first place, and it remains my key point in assessing the role of the Supreme Court.

So long as the framework statute is in place, it makes perfect sense for the Court to defer to Congress when it votes for a partial suspension of habeas corpus. The supermajoritarian escalator provides institutional recognition that suspension is a very serious constitutional matter, and that Congress is perfectly cognizant of its limited power to act in cases of "rebellion" or "invasion." Within this institutional context, it would be silly for the Court to second-guess particular contextual judgments made by supermajorities in response to particular terrorist attacks.

But the destruction of the framework statute radically transforms the Court's situation and raises a question of fundamental principle. Although the historical material is sparse, and there is an enormous gap between our twenty-first-century problem and the experience of our eighteenth-century Founders, one thing is clear: that the Constitution sets its face against *any* suspension of habeas corpus, insisting that this action should be reserved *only* for the gravest ongoing crises, comparable to traditional "rebellions" and "invasions." The easy and extended suspension of the Great Writ by a simple majority in Congress threatens the very foundations of freedom in this country. Call this the antinormalization principle, and it lies at the very foundation of the American constitutional tradition. If Congress ever destroyed the supermajoritarian escalator at a moment of high panic, the Court should safeguard this principle at all cost.

Great Cases

The great case is *Ex parte Milligan,* decided immediately after the Civil War. Lincoln had suspended the writ unilaterally early in the war, when Congress wasn't in session. After his decision was challenged in the courts, Congress ratified the president's actions when it convened in special session on July 4.[38] During its next regular session, it stabilized the situation further with a framework statute, which sharply distinguished between zones of insurrection and loyal areas where the courts were still in session.[39] In Unionist states like Indiana, the statute suspended the writ only in a limited fashion, granting military commanders the authority to arrest and detain until the government had a chance to make its case before a grand jury—but if the jury refused to indict, the statute required the release of the detainee within twenty days.

Indiana's military commander simply ignored the statute when it came to Lamdin Milligan, a longtime resident of the state without any ties to the military. Accusing him of inciting insurrection and violating "the laws of war," he seized Milligan and brought him before a military commission, which proceeded to sentence him to death. Milligan responded with a writ of habeas corpus, which reached the Court in 1866, the year after the war ended.

The Court ordered his immediate release, unanimously rejecting the president's claim, as commander in chief, to defy the statute. The justices unanimously upheld the authority of Congress to provide a suspension framework that required strict presidential obedience. Indeed, five of them went further to deny Congress all authority to suspend the writ entirely: "Martial law cannot arise from a threatened invasion. The necessity must be actual and present; the invasion real, such as effectually closes the courts and deposes the civil administration." The other four judges were not willing to go this far. On their view, Congress did have the power to authorize martial law in states like Indiana, which "had been actually invaded, and was constantly threatened with invasion."[40] But the decisive point, for them, was that Congress hadn't done so.

Our repeal scenario would force the Court to revisit the issues that divided the five from the four—but in a context that would permit it to split the difference. Although the five-judge majority categorically denounced presidential unilateralism, it upheld a significant, if limited, suspension of habeas corpus. Though the point is rarely noted, the framework statute of the Civil War era authorized the military to hold Milligan not only for the period it took to convene a grand jury but for twenty days after the jury refused to indict. Despite its broad dicta, the *Milligan* majority gave its imprimatur to a carefully controlled Congressional enactment that imposed a limited suspension of habeas corpus.

Similarly, it is wrong to read the more permissive minority opinion in *Milligan* to support anything like an open-ended congressional authorization of long-term emergency detentions. When Chief Justice Salmon P. Chase, speaking for three other colleagues, speaks of a "constant threat" of "invasion," he is gesturing not toward an uncertain prospect of a terrorist second strike but toward well-organized Confederate armies that once, briefly, actually invaded Indiana. Chase is disagreeing with the majority in upholding suspension only when it comes to the power of Congress to confront a massive civil war. But such cases of existential crisis are not to be confused with the very different threats posed by terrorism. It is an historical mistake to interpret Chase's opinion as supporting a panic-driven decision by Congress to destroy a carefully controlled framework statute and to authorize lengthy periods of emergency detentions.

So far as twenty-first-century terrorism is concerned, the two *Milligan* opinions are more similar than different. Both endorse a framework statute that will fill in the gray areas of the Suspension Clause; neither endorses congressional action that permits the normalization of open-ended emergency detentions—though, of course, the more emphatically restrictive position adopted by the majority deserves more weight in contemporary Court deliberations: 5 beats 4, after all. Taken together, the two opinions make *Milligan* into a crucial resource for future Courts confronting future Congresses at moments of panic.

To drive this point home, a well-drafted framework statute should go out of its way to invite judicial intervention in defense of the antinormalization principle. Its preamble should affirm *Milligan* and declare that the supermajoritarian escalator plays a crucial role in keeping Congress's suspension powers within their narrow constitutional limits. It should then expressly authorize the Supreme Court to strike down later statutes that seriously threaten the normalization of emergency powers by undermining the operation of the escalator. But even if the statute is silent on this score, *Milligan* makes it plain that the Court, not Congress, is the ultimate arbiter of the limits of the Suspension Clause.

Milligan is the great historical statement, but a second case, almost a century later, also serves as a key reference point: *Youngstown Sheet & Tube v. Sawyer.*[41] This decision doesn't squarely involve the Suspension Clause, but it raises larger issues posed by the president's assertion of war powers in domestic settings. It comes from the Korean War era: With a strike threatening the nation's steel production, President Truman asserted his power as commander in chief to seize most of the country's steel mills, and to order their continued operation. In response, the Court intervened decisively to protect the framework statutes that Congress had enacted to regulate labor relations. In drafting the National Labor Relations Act and related laws, Congress had self-consciously rejected government seizure as a solution to strikes, providing other methods for mediating conflicts in industries of national importance. The Court refused to allow the president to ignore this framework statute, despite Truman's finding that a strike posed a serious threat to the war effort.

In supporting the Court's decision, Justice Robert Jackson wrote a concurring opinion that made some commonsense distinctions that have had a big impact on later thought. He isolated three basic forms of legislative-executive relationship: in the first, Congress gives statutory support to the exercise of presidential power; in the second, it is silent; and in the third, "the President takes measures incompatible with the

expressed or implied will of Congress." Unsurprisingly, Jackson con-
cluded that "presidential power is at its lowest ebb" in this last category:

> [The President] can rely only upon his own constitutional pow-
> ers minus any constitutional powers of Congress over the matter.
> Courts can sustain exclusive Presidential control in such a case
> only by disabling the Congress from acting upon the subject.
> Presidential claims to a power at once so conclusive and preclu-
> sive must be scrutinized with caution, for what is at stake is the
> equilibrium established by our constitutional system.[42]

Equilibrium—that is the watchword, and the Court has a crucial role in
sustaining it: forcing the president to accept his role within the framework,
and forcing Congress to accept its limited role under the Suspension Clause.

Some Practical Principles

As an operational matter, the Court's actions should depend on the
branch seeking to destroy the equilibrium. Suppose, first, that a bare majority of Congress attempted a double-fisted assault—repealing the framework
statute on the one hand and enacting large new emergency powers on the
other. The Court's response should focus on the second hand. It should
concede that repeal of the framework statute is constitutional—after all, it
took a bare majority to enact in the first place, and what a majority can
enact, it can also repeal. But the Court should insist that repeal is of the first
importance when it comes to evaluating new grants of emergency powers.
Unless and until Congress restores such an institutional check, the Court
should hold fast to *Milligan*'s insistence that "martial law cannot arise from
a threatened invasion. The necessity must be actual and present; the invasion real, such as effectually closes the courts and deposes the civil administration." As a matter of institutional competence, the Court should explain,
it lacks the capacity to engage in subtle assessments of less obvious threats.
After all, there will *always* be a risk of a terrorist strike for the indefinite
future. If Congress wishes to distinguish those that rise to the gravity of a
real "rebellion" or "invasion," it should be allowed to do so only through a
procedure, like the escalator, that will prevent it from riding the slippery
slope down to an unending state of emergency. In short, the Court should
applaud the constitutional responsibility of the earlier Congress that enacted

the framework statute, and stand by the strong words of the *Milligan* Court until a future Congress demonstrates a similar constitutional sensitivity and restores an escalator.

A variation on this theme will be required under a second disequilibrating scenario: Here Congress repeals the framework but doesn't go further to authorize new emergency powers. It stands idly on the sidelines as the president fills the statutory void by issuing emergency decrees as commander in chief. It should be plain that the threat of permanent emergency is even greater in this case: If the Court insists on *Milligan* when Congress breaks free of supermajoritarian constraints, it should impose even more rigorous review of unilateral presidential actions which carry an even greater risk to liberty. The justices should, of course, allow the president to act alone in response to an attack until Congress can assemble and deliberate. But even Lincoln and Roosevelt gained express Congressional authorization for their use of emergency powers during times of all-out war; and nothing less should be required in the more uncertain cases posed by terrorism.

The case for judicial intervention is yet more compelling when Congress remains steadfast behind the framework statute, but the president refuses to accept a termination of the emergency, ordering its continuation under his sole authority as commander in chief. Here is where *Youngstown* gives additional support to *Milligan:* whatever the scope of the president's power to act as commander in chief abroad, the Steel Seizure Case makes it clear that he can't extend these powers domestically in the face of contrary framework statutes.

The signposts provided by *Milligan* and *Youngstown* can't prevent some future Court from losing its way. And even if the justices prevent the first panic-driven effort, and the second, and the third, they will only be buying time for sober second thought. Nobody can save our great tradition of freedom in the long run except the American people; but in the middle run, the courts can make a big difference.

Exceptionalism Reconsidered

We began with a puzzle: given the difficulty of formally amending the U.S. Constitution, could a way be found to entrench a good emergency framework into our governing arrangements?

My constructive argument relies on one crucial point: the Constitution already expresses a profound opposition to the normalization of emergency powers. Given the narrow reach of the Suspension Clause, it is constitutionally imperative for Congress to reassure the country, and the Court, that the danger of a second strike is comparable to those confronted by an ongoing "rebellion" or "invasion." While an initial major attack may justify such a finding in the short run, first impressions won't necessarily stand up over time, and there is a need for constant, and sober, reassessment. This commonsense point provides a constitutional anchor for congressional adoption of a supermajoritarian escalator and for aggressive judicial review in case of its later repudiation. And if Congress fails to build special checks into its own decision making, the Court should intervene in the future, as it did in *Milligan* and the Steel Seizure Case, to protect the American tradition of freedom.

This conclusion suggests that American exceptionalism may turn out to be an advantage, not a liability, in the longer run. Instead of fixing the precise terms of the "emergency constitution" in the formal Constitution, a framework statute provides more flexible opportunities for midcourse corrections over time. Our experience with the Emergencies Act of 1976, after all, revealed disabling weaknesses; and others—less serious, we hope—will doubtless emerge as the new framework statute confronts reality tests. Although the Court should be profoundly skeptical of panicky efforts to smash the framework in the midst of crisis, it should be more sympathetic toward serious congressional efforts, at moments of relative calm, to learn from accumulating experience.

If we are lucky, we will be in a position to hand to the next generation a more resilient emergency constitution than anything currently on the drawing board.

7

IF WASHINGTON BLOWS UP?

Although the next attack may devastate Chicago or Los Angeles, it may not touch Washington, D.C. On the morning after, there will still be a president, Congress, and Supreme Court to take charge.

Yet fate may not be so kind, and decapitation poses distinctive challenges. The emergency constitution must move fast to select leaders who can gain the confidence of the country. By the next morning, we should know who will be serving as president, and before the week is out, an anxious citizenry should see new leaders converging on a makeshift Capitol and Supreme Court to continue the work of government. Further delays will profoundly demoralize the nation, and yet that is what we will get from our current system.

Under existing law, only the Senate will reliably resurrect itself in a timely and credible fashion; as to the presidency, we may wake up to hear the unknown voice of the secretary of transportation assuring the country that it is in good hands—only to find that he is quickly displaced by other nonentities from the House or Senate in a series of partisan power plays.

The House of Representatives and the Supreme Court also raise grave problems. It will take many weeks before a satisfactory House can reestablish itself, and reconstructing the Supreme Court will pose great difficulties.

This is unacceptable: the government can't pass any laws without a functioning House, and a credible Court plays a key role in assuring the country that the ensuing state of emergency won't spin entirely out of control. Without an operational system of separation of powers, an untested president will have no choice but to discard the rule of law and govern by emergency decree. Given his inexperience, he will be under special pressure to prove that he's "in charge" even at the cost of erasing the line between decisiveness and ruthlessness. We cannot afford to retire our tradition of checks and balances. My emergency constitution gives the president extraordinary powers to prevent a second strike, but given his inexperience, it is especially important to require him regularly to gain the assent of Congress under the supermajoritarian escalator.

There are hard choices involved in designing a better system, but the status quo is plainly inadequate, and everybody should be willing to compromise on a reasonable proposal before terrorists put us to the test. I will be clarifying basic principles and searching for institutional fixes that are within the realm of political possibility. I will be on the lookout for solutions that don't require formal constitutional amendments. If statutes can get the job done, they should be enacted quickly. Some readers may believe that further major improvements should be sought through constitutional amendment—though I don't share this opinion. In any case, it is important to pass good statutes now, and then debate the need for, and nature of, further perfecting amendments. Although this is the only area where a formal amendment is a serious political option, its consideration should not serve as an excuse for doing nothing in the short term. The best should not become an enemy of the good, and good statutory alternatives are currently available.

Once we have gotten the government back in business, there is a second problem. The new office holders may be rookies, with problematic legitimacy under ordinary constitutional norms, but they will try to consolidate their hold on power and make long-lasting decisions that can reverberate for decades. Should special steps be taken to rein in their desire to transform a tragic opportunity into long-term political gains?

This problem of entrenchment, as I shall call it, takes different forms in different branches. If the attack occurs early in a presidential term, do we really want the late president's replacement to serve for almost four years before the next election, or should we reschedule the vote so that it occurs at the next biennial selection of senators and representatives? Should we bar the acting president from seeking another term, encouraging him to focus his energies on the immediate emergency, and giving the competing political parties an equal chance at the open seat?

Analogous questions arise with the other branches, leading to a series of tough choices. But first things first: before taking aim at the problem of entrenchment, we must get the government up and running again.

What Do We Want?

Speed is important, I can hear you say, but so is legitimacy—isn't it okay to delay matters a bit to get a more legitimate result in the middle run?

I don't think so. Speed is itself a crucial element of legitimacy: Power abhors a vacuum, and if the emergency constitution doesn't fill positions quickly, the military may take charge, and this is a lot worse than the secretary of transportation. Unless and until there is a House and Supreme Court, government will lose its capacity to make laws and assure their uniform administration. The power vacuum will also be sending a terrible message to American citizens, who have seen their institutions withstand two centuries of crises without missing a beat. So far as they are concerned, no Congress and no Court means no constitutional government in America—and this is a very illegitimate state of affairs, which may readily breed further lurches into the dark rather than a return to constitutional government in the middle run.

So delay should be treated as a last resort, and we should aim for a scheme that permits as much legitimacy as speedy reconstruction will allow. If the interim government doesn't seem legitimate enough to last for a long time, we can respond by restricting its capacity to entrench itself.

If speed is all-important, other aspects of legitimacy raise different, and potentially incompatible, notions of good government. The first ideal is policy continuity: Other things equal, it is a bad thing if a terrorist bomb leads to a big change in political direction—with a right-wing acting president substituting for a left-wing predecessor, or vice versa. Such a shift will hand the terrorists a victory by disrupting the basic American expectation that government tracks democratic will.

Policy continuity may work at cross purposes with a second aim: the new officials should be seasoned statesmen, with track records of visible political accomplishment. This point is recognized, for example, in the existing statute that governs succession to the presidency—if the president and vice president are dead or disabled, the statute doesn't designate the secretary of state as next in line, continuing government in the hands of one of the old president's most trusted associates. It passes the presidency to the speaker of the House and then to the president pro tem of the Senate before turning to the secretary of state and other members of the cabinet. Since there is no guarantee that the House or Senate is controlled by the president's party, the statute is choosing statesmanship over continuity as its governing criterion.

And plausibly so.[1] Whatever their vices, House and Senate leaders have two virtues. They gain and keep their positions only by mastering the art of politics; and their many years of public service make their names relatively familiar to the American people. Perhaps it is too much to call them statesmen, but they are men and women whose political leadership has stood the test of time. There is no similar guarantee for cabinet officers—there have been many distinguished secretaries of the leading departments, and some have become household names, but very few modern secretaries have had genuine political experience before assuming their office, and they may be ill prepared for the rough-and-tumble of political life.

Apart from policy continuity and experienced statesmanship, there is also the critical issue of constitutional continuity: the replacement should be selected, as much as possible, in a fashion that tracks established constitutional principles. Consider, for example, how Senate vacancies are handled under existing law. The Constitution authorizes governors to fill vacancies immediately with temporary appointments, allowing the state to remain fully represented in the Senate. This selection mechanism expresses the Senate's distinctive claim to federalist legitimacy by giving the state's governor, and not some national officer, the power to make the interim appointment.

Finally, a couple of criteria should go without saying, but unfortunately, the present ramshackle system fails even these minimal requirements. First, the rules of succession should be absolutely clear—everybody should know who is in charge of each of the critical institutions; and second, they should not create unnecessary instability by allowing the rump Congress to engage in partisan coups that displace the acting president with another untested official. Political gamesmanship is simply unacceptable at a time when the American people desperately need a steady hand on the tiller. And yet, as we shall see, it is all too likely.

I propose to explore our grim situation in a deliberate fashion, canvassing each of the four departments of government—House, Senate, presidency, and Court—and see what we can do get each back in business in a timely and credible fashion. My tour begins with the Senate, since it is the institution in least need of repair.

The Senate

Under the Seventeenth Amendment, the state legislature may authorize the governor to fill vacancies on an interim basis, pending a special election to fill out the old senator's term. Within days of a devastating attack, the nation will see a new Senate rising from the ashes, which easily satisfies the Constitution's requirement that "a majority of each [House] shall constitute a quorum to do business."[2]

The Senate system of gubernatorial replacement also scores well on the political continuity test—if a devastating attack required all fifty governors to make one hundred interim appointments, it is unlikely for the party breakdown of the new Senate to depart radically from its predecessor.[3] The current procedure seems more problematic when it comes to the newcomers' stature as visibly accomplished political leaders—governors have, in the past, rewarded old buddies, or big contributors, or even family members, with the job.[4]

But nothing is perfect, and here the existing constitutional rule against entrenchment plays a meliorating role. When the Seventeenth Amendment was enacted in 1913 to require the popular election of senators, its draftsmen had the wit to require the governor's appointee to face a special election before he has had a chance to gain too large an advantage from his incumbency.

All in all, the existing system does a perfectly good job in a difficult situation. There is only one hole worth filling. The terrorist blast may have left some senators with their lives, but in a grievously impaired condition, unable to function as competent representatives. The Seventeenth Amendment speaks of "vacancies," leaving it open for Senate Rules or congressional statutes to determine when these occur. The present definition should be expanded to take the problem of incompetence explicitly into account, at least in the case of a major terrorist attack.[5] The rules should, of course, be careful to respect the rights of invalided senators to a full medical determination of their condition. But if any senator is medically incompetent and shows no significant prospect of recovery, his seat should be declared conditionally "vacant" to allow an interim appointment; and if the senator remains in his tragic condition, the seat should be declared permanently vacant after six months.

Under the amendment, the next move is up to the state legislatures, which are vested with authority to determine the conditions under which the governor makes interim appointments, and to fix the time for the special election. Upon receipt of a notice of interim vacancy, two options are open. The legislature can elect to do nothing, allowing the state to suffer the loss of Senate representation for six months pending a final competency determination. Or it can authorize an interim appointment, pending the senator's recovery, and authorize a special election if he does not recover. This will allow the legislature to fulfill the amendment's plain purpose—to assure the full representation of the state on an ongoing basis when the previously elected senator cannot cast a ballot, and so has, functionally speaking, left the seat vacant.

From the federal point of view, all that is required is a statute redefining the constitutional concept of vacancy to give the state legislatures an option.[6] Such a statute might have seemed an over-elaborate response to the occasional case in which a senator suffers a terminal decline in his faculties. But the terrorist threat creates a significant risk that a substantial number of states might be deprived of representation in a single attack. It is both "necessary" and "proper" for the Congress to use its constitutional powers to implement the Seventeenth Amendment to rectify this inadequacy in the existing scheme.

But even without this legislative repair, the Senate should regain its status as a functioning body within days of the attack. And this, as we shall see, is not something that readily can be taken for granted.

The House

At present, there is no way to fill House seats on an interim basis. They remain vacant until there is a special election, leaving the House of Representatives in a potentially desperate condition.

Suppose that a blast kills 375 Representatives, leaving only 60 alive. Can these members meet as an organized body when the Constitution says that "a majority of each [House] shall constitute a quorum to do business"?

One obvious answer is No: a majority of a 435-member House is 218, and the remaining rump has no constitutional authority; undoubtedly, this is the answer that lots of Americans will give, especially if the remaining 60 living members fail to represent a geographic and political cross section of the country. But over the centuries, the House has come up with a less obvious interpretation of the Constitution's quorum requirement. For the past century or so, its rules defined a quorum as a majority of Representatives "chosen, sworn, and *living,* whose membership has not been terminated by resignation or by action of the House."[7] When it eliminated the dead from the quorum requirement in 1891, the House was treating the matter as a minor bookkeeping measure and did not contemplate the almost unthinkable prospect of mass decapitation.[8]

So matters stood until January 4, 2005, when the 109th House of Representatives confronted the prospect of a massive strike in an extraordinary fashion. Every two years, each new House votes on its Rules on opening day, and the leadership took the opportunity to make a dramatic change in the traditional definition of a quorum. In the event of "catastrophic circumstances," a "provisional quorum" will be established by determining how many representatives show up on the floor of the House within seventy-two hours after they have been summoned. Under my scenario, if 375 representatives were killed, 30 were incapacitated, 10 were safe but far away from Washington and unable to return, the 20 members responding to the call would represent the basis for future quorum calls—so that 11 members would suffice to constitute a quorum, and 6 would be enough to pass legislation, declare war, or authorize a state of emergency.[9]

To his very great credit, Congressman Brian Baird rose to raise a point of order on the ground that this remarkable rule change was unconstitutional. But Speaker Dennis Hastert ruled this objection out of order, and the proposal was virtually ignored in the debate on the Rules that followed.[10] The members were far more interested in the efforts by Majority Leader Tom DeLay to change the rules governing the House Ethics

Committee, which had been a consistent critic of his behavior during the previous session.[11]

This remarkably casual treatment will guarantee blistering constitutional criticism on the morning after the decapitating strike. However the debate is resolved, we are in a terrible situation. Perhaps the rump House will simply retreat before popular outrage and refuse to meet on the basis of the arbitrary decision of 2005. In this case, Americans are stuck without a functioning Congress, leaving an entirely inexperienced acting president little choice but to rule by decree in defiance of the most basic constitutional norms—until such time as a more satisfactory House, containing at least 218 members, and preferably lots more, can assemble. Or the rump House may claim a contestable legitimacy, and together with a gubernatorially selected Senate and the novice president, enact laws that may or may not have much relationship to majority sentiment in the country.

Worse yet, the Constitution presently precludes a Senate-like solution, in which state officials—perhaps governors, perhaps members of the state legislatures—make interim appointments: "The House of Representatives shall be composed of Members chosen every second Year *by the People* of the several States."[12] These words inscribe a constitutional understanding that is deeply engraved on the national consciousness: membership in the "People's House" is, and should be, based on a direct connection between voters and representatives. No formal amendment challenging this idea has a ghost of a chance of enactment, and I myself am firmly committed to retaining a direct linkage between the House and the people.

Especially when there is a straightforward solution that is perfectly compatible with existing constitutional commitments: Congress should create a new office of vice representative, who will serve in the event of the death or disability of the representative. Henceforth, the major political parties would regularly nominate a two-person "ticket" in each House race, and voters would cast ballots for *both* positions at each election, enabling the vice representative to take over immediately in the event of a decapitating strike.[13]

This system transparently complies with the constitutional text, since both representative and vice representative will be "chosen every second Year by the People." Rather than violating this command, Congress is complying with its literal terms. It is simply changing the mode of its compliance—replacing the current system of special elections with a more regularized mechanism for filling potential vacancies in advance.

A straightforward statute will suffice for this change—no formal amendment is needed. The Constitution nowhere requires special elections to fill vacancies; indeed, the text tilts in the direction of my proposal, since it speaks of the people going to the polls "every second year" to select the men and women who will be serving during the biennium. It is the existing practice of holding irregular special elections that doesn't quite square with the text's command that House selection should occur "every second year." I do not suggest that special elections are unconstitutional—there is a lot more to constitutional law than the "plain meaning" of the text, and in the days before September 11, special elections seemed a far more sensible way to respond to the occasional House vacancy. But the language of the Constitution suggests that critics of my proposal—and there are sure to be some—shouldn't convert their doubts about its wisdom into complaints about its unconstitutionality.

My proposal may be novel, but it conforms to the Founding approach to the analogous problem raised in connection with the presidency. When confronting the prospect of the president's death—by assassination or otherwise—the Framers could have dispensed with the vice presidency entirely and designated some interim figure, like the secretary of state, to call a special election to fill the office as soon as possible—this is the system used to fill the presidency in Mexico, for example.[14] What is more, when the First Congress confronted the problem of presidential succession, it actually required a special election, supervised by the secretary of state, in the unlikely event that both president and vice president proved unable to serve.[15] But so far as the Founders were concerned, the death of the president seemed sufficiently likely, and sufficiently disturbing, to warrant the selection of a replacement in advance. Although they didn't give the vice president very much to do, they thought it was important to have him hanging around.

During the eighteenth century, the technology for a massive sneak attack wasn't available—nobody took the possibility seriously that the House, like the presidency, could be decapitated by a single blow. So the Framers didn't seriously consider the creation of a vice representative, on analogy with the vice president. But there is no reason to suspect that they would have objected as a matter of principle.[16] So far as the Constitution is concerned, Congress has ample authority to pass a statute creating the office of vice representative as "necessary and proper" for assuring the continuing existence of government in the United States.[17] The only serious question is whether, all things considered, such a move is wise.

This involves weighing up imponderables. As we shall see, creating 435 new vice reps may involve some political difficulties—though steps can be taken to ameliorate them. But if disaster strikes, the vacuum of legitimate lawmaking power could generate tremendous evils. It's silly to proffer precise estimates of the probability that a doomsday scenario will occur, say, over the next half-century: is it one chance in a thousand, or five hundred, or one hundred?

Hard to say, but it isn't one in a million. For one thing, the costs of producing a miniaturized weapon will be going down throughout the period. For another, technological improvements will allow terrorists to wreak destruction at a distance: they won't have to get to Pennsylvania Avenue before launching a decapitating strike. It may suffice to strike from Georgetown on a day when the power elite is in town. And finally, Washington is an obvious target of choice, precisely because of the disastrous consequences of a decapitating strike. To be sure, the security services will be in a position to offset the increased threat by the clever use of better surveillance technology. But it would be blind to ignore the residual risk.

So let's move on to consider the proposal in further detail, comparing it with other options. Most obviously, it passes the test of policy continuity: a House of Vice Representatives will have the same political complexion as the one it replaces. Since the major parties will be running two-candidate slates in each House district, the winning vice representative will almost invariably have the same political affiliation as the representative at the top of the ticket.

But the system scores less well when it comes to experienced statesmanship: the candidate at the top of the ticket won't be interested in giving a platform to somebody with sufficient stature to launch a primary challenge during the next election cycle. He will predictably ask a longtime political associate, or a trusted staffer, to serve as his running mate—and arrange with his local political party to rubber-stamp the nomination; or if there is a primary, he will launch a joint campaign with his running mate.

The need to stand jointly before the voters, however, will force the representative to think twice before making an egregious choice for vice rep. As presidential candidates have learned, the selection of a bad vice presidential nominee starts the campaign off on a very bad note—giving opponents a field day in the press. This will restrain the selection of a spouse or a child, or a notorious incompetent. Even if one takes a pessimistic view of likely candidate quality, a House of Vice Representatives will provide valuable ballast in a doomsday scenario, in which the presidency is held by an unknown novice and the Senate is dominated by interim members selected by state governors.

Not a pretty picture, I confess, but surely a lot less grim than a scene in which the acting president must rule by decree, or a rump House sits in defiance of bitter challenges to its constitutional legitimacy. Though concerns about the political statecraft of the typical vice rep may be justified, they should not be exaggerated—as a comparison with the interim appointments to the Senate makes plain. While the major parties will make their selections for vice rep clear to the voters in advance, the governors never tell the electorate who they will select if a senate seat becomes vacant—and as a consequence, governors pay much less of a political penalty if they appoint a crony or a relative to an empty seat. Although the vice reps may not shine, the interim senators may well look more problematic as a group—though I suspect that, even here, the prevailing sense of national unity will encourage the nation's governors to avoid egregious selections.

If, however, the quality of vice reps seems a serious concern, a modification of the proposal might be worth considering. Perhaps the statute should not merely authorize vice representatives to replace the fallen Reps when a major terrorist attack kills forty or fifty members in a single episode. Perhaps it should go further and stipulate that the vice rep should begin voting whenever his or her representative vacates the office. By making it more likely that the vice rep will exercise real power, this modification will increase the political cost involved in presenting an obvious lightweight to the voters on election day.

But alas, there is a danger lurking in this seemingly sensible proposal. Once the vice rep succeeds as a matter of course, elderly representatives will use their effective political control over their district's vice rep nomination to designate a political heir apparent. This would be a serious evil, I think, since incumbents already have too many advantages in their competition against the out-party, and it would be a shame to allow the vice rep to run for his first election without the normal testing that occurs when a seat is vacated.[18] Though reasonable people can certainly disagree, I think it's more prudent to limit the vice reps to service in dire emergencies, and to continue to rely on special elections to fill other vacancies.

Given this limitation, there will always be one disadvantage to the office of "emergency vice representative"—it will serve as a constant reminder of the real possibility of a devastating terrorist attack, and provide a demoralizing undertone to ordinary politics. But demoralizing or not, the truth is that we do face a low-level but palpable terrorist risk. Rather than burying our heads in the sand, isn't it better to deal with the truth in a sober fashion, and in a way that seeks best to sustain our democratic ideals?

Since September 11, more and more serious people have been confronting this question. A special commission, organized by the American Enterprise Institute and the Brookings Institution, has done some important preliminary work, and as we have already seen, the House is already taking ad hoc actions to fill the potential legitimacy gap. My particular proposal hasn't been considered, but it might resolve some of the difficulties that perplex the leading initiatives of the moment.

In addition to its precipitous change in quorum requirements in January 2005, the House has been considering other responses more deliberately. In June 2004 Congressman Brian Baird obtained a floor vote on his proposed constitutional amendment requiring each representative to submit a list of two to five replacements to his state's governor— who would then draw from the list in appointing a successor in response to a decapitating attack.[19] After a spirited debate, the proposal was overwhelmingly defeated, and for good reason. The Baird Amendment shut the voters out of the entire process, even failing to require the candidate to announce his choices before election day.[20] This assured its overwhelming defeat by members who rose to preserve the "People's House" from elite manipulation.[21] Nevertheless, Baird was on the right track in seeing a need to devise a procedure for filling vacancies in advance.

Baird's opponents missed this point when making their own proposal. Led by Representative David Dreier, the House overwhelming passed a Continuity in Government Act that would require special elections within 49 days.[22] When the Senate failed to hold hearings on the measure, the House leadership kept up the pressure by tacking Dreier's initiative onto a key appropriations bill, which finally assured its passage—without any serious consideration by the Senate.[23] While the new law serves as a gesture at the problem, it is not a real solution. Although it may insist on a vote within 49 days, it takes about four months, on average, to hold special elections under normal conditions. Perhaps a month could be cut from the 120-day norm, but even this is asking a lot given the chaos following a massive terrorist attack.[24] And it is hard to think of worse conditions for rushing an election. Since the seat has been vacated without warning, potential candidates will have had no notice of the need to campaign for the job. The nomination will fall to local party bosses, who will have neither the time nor inclination to test their favorite's broader support. Once the major parties manage to name candidates, they will confront constituents who are reeling from the attack—a recipe for demagogy.

This dark scenario puts my alternative proposal in its best light: it seems more sensible to enable the voters to select vice representatives at a calmer moment, giving the local parties the time they need to recruit their best candidates for the next regular election. By this point, it is even possible that panic might have died down a bit, allowing for a more sober choice. Although the Dreier Act admirably defends the principle of popular election, it gets a failing grade on follow though. Despite its forty-nine-day schedule, it will take several months before a replacement House can assemble to join the Senate in attending to the nation's pressing business; and in its haste to reduce this delay, the act encourages the selection of political hacks who have successfully played the demagogue. In the meantime, the House's precipitous quorum change authorizes a rump to assert its prerogatives, catalyzing a heated constitutional debate at a time when clear lines of authority are imperative.

In contrast, my proposal marries Congressman Dreier's democratic principles with Congressman Baird's strategic insight—let the voters, not their representatives, choose replacements in advance of an attack, so that they can meet immediately without raising any challenge to the House's constitutional legitimacy. Since my proposal is entirely compatible with the principles and text of the current constitution, there is no need for a formal amendment. A statute will suffice to bring the House of Representatives into the twenty-first century.[25]

The Presidency

Under current law, presidential succession is a three-tier affair: the vice president is in his own tier, and if he is killed, he may be replaced by a presidential nomination, when confirmed by the Senate.[26] But if a terrorist blast kills both president and vice president, Congress has passed a statute that moves the acting presidency into a second tier that currently gives priority to the speaker of the House, and then to the president pro tem of the Senate.[27] Neither of these officers is required to assume the acting presidency—it is up to each of them to decide whether he will resign his office and take the job. But if one does, and if he otherwise qualifies, he has priority over the officers in the third tier, comprising the deceased president's cabinet, beginning with the secretary of state and proceeding through the others in the historical order in which their departments were created.[28]

We owe this statute to Harry Truman, who, upon succeeding Franklin Roosevelt, was dismayed to learn that the secretary of state was next in line to succeed him under existing law. Truman believed that his successor should be an elected official with deep political experience, and he successfully lobbied Congress to adopt this position.[29] But the resulting statute is a technical monstrosity that virtually guarantees presidential instability after a massive attack.

Suppose, for example, that the blast kills both House and Senate leaders in the second tier, and the secretary of state becomes acting president. A week later, the Senate convenes with a host of gubernatorially selected interim appointments and selects a new president pro tem. The statute gives him the right to supplant the secretary and become the new acting president if he chooses to resign his new position and is otherwise qualified for the presidency. Even more remarkably, the statute allows him to keep his options open: he may choose to remain in his Senate job for the moment, but he can exercise the privilege to bump the secretary out of office *whenever he wants to*. The plot thickens when the House returns to operation—either as a rump body or as a 435-member institution after a round of special elections. The statute puts the speaker at the top of the second tier and allows him to bump either the secretary *or* the Senate's president pro tem, simply by resigning his speakership and assuming the acting presidency—he, too, can exercise this privilege any time during the remainder of the presidential term. However, if the speaker does choose to bump his predecessors, he can't be bumped by the next speaker of the House, but stays in office until the end of the presidential term. (Bumping does not extend to members of the third tier: if the secretary of transportation becomes acting president, he can't be removed by the secretary of state if she emerges later from the rubble.)

The pathological possibilities are breathtaking. Suppose the rump chooses a speaker during the interval it governs before special elections. The new speaker is a political unknown, whose only distinction is that he has survived the blast. Nevertheless, the statute gives him the right to resign and demand the presidency from the secretary of state, who may be a distinguished statesman. Suppose the secretary refuses on the ground that the rump lacks a constitutional quorum of 218 members, and its designation of the speaker is a legal nullity. While the country is reeling from the massive attack, it looks on helplessly as the impasse continues. If the rump speaker somehow emerges on top in this power struggle, the statute doesn't allow his replacement by the speaker selected by the 435-member House of Representatives when that body comes to Washington in three or four months. Instead, he can hang on for years as the country deals with a state of emergency.

Or perhaps the congressional leaders in the top tier show restraint and allow the acting president to govern—so long as he panders to their every wish. Rather than decisive presidential action, checked and balanced by congressional oversight and the supermajoritarian escalator, we will get executive dithering by an unelected president under the thrall of irresponsible politicians.

Congress was aware of the bumping mechanism built into the statute, and endorsed it.[30] But it didn't take doomsday scenarios seriously—in

1948 the United States possessed a nuclear monopoly, and terrorists had access only to primitive weapons. The debate on the floor suggests that Congress supposed that a cabinet officer would serve as acting president for a very brief time before he would be displaced by the speaker selected by a House of Representatives constituted by a constitutionally unproblematic quorum.

But this is 2006, and the statute is in obvious need of overhaul. The bumping mechanism must be eliminated: whoever is initially placed in the presidency should stay there until the next election (with impeachment as a last resort during the interim). The line of succession also should be reconfigured. President Truman was right, I think, in preferring seasoned political leaders over cabinet officers, but there are two problems with the current designations. Although the speaker of the House is almost invariably a powerful and seasoned politician, this isn't true of the president pro tem of the Senate. The central figures in today's Senate are the majority and minority leaders—the president pro tem is an honorific position that, for example, was held by Strom Thurmond into his nineties. The statute should take these realities into account, and replace the president pro tem with a Senate official whose leadership skills have gained the support of his colleagues.

My second change is more controversial, but it shouldn't be. By putting the speaker first in line after the vice president, the current statute assures us that a skilled politician will assume the presidency, but he may well be a member of the opposing political party. Policy continuity is a key value, however, and a statutory tweak will suffice to satisfy its imperatives. The statute should instruct each president, at the start of each congressional session, to designate either the speaker or the minority leader as the successor to the vice president; and the president should have the same privilege when it comes to choosing between the Senate majority and minority leaders.[31] He will, of course, choose the leader of his political party, permitting us to avoid the unnecessary choice that the current statute forces us to make between seasoned statesmanship *or* policy continuity. With this minor statutory tweak, we will have both: the first three positions in the line of succession will be occupied by politicians of national stature from the political party that won the preceding presidential election.

We run into serious trouble only if some unspeakable disaster eliminates all three of these stand-ins, as well as the secretaries of state and the treasury. This puts the secretary of defense next in line, since the War Department was created next in time, when George Washington was setting up the executive branch. But it would be a mistake to allow the accidents of history rule us. The principle of checks and balances is far more important, and it suggests that the defense secretary should be placed at the bottom of the list. As civilian chief of the military, he will inevitably—and justifiably—have a large role in emergency decision making, but he should be obliged to make his case to an acting president whose past experience has exposed him to a different perspective. If the defense secretary is made president and promotes his deputy to his old job, their conversations in the Oval Office will be dangerously parochial—one Pentagon guy talking to another. The succession statute should skip to the next officer in line, the attorney general.

At this point, we confront a final problem. The attorney general, as well as the secretaries of state and treasury, is obliged to take a large view of national problems, and as a consequence, these officers regularly become prominent figures in political life. But the other secretaries are in charge of narrower sectors—agriculture, public lands and resources, and the like. They often owe their appointments to well-organized interest groups, and rarely win a national reputation during their time in office. It would be terrible if any of these worthies were called upon to exercise presidential power.

To its credit, the Senate has recently recognized this problem and has passed a small amendment to the existing statute that would promote the secretary of homeland security, authorizing him to follow the attorney general in the line of succession.[32] The Senate's interest in revisiting the statute is to be applauded, but its particular intervention is misguided. Like the secretary of defense, the secretary of homeland security isn't a good choice for the job—he shouldn't be in a position to become acting president, appoint his deputy as the new secretary, and then engage in an extremely parochial conversation about the use of emergency powers. Rather than promoting him to prominence, he should be placed at the bottom of the list, with the secretary of defense.

Perhaps there is no need for further worry. We already have six strong replacements in the line of succession: vice president, the leaders of the president's party in the House and the Senate, the secretaries of state and the treasury, and the attorney general, and that should be enough. Nevertheless, it is worthwhile to consider a proposal by my colleague Akhil Amar. He suggests the creation of a new position—minister without portfolio—whose sole function would be to serve as acting president in the case of a dreadful decapitation.[33] Once confirmed by the Senate, the minister would live outside Washington, D.C., and receive regular briefings that would enable him to act effectively if disaster struck. Amar hopes that the president would appoint a retired senior statesman—a George Mitchell or a Colin Powell—to this post and give the country a figure in whom it has confidence at its hour of need.[34] The danger, of course, is that the president would use the appointment to score points with a particular interest group or to reward a crony. And there is always the risk that the senior statesmen will suffer a sudden decline in vigor before he is suddenly placed in command.

To be sure, the minister would have to be confirmed by the Senate, but I don't put much weight on this point. When nominated, he will have a very small chance of actually wielding power, and the Senate won't raise much fuss unless the president's choice is truly egregious. All in all, we should use this device only as a last resort, when a terrorist attack has taken out all six of the officials at the top of our lineup. Whatever the differences between the speaker of the House and the attorney general, all of them are wielding serious power on a day-to-day basis—and you don't stay in this position for long unless you are in the prime of your political life. But if it's a choice between Amar's minister and, say, the secretary of agriculture, I go with the minister.

Reconstituting the Court

The decapitation of the Court will predictably generate two sequential responses—one temporary, one permanent, both terrible. In the intermediate aftermath, the acting president could first move to fill the Court, on an interim basis, when the Senate is in recess. The Constitution gives him this authority, though any appointment can remain on the bench only until the end of the congressional term.[35] During this time, the Senate will insist on its right to give its "advice and consent" to nominees for permanent positions—and this threatens a bitter series of confirmation struggles. If, as is likely, the Senate falls short of confirming all the president's nominees, the agony will continue during the next session of Congress. Once the newly elected Senate comes to town, the president can wait for its first recess to refill the bench unilaterally as the confirmation battles rage on.[36] The entire affair will be a giant distraction during a tragic period, diverting the president, the Senate, and the country from many pressing matters.

This is not the worst of it. The entire two-wave cycle—first interim, then permanent, appointments—threatens two great constitutional values. The first is judicial independence. The interim appointees will be on probation at a time when the emergency constitution assigns them crucial tasks. If the interim justices exercise these functions with vigor, they may easily antagonize key politicians on Capitol Hill, jeopardizing their future careers on the Supreme Court. If they roll over and rubber-stamp, constitutional safeguards will crumble, with long-lasting consequences.

The second great value returns us to the problem of entrenchment. Ordinarily, the Supreme Court's membership turns over slowly—over the past half-century, a position has opened up every three years, on average, and with increasing longevity, turnover is getting slower.[37] This all-too-deliberate pace is getting to be a problem, creating the prospect of a Court that has lost touch with its many publics. But the decapitation scenario promises something worse: a problematic acting president, together with a Senate composed of gubernatorial appointees, makes a series of lifetime appointments who will decisively shape constitutional law for decades. Even if the acting president contents himself with interim appointments, and waits for an elected Senate to come to Washington, the country will still be reeling from the tragedy. This is hardly a propitious moment for selecting all nine justices, freezing the doctrinal orthodoxy of the day into a rigid pattern for thirty or forty years.

We confront a paradox—loss of judicial independence over the short run, excessive rigidity over the long run. Whichever way you look at it, this is a recipe for disaster, especially in a country that depends so heavily on the Supreme Court in its governing arrangements. It is only by taking steps now that we can eliminate this grim scenario, once and for all. Once again, it won't be necessary to change the Constitution in order to get us out of this hole—a statute will be enough, though a subsequent amendment might further improve the situation.

Here is what the statute should say: if the Court is deprived of its quorum, some of the chief judges of the courts of appeal should be immediately reassigned to the high court to serve as justices.[38] The reassignment would take place through a lottery: there are twelve courts of appeal; the names of each chief judge would be dropped into a hat, and the identity of the new justices will be called out after the random draw.[39] Judges become chief of their appellate circuits through seniority, and they must resign this position when they reach seventy.[40] By promoting them to the Supreme Court, we are guaranteed experienced jurists whose powers have not yet been dulled by great age.

Randomized selection will minimize the political spin—most judges on a particular circuit might be appointed by Democratic presidents, but this won't prevent the chief judge from being a Republican if seniority marks him out, and vice versa.[41] Finally, the replacements won't occupy their seats for extremely long periods. Chief judges of the appeals courts are almost invariably in their middle or late sixties, and even in this day of medical miracles, the grim reaper can't be indefinitely postponed.[42] The statute, however, might go further and require the chief judges to return to their circuit courts on a staggered schedule—guaranteeing the president and Senate at least one appointment every two years, say, if a vacancy doesn't otherwise arise through death or resignation.

But we are now descending into (important) details, and it is more important to see how the basic proposal resolves the egregious difficulties of the status quo. Rather than diverting the president and the Senate into a protracted battle over the Supreme Court at a time of emergency, the statute renews the court immediately with the nation's surviving senior jurists, without any partisanship involved. And it immediately assures judicial independence—in contrast to "recess appointments" by the president, the tenure of the new justices won't depend on pleasing the powers that be in the White House and the Senate. At the same time, the happenstance of a successful terrorist assault won't freeze constitutional jurisprudence for thirty or forty years: the Court will evolve with the changing temper of public opinion. Is there any fair question that this is a *lot* better than we can hope from the status quo?

Of course, there may be better solutions available, and I invite my friends in the legal academy to join in the hunt.[43] For now, let's move on to the key question of implementation: whether the lengthy process of constitutional amendment is required before my proposal—or something like it—can become the law of the land. With one exception, I think a statute will suffice. After making my case, I turn to the possible exception.

The Constitution says that there shall be "one Supreme Court," but it gives Congress broad discretion in determining its organization. For example, it does not require nine justices to serve on the Court, and in fact, Congress expanded and contracted the Court's size repeatedly during the nineteenth century—with the number of justices varying from five to ten before it settled down to nine.[44] Nor does the Constitution expressly limit positions on the Supreme Court to justices who were named to that body. It simply requires that members of all federal courts be confirmed by the Senate, but it leaves open the question whether Congress can reassign a judge initially appointed to one court for service on another if it finds this to be in the public interest.

Though the text is silent, historical practice is eloquent: from the earliest days, the Supreme Court has upheld Congress's authority to reassign judges from one court to others. The Court's first major decision on this subject, rendered in 1803, involved its own prerogatives. The official commissions granted Supreme Court justices do not grant them general authority to conduct trials. Nevertheless, when Congress ordered the justices to engage in trial work, they went along, upholding congressional authority in an early decision by the Marshall Court.[45]

Congress's use of its reassignment authority has taken a different turn in the modern era. While the Supreme Court doesn't conduct many trials nowadays, Congress has now created a system for reassigning lower-court judges to overloaded and undermanned judicial districts. Under this well-established procedure, appeals judges regularly leave their regions to serve in other courts of appeal. More relevant to the present point, so do district judges. Even though the Senate has confirmed these men and women only to preside over trials in the lowest rung of the federal courts, they frequently travel elsewhere to serve on courts of *appeal*.[46]

These precedents establish the general legitimacy of congressional reassignment, but they don't expressly cover the present case: Congress has reassigned Supreme Court justices to serve on trial courts, and it has reassigned trial court judges to serve on the intermediate courts of appeal, but it has never reassigned appeals judges to serve on the Supreme Court. I do not suggest, moreover, that Congress's powers in this sensitive area are entirely unlimited. For example, it would be plainly unconstitutional for Congress to reassign Supreme Court justices to the lower courts in retaliation for unpopular decisions.

But retaliation isn't in question here. Rather than attacking judicial independence, my proposed statute seeks to preserve it. It avoids the prospect of an interim Court of recess appointees who are anxiously looking over their shoulders at the powers that be. And it provides an orderly process through which the president and Senate can, with deliberate speed, reconstitute a Court that is worthy of its central role in the American system. The constitutional case is compelling: If it is constitutional for Congress to reassign district judges to appeals courts that are overwhelmed by overloaded dockets, it is also constitutional to reassign appeals judges to the Supreme Court when the Court is otherwise unable to do its work.

It is also hard to see who could plausibly launch an effective constitutional attack on the statute once the terrorists have struck. Surely the president will have lots of better things to do than insist on making recess appointments in defiance of a congressional framework statute. And if a challenge were launched in the federal courts, I doubt that any lower court would challenge the constitutionality of a Supreme Court— composed of the appellate judges—once it was up and running.[47]

So it would appear that the existing problems confronting the emergency constitution aren't insuperable. Four statutes will suffice to fill the existing vacuum—one reassigning appeals judges to the Supreme Court, a second tweaking the order of presidential succession, a third creating the office of vice representative, and a fourth resolving the problem posed by Senators who have been profoundly disabled by the terrorist blast. Or better yet, perhaps Congress and the president could lead a sober debate on a single framework statute. This would allow them, and the country, to see more clearly how each piece of the puzzle fits together, and thereby eliminate superficially attractive proposals that fail to survive critique once placed within a broader framework of the separation of powers.

The Entrenchment Problem

Now that we have gotten the government up and running, we can indulge the luxury of considering a second problem: given the compromises made to achieve speedy reconstitution, should we impose special restrictions on the new incumbents' capacity to entrench themselves in power?

Turning to the Supreme Court, I have provided a rather complicated answer. The chief appellate judges serving on the Supreme Court will indeed suffer a legitimacy deficit. These men and women were never subjected to the extraordinary scrutiny that the president and the Senate give Supreme Court nominees, and yet they are wielding great power during tough times. It may well be wise to make their stay on the Supreme Court temporary, permitting the president and Congress to replace the emergency judges with normal appointments in a deliberate fashion—if a vacancy doesn't open up through death or resignation, one of the emergency justices should create an opening every second year by returning to the circuit from which he came. Yet these openings should not be created too rapidly, lest the president and Senate seize the opportunity to create a judicial orthodoxy that freezes constitutional development for thirty or forty years.

If you agree, then this is the place for a formal constitutional amendment. Consider this scenario: Once the smoke begins to clear and Congress arrives on the scene, the currently dominant political coalition may chafe at its restricted power to make Supreme Court appointments imposed by the framework statute. After consulting his constitutional gurus, the president calls for the enactment of a new statute, ordering these judges back to service on their courts of appeal and opening up their slots on the Court. If he is successful, he will then fill the openings with a bunch of true believers in the reigning constitutional orthodoxy of the moment.

Only a formal amendment can decisively preempt this maneuver.[48] Without it, we will have to depend on a tradition of congressional restraint that has survived many tests over the past two centuries. Congress passed its greatest test of the twentieth century in 1937, when Franklin Roosevelt tried to consolidate his New Deal by adding six new justices to the Court. Though the president was at the height of his popularity, his Court-packing statute was rejected by Congress, reflecting broader popular support for the principle of judicial independence.[49] My hypothetical scenario is very different: a problematic president calling on a problematic Congress to pass a different kind of Court-packing statute. It is too quick to suppose that public opinion will tolerate this entrenching maneuver. All things considered, however, it would be best to enact an amendment as a safeguard.

Turning next to the presidency, the entrenchment question takes a different form. The acting president probably could never have reached this office on his own steam: he might have been a good attorney general, but this would not have qualified him as a serious candidate for the White House. Nevertheless, he is now occupying the presidency, with all the advantages of incumbency. If we allow him to run again in his own right, the terrorists will have had a big say in determining one of the major party's nominations. By giving him the advantages of incumbency, moreover, the terrorists also will have helped him out in his campaign against his major-party rival. The sting will be all the greater if the acting president comes from the political party that *lost* the last presidential election—as can readily happen, under present law, if he formerly served as speaker of the House or president pro tem of the Senate. Given all these points, shouldn't we forbid the acting president from seeking an elected term in his own right?

I say No, but reasonable people may certainly disagree. I don't wish to minimize the case for limitation, but a countervailing point seems more important: if the acting president is barred from further office, his influence over Congress will be strictly limited—and this is especially important, given the supermajoritarian escalator that provides the key to extensions of emergency power. It may prove too easy for a minority in Congress to deprive a lame-duck president of emergency powers. There is also the matter of democratic principle: it is a very serious thing to deny *anybody* the right to seek the support of the American people at a popular election, and it is especially problematic to deny this right to an acting president who has already occupied one of the leading offices of the land. This democratic principle, together with my more instrumental concerns, leads me to reject the case for constitutional amendment.

I would support a lesser restriction, however. If the attack occurs early in the presidential term, there is no sense allowing the acting president to remain in office for three whole years. The presidential election should be accelerated to the next even-numbered year, concurrent with congressional races. This will assure the earliest feasible return of a president with the explicit backing of the American people. This emergency reform might readily be accomplished through statute. During the first 150 years of American history, a congressional statute did provide for a special election in cases when both the presidency and vice presidency had become vacant. The last of these provisions was repealed only as a part of President Truman's initiative revising the order of presidential succession.[50] It is time for Congress to reinvigorate this authority, and provide for a popular election at the earliest feasible time.[51]

Turning finally to Congress, the entrenchment problem takes another spin. As we have seen, the Constitution authorizes governors to appoint interim senators, pending special elections; and under my proposal, vice representatives, selected at the previous election, would constitute the House until the next regular election. In the short run, this regime provides constancy in the House while the Senate turns over as the results of special elections are announced. And after the next scheduled election, everything returns to standard operating procedures, stabilizing an otherwise chaotic political environment.

Interim senators and vice representatives will have the advantage of incumbency when facing the voters. But I don't think that this remotely justifies their exclusion from congressional races—the same democratic principles apply here as in the case of the presidency. Moreover, it would require a formal constitutional amendment to bar them from the competition.[52]

A second problem is more interesting: until the interim Congress is replaced by a regularly elected body, it does suffer a democracy deficit which should be reflected, I suggest, in a limitation on its lawmaking powers. Although it should be fully empowered to act on all matters of immediate concern, the framework statute creating vice representatives should impose a "sunset" provision on all statutes enacted by the interim Congress: unless the House of Vice Representatives explicitly stipulates otherwise in passing a statute, its enactments should lapse six months into the term of the next, regularly elected, Congress. Note the condi-

IF WASHINGTON BLOWS UP?   167

tional character of this proviso: the emergency Congress can, if it wishes, enact permanent legislation if it thinks this is truly required. Nonetheless, the framework provision announces a norm against entrenchment and places the burden of persuasion on those who would break it.

I would not go further and impose an absolute bar on permanency: it is just too hard to predict what will be sensible in the chaotic conditions of the time—and in any event, an absolute prohibition would require a constitutional amendment. In contrast, a more conditional measure can be passed by statute: it simply instructs the courts to interpret legislative silence with a presumption in favor of sunsetting, leaving it up to the emergency Congress to make its contrary intentions clear if it thinks that permanency will serve the public interest.

To sum up my assessment of the entrenchment problem: It isn't much of a problem. The most serious issue involves the appeals judges on the Supreme Court, and even here the case for a constitutional amendment isn't utterly compelling. The other issues can be fixed by ordinary statutes: rescheduling the next regular election for the presidency when an attack occurs early in the term, creating a presumption against the permanency of legislation enacted by the interim Congress.

A decapitating terrorist strike will, of course, deal the government a crushing blow. But the emergency constitution shouldn't make the blow even more devastating. At least it can provide the country with the tools it needs slowly to regain a sense of self-confidence.

Two Emergencies

There are two kinds of emergency. One kind is created by a terrorist attack—an atomic blast, a killer epidemic—another when the government is paralyzed and can't respond in a credible fashion.

The first kind of emergency is an inevitability of twenty-first-century life—it will be a miracle if we can prevent all terrorist attacks, and I don't believe in miracles. But the second kind is merely a product of an ostrich-like refusal to confront the obvious inadequacies of our present arrangements. It doesn't take a rocket scientist to come up with a better solution; it just takes a little foresight and a bit of political will—not a lot, since there is little reason to expect significant political resistance.

There have been encouraging signs that Washington is beginning to pay attention to the prospect of its decapitation. As we have seen, there have already been ad hoc efforts to cure some of the obvious problems currently afflicting the House of Representatives, and a bipartisan commission, organized by AEI and Brookings, has played a useful role in raising consciousness about the issue's importance. But the time is ripe to take the next step and fashion a bipartisan coalition with the discipline to enact a package of sensible statutory solutions to the most pressing problems.

A success will also promote the larger conversation we so urgently need. Governmental paralysis is only the tip of the iceberg. We need not only a functioning government in Washington but an emergency constitution that will give it special powers to prevent a second strike—on terms that assure against the permanent destruction of our freedoms. Making progress on one front will encourage Americans to take the larger agenda seriously.

It is never pleasant to think about the unthinkable. But once we start, perhaps we will systematically prepare for the worst as we hope for the best.

8

THE MORNING AFTER

Born in the American and French Revolutions, liberal democratic constitutionalism has struggled against the odds for two centuries—against monarchy, against Nazism, against Communism—to achieve an uncertain hegemony. No competing ideal has the same universal appeal. Only the most fervent fanatic dreams of the day when all mankind worships Christ or Allah, but the most pragmatic pragmatist cannot dismiss the possibility that, in a century or two, the entire world will be governed by variations on themes first elaborated by John Locke and Immanuel Kant.

We are dealing only with a possibility, not a probability, much less a certainty. But for the first time in world history, the fate of Enlightenment constitutionalism depends more on us than our enemies. The greatest threat is the implosion of liberal democratic values in the heartland, not their destruction by hostile forces from the periphery. The twenty-first century will be littered by episodic terrorist outrages, but we cannot allow ourselves to lose our heads as we strike back.

September 11 was a wakeup call, an augury of much more terrible events to come. America overreacted both at home and abroad, but not—one may hope—in ways that preclude reflection and recuperation. There is still time to take steps that will safeguard against much worse forms of overreaction the next time around, and the next, and the next. Or so I have argued.

I have been searching for a third way. September 11 hasn't "changed everything," but civil libertarians shouldn't pretend that it has changed nothing. Terrorism is real, it will not go away, and it requires a strong response. It is self-indulgent to deny this: the future of civil liberties isn't best defended by the tribe of the ostrich, but by the friends of the fox. The partisans of a free society should not seek to draw a line in the sand and suppose it is secure. They should aim to deflect the thundering demagogue by artful constitutional maneuvering at moments of great peril.

The place to begin is with the language we use to describe our current predicament. Neither *war* nor *crime* captures the special challenge to effective sovereignty that follows a massive terrorist strike. This false dichotomy—war or crime—should be replaced by a trichotomy that gives a new prominence to a familiar idea: the state of emergency. Familiarity is a great advantage. In times of crisis, the last thing we need is Newspeak. The "state of emergency" requires reworking before it can serve its proper function under modern conditions. Yet we have faced similar intellectual challenges many times before. The life of the law is a constant effort to renovate received ideas to confront new problems, and we should not falter before the challenges involved in critical reconstruction.

But we can gain insight by putting the evolving concepts of our tradition—war, crime, and emergency—under a more analytic microscope. I have made lots of points in arguing my case, but only two themes are fundamental. And if we recall them one last time, we can grasp the distinctive features of the argument more clearly, as well as their relationship to other problems.

I have been urging historical perspective: September 11 was terrible, but there have been worse moments in our history. During World War II, the Axis powers not only were killing millions, they were jeopardizing our survival as an independent nation: the Japanese were threatening an invasion from the Pacific, while German U-boats were cutting off our links across the Atlantic. It was reasonable, at least for a time, to believe that our future political existence was at stake. The same was true of the Civil War: Jefferson Davis and the Confederacy were aiming to destroy the Union and create a rival republic. Osama and his many successors do not pose these existential threats, and if we pretend otherwise, we will only succeed in destroying our freedom in an endless "war on terrorism." We must distinguish, in short, between *existential struggles,* which threaten utterly to destroy the polity, and *momentary affronts to effective sovereignty,* which don't.

Both kinds of traumatizing assault can occur domestically and abroad, yielding four conceptual possibilities: the Civil War (domestic) and World War II (foreign) are paradigmatic existential struggles, but we use the same word—*war*—to describe them. To increase the confusion, scholars have often used "states of emergency" to describe responses to other forms of existential assault, like attempted coups d'état, that seek to supplant the established constitutional order.

But there have been many "wars"—from the Spanish-American through the Iraqi—which did not endanger the nation's political existence. They were provoked—rightly or wrongly—by the perception that a foreign country was threatening the effective pursuit of America's sovereign interests. One might mark this distinction by restricting "war" to cases in which a country is battling for its political independence, and using another word to describe the coercive use of force to pursue other sovereign interests. To adapt a term popularized during the Korean conflict, I will call such conflicts police actions and note their conceptual similarity to our own problem. Quite simply: police actions involve coercive force when a state's interest in the exercise of effective sovereignty is threatened abroad, while states of emergency arise when effective sovereignty is challenged by terrorist assaults at home.

Table 1 plots a fourfold table of possibilities.

Table 1. Varieties of Conflict

	Type of Threat	
Locus of Threat	*Existential Danger*	*Assault on Effective Sovereignty*
Foreign	War	Police Action
Domestic	Civil War	State of Emergency

The chart helps clarify precisely what this book is, and is not, about. Most important, it is not about terrorist campaigns of the kind launched by the Palestinians against the Israelis or by the IRA against the British government of Northern Ireland. These involve existential struggles in which the Israeli and British states are fighting for their very existence (in the latter case, only in part of its territory). In terms of my categories, they are civil wars, de facto if not de jure.

I have not been trying to write a book on civil war, let alone a book on some vast subject called "terrorism." I have been focusing on a very particular problem, albeit one of great importance: how to respond to attacks, like September 11, which *don't* involve a serious threat of political takeover by the attackers. From this vantage, recurrent references to places like Iraq, Israel, and Northern Ireland would muddle, not clarify, my argument. It's true, of course, that terrorist bombs go off in Baghdad and the West Bank as well as in London and Oklahoma City. But the entire aim of this book has been to move beyond a superficial view of terrorism as a technique, and insist that we can't assess *any* technique without a close attention to the political context in which it arises. When a terrorist bomb detonates as part of a civil war, it raises existential issues that simply don't arise when it goes off in a stable country that does not confront a grave threat to its political integrity.

America's "war on terror" is a signal example of the larger failure to appreciate this key point. The same blindness helps account for Britain's extremely repressive responses to September 11. Even before the London attacks of July 2005, the Blair government had passed antiterrorist legislation requiring it to derogate from the fundamental rights guaranteed by the European Convention on Human Rights—the only signatory nation to avail itself of this extreme measure. After decades of fighting an existential struggle for mastery in Northern Ireland, it was all too easy for the British to suppose that September 11 represented a similar problem.

But it doesn't: Osama and his followers aren't trying to occupy and govern Britain any more than they are trying to take over the United States. By wreaking havoc, they are destabilizing established institutions, demoralizing the citizenry, and killing innocent people—big problems, to be sure, but not the *same* problem raised by the IRA's decades-long struggle for the independence of Northern Ireland. But alas, the London attacks of July 2005 will only encourage the British to continue ignoring the big difference between civil wars and states of emergency, making another cycle of repressive legislation a virtual certainty.

The sad British story should serve as a cautionary tale for the rest of us. The ease with which a country with such a proud tradition of freedom can take the wrong course should encourage the rest of us to pause, reflect, and take decisive action to avoid similar cycles of repression.

Here is where a second recurring theme has entered my argument— the importance of distinguishing rigorously between the short term and long term in responding to terrorist attacks. This distinction isn't so important in dealing with existential threats. When fighting a powerful enemy seeking to destroy the state, leaders rightly suppose that they shouldn't spend much time on the long run—if they can't respond effectively in the short run, there won't be a long run: somebody else, very different, will be taking charge. And if they do succeed in destroying the enemy, the victory will be clear and decisive. With the enemy surrendering on the field of battle, it will be clear to the relieved citizenry that the time has come to return to the normal protection of individual rights.

But the distinction between short and long term becomes crucial when the state isn't struggling for its very existence. Perhaps this point is recognized more clearly when it comes to the international use of force in "police actions" like Kosovo or Iraq.[1] Since the foreign enemy doesn't really pose a clear and present danger of taking us over, we have all come to recognize the imperative need for an exit strategy: we will forever be bogged down in a quagmire unless we define very clearly the precise character of the threat and declare victory once it has been controlled or eliminated.

By parity of reasoning, we also must have a well-developed "exit option" in dealing with terrorist attacks at home—otherwise, short-term emergency responses will morph into the long-run destruction of freedom. The emergency constitution takes this insight and runs with it, keeping extraordinary powers on a short leash by insisting on short-term renewals with increasing majorities.

More generally, my two basic distinctions organize the book's larger thesis: by differentiating between threats to effective sovereignty and threats to our very political existence, by distinguishing the short term from the long term, we may yet manage to sustain a sober response to the crises that are sure to come. Without minimizing the dangers of terrorism, we must keep our heads and refuse to confuse them with existential contests like the

Second World War. The prospect of existential struggle may reemerge in the fullness of time, but for the foreseeable future, our challenge is very different: we must reject the presidentialist logic of the war on terrorism and creatively build upon our system of checks and balances.

As we try to regain equilibrium after September 11, we are beginning to learn this lesson. In enacting the Patriot Act, Congress had the foresight to place a "sunset" clause on some provisions, requiring them to lapse after four years unless reenacted. This has had a salutary effect: when forced to reconsider the matter, Congress refused to rush. It extended the sunset for a brief period to craft a new Patriot Act with more libertarian guarantees, and further sunset clauses.[2]

This is a very small, but promising, step toward the emergency constitution.[3] But time is not on our side, and it would be tragic if a serious effort must await the morning after the next major attack. By then it will be much harder to deflect the presidentialist logic of war that leads inexorably down the path to despotism. The present moment of relative calm will not last, and yet we are currently in denial, pretending that the next attack will never come.

We all know better. No framework for a "state of emergency" will assure success—nothing can substitute for good leadership at the moment of crisis. But institutions matter tremendously, and ours are in need of repair.

We are the happy beneficiaries of a great historical legacy. We have inherited a gift that celebrates the freedom of the individual, protecting each person's right to life, liberty and the pursuit of happiness. We owe it to past and future generations to preserve what we have been so generously given. The emergency constitution will not succeed without sober leadership and enduring popular commitment to the fundamental values of our tradition. But on that grim morning after the next attack, it will give us a better chance to survive as a free people.

NOTES

Introduction

1. The USA Patriot Act was enacted on October 26, 2001 (Pub. L. No. 105-56). The act was first mentioned in the *Congressional Record* for October 2, 2001. But focused consideration began when Attorney General Ashcroft presented a proposal to the House Committee on the Judiciary on September 24, 2001.

2. The quoted assessment comes from two of our most thoughtful legal analysts. Philip Heymann and Juliette Kayyem, *Protecting Liberty in an Age of Terror* 5 (2005).

3. Eric Posner and Adrian Vermeule provide a Panglossian view of the problem: "It is not clear that panics and ratchets, if they occur, are bad things. Fear is often the correct response to a threat; panics can shatter constitutional structures, but sometimes constitutional structures should be shattered. Ratchets put the status quo out of reach, but sometimes that is where it should be." Posner and Vermeule, "Accommodating Emergencies," 56 *Stan. L. Rev.* 605, 610 (2003). The authors also pooh-pooh the likelihood of panic and profess confidence in the recuperative capacities of the legal system. Although I won't cite this article again in these notes, I have kept it in mind in developing my contrary arguments. If you turn to this essay after reading the book, I hope you will come to view it as a cautionary tale, suggesting how easily bright legal scholars can lose their way in a maze of speculative possibilities.

4. *The Federalist* No. 10, at 60 (James Madison, James E. Cooke ed. 1961).

5. Jackson left the explicit warmongering to his political lieutenants, most notably Senator Thomas Hart Benton, who presented a then-famous defense of the president's veto: "The bank is in the field; enlisted for the war; a battering ram—the catapulta, not of the Romans, but of the National Republicans; not to beat down the walls of hostile cities, but to beat down the citadel of American liberty; to batter down the rights of the people." See Thomas Hart Benton, 1 *Thirty Years' View* 256–63 (D. Appleton 1859). On the problematic legality of the president's actions, see Gerard Magliocca, "Veto! The Jacksonian Revolution in Constitutional Law," 74 *U. Neb. L. Rev.* 205, 236–37 (1999).

6. See Dana Priest and Douglas Farah, "Terror Alliance Has U.S. Worried," *Washington Post,* June 30, 2002; Susan Schmidt and Douglas Farah, "Al Qaeda's New Leaders," *Washington Post,* October 29, 2002.

7. Michael Ignatieff, *The Lesser Evil* (2004)

Chapter 1: This Is Not a War

1. For a good defense of this definition of terrorism, see C. A. J. Coady, "Terrorism, Morality, and Supreme Emergency," 114 *Ethics* 772, 772–75 (2004).

2. I owe the analogy to the Blitzkrieg to Zbigniew Brzezinski, *The Choice: Global Domination or Global Leadership* 28 (2004), who provides a skeptical treatment of the war metaphor. My critique also complements that of Philip Heymann, *Terrorism, Freedom, and Security* (2003). Heymann shows how war talk distorts priorities when it comes to preventing future attacks; I complement this analysis by exploring the pathological consequences of the "war on terror" once an attack has occurred.

3. During the Vietnam War, only Justices Stewart and Douglas raised their voices in protest, failing to gain the four votes needed for the Court to hear a case. See Edward Keynes, *Undeclared War: Twilight Zone of Constitutional Power* 84 (2d ed. 1991). Nobody supposes that the present Court will act any differently. Ryan C. Hendrickson, *The Clinton Wars: The Constitution, Congress, and War Powers* 3 (2002).

4. See the official White House press release at http://www.whitehouse.gov/news/releases/2003/05/iraq/20030501-15.html.

5. For a thoughtful discussion of the role of public opinion in foreign policy, see Bruce Russett, *Controlling the Sword: The Democratic Governance of National Security,* chap. 4 (1990).

6. John Yoo, "War, Responsibility, and the Age of Terrorism," 57 *Stan. L. Rev.* 793, 816 (2004). Professor Yoo was a principal architect of the "torture memos" issued by the Ashcroft Justice Department, which I discuss in Chapter 5. As his recent essay suggests, the shock waves generated by the publication of these memos hasn't encouraged him to rethink his extreme positions upon his return to academia from his active engagement in Washington.

7. The first President Bush couldn't have been clearer: "I didn't have to get permission from some old goat in the United States Congress to kick Saddam Hussein out of Kuwait." Remarks of President George Bush to the Texas State Republican Convention in Dallas, Texas, 28 *Weekly Comp. Pres. Doc.* 1119, 1120–21 (June 20, 1992). During the run-up to the second Gulf War, the Bush administration made a variety of legalistic arguments for unilateral action, but aides conceded, off the record, that political pressures might compel the president to seek explicit congressional backing. See, e.g., Neil A. Lewis, "Bush May Request Congress's Backing on Iraq, Aides Say," *New York Times,* August 29, 2002.

8. Todd S. Purdum, "Bush Seeks Power to 'Use All Means' to Oust Hussein," *New York Times,* September 20, 2002.

9. The remarks of Republican Senator John Warner of Virginia were typical. The resolution, he assured the nation, was "not an act of war. It is an act to deter war, to

put in place the tools for our President and our Secretary of State to get the strongest possible resolution in the United Nations." 148 *Cong. Rec.* S10240. For similar sentiments by leading Democrats, see 148 *Cong. Rec.* S10290 (Senator Joseph Biden of Delaware), 148 *Cong. Rec.* S10289 (Senator Hilary Clinton of New York).

10. See, e.g., Bruce Ackerman, "The Legality of Using Force", *New York Times,* September 21, 2002.

11. Congressman John Spratt of South Carolina and Senator Sander Levin of Michigan led the opposition. Their proposals required the president to obtain another United Nations resolution before proceeding with an invasion. These resolutions failed by votes of 270–155 in the House and 75–24 in the Senate. See 148 *Cong. Rec.* H7769 (2002), 148 *Cong. Rec.* S10264 (2002). The administration's resolution won by votes of 296–113 in the House and 77–23 in the Senate. See 148 *Cong. Rec.* H7799 (2002), 148 *Cong. Rec.* S10342(2002).

12. See the *Washington Post*–ABC News poll from March 17, 2003, of 510 randomly selected adults, which found that 71 percent supported going to war with Iraq, 66 supported it without another Security Council resolution, and 72 percent supported the president's ultimatum. Poll available at http://www.washingtonpost.com/wp-srv/politics/polls/vault/stories/data031803.htm.

13. In fairness to the reader, I should mention my very public stance as an opponent of the Iraqi invasion. During the run-up to the war, I argued that it was illegal under international law (Bruce Ackerman, "But What's the Legal Case for Preemption?" *Washington Post,* August 18, 2002); that the constitutional methods used to gain congressional authorization were problematic (Bruce Ackerman, "Bush Must Avoid Shortcuts on Road to War," *Los Angeles Times,* May 31, 2002; "The Legality of Using Force," *New York Times,* September 21, 2002); and that military adventurism in response to terrorism is massively imprudent (Bruce Ackerman, "On the Home Front, a Winnable War," *New York Times,* November 6, 2001).

The merits of the war in Iraq really doesn't much matter in the arguments presented by this book. Whatever you may think of the last invasion, the problems raised by the next one will be different, at least on the surface.

14. For a fine review, see Geoffrey Stone, *Perilous Times* (2004).

15. Abraham Lincoln, Message to Congress in Special Session (July 4, 1861), in 4 *The Collected Works of Abraham Lincoln* 421, 430 (Roy P. Basler ed., 1953). Lincoln ultimately did gain congressional consent for his actions.

16. President James Buchanan, Fourth Annual Address Before Congress (December 3, 1860), in 5 *Messages and Papers of the Presidents,* 1789–1897 635–36 (James D. Richardson ed., 1899).

17. The story is well told by Pierce O'Donnell, *In Time of War* (2005). He describes the landing in chapter 5.

18. Ernest Peter Burger, a second saboteur, was also a U.S. citizen, but prevailing law stripped him of this status when he volunteered in the German army and swore an oath of loyalty to the Reich; see 8 U.S.C. §801. The saboteurs' lawyers actively defended only Haupt's citizenship. See Ex parte Quirin, 317 U.S. 1, 20 (1942).

19. Roosevelt himself made the final decision in his capacity as commander in chief, with his handpicked commission forwarding the testimony and their recommendations. See O'Donnell, *In Time of War,* 244–46.

20. Letter from Stone to Frankfurter, September 10, 1942; Frankfurter Papers quoted by Louis Fisher, *Military Tribunals: The Quirin Precedent,* Congressional Research Service Report 28 (March 26, 2002).

21. The Court announced its decision orally on July 31. The executions took place on August 8. O'Donnell, *In Time of War,* 228, 247.

22. Quoted by Fisher, *Military Tribunals,* 27.

23. According to Justice William Douglas, Biddle "told the Court that the claims of the saboteurs were so frivolous, the Army was going to execute the men whatever the Court did; that the Executive would simply not tolerate any delay." William O. Douglas, *The Court Years, 1939–1975,* 138–39 (1980).

24. See, for example, the government's brief in *Padilla v. Rumsfeld* in the Supreme Court: "The settled authority of the military to capture and detain enemy combatants fully applies to a combatant who is an American citizen and is seized within the borders of the United States. In *Quirin,* supra, this Court upheld the President's exercise of military jurisdiction over a group of German combatants who were seized in the United States before carrying out plans to sabotage domestic war facilities during World War II."

25. The affidavit was sworn by Michael H. Mobbs, who was not even a regular employee of the U.S. government, but a special adviser to the Pentagon. Worse yet, Mobbs was not advising the judge advocate general but the undersecretary of defense for policy—an official who is more concerned with planning for the future than fact-finding about the past. Though Mobbs provided the government's "sole evidentiary support," he has never been cross-examined in any forum. *Hamdi v. Rumsfeld,* 124 S.Ct. 2633, 2636–37 (2004).

26. Dan Eggen and Susan Schmidt, "'Dirty Bomb' Plot Uncovered, U.S. Says," *Washington Post,* June 11, 2002. By late summer, anonymous administration officials were telling reporters that Padilla was a "small fish." "'Dirty Bomb' Suspect a Nobody?" *CBS News,* August 14, 2002, http://www.cbsnews.com/stories/2002/08/27/attack/main519996.shtml. When called to defend its decision in court, the government once again relied on an affidavit by Michael Mobbs to provide its evidence against Padilla. Like Ashcroft, Mobbs relied on "multiple intelligence sources," but he admits that two key sources "have not been completely candid about their association with Al Qaeda," that some of their information "may be part of an effort to mislead or confuse U.S. officials," and finally, that "one of the sources was being treated with various types of drugs." See Declaration by Michael H. Mobbs, Special Advisor to the Under Secretary of Defense for Policy, August 27, 2002, available at http://www.cnss.org/Mobbs%20Declaration.pdf.

27. Padilla arrived at O'Hare on May 8, 2002, wearing civilian clothes and without weapons or explosives of any kind. He was initially detained as a material witness, but when his lawyer sought his discharge through a writ of habeas corpus, the president declared him an enemy combatant on June 9 and transferred him to a naval brig in Charleston, South Carolina, where he has been held in isolation ever since.

28. *Hamdi v. Rumsfeld*, 124 S.Ct. at 2641. (O'Connor, J.)

29. See Transcript of Proceedings before the Military Commission to Try Persons Charged with Offenses against the Law of War and the Articles of War, Washington, D.C., July 8 to July 31, 1942 (Joel Samaha, Sam Root, and Paul Sexton eds.), available at http://www.soc.umn.edu/~samaha/nazi_saboteurs/indexnazi.htm. The proceedings are analyzed by Louis Fisher, *The Nazi Saboteurs on Trial* 43–80 (2003); and David Danielski, "The Saboteurs' Case," 1 *Journal of Supreme Court History* 61–82 (1996).

30. In both Hamdi and Padilla, the government's evidence, such as it was, was transmitted to the court by Michael Mobbs, who did not even have a regular position in the United States government. See notes 24–27.

31. In defending its position before the courts, the government asserted that Padilla was "closely associated" (*Padilla v. Rumsfeld*, ¶5) with Al Qaeda leaders as he moved to Egypt in 1998 and traveled to Afghanistan and Pakistan in 2001 and 2002 (¶¶4, 6, 8). While in Afghanistan in 2001, Padilla allegedly discussed a plan to explode a "dirty bomb" in the United States with Osama bin Laden and his lieutenant Abu Zubaydah (¶¶6, 8). He also allegedly engaged in research on explosive devices at an Al Qaeda safehouse in Lahore, Pakistan (¶¶6–7), meeting with senior Al Qaeda operatives, before finally returning to the United States to engage in terrorist operations (¶¶9–10). See Declaration by Michael H. Mobbs, Special Advisor to the Under Secretary of Defense for Policy, August 27, 2002, available at http://www.cnss.org/Mobbs%20Declaration.pdf. As we shall see, these allegations were significantly revised at a much later stage in the judicial proceedings.

32. *Padilla ex. rel. Newman v. Bush*, 233 F.Supp.2d 564 (S.D.N.Y. 2002)(Michael Mukasey, D. J.).

33. District Judge Mukasey's opinion on this point was reversed by a divided panel of the Court of Appeals for the Second Circuit, *Padilla v. Rumsfeld*, 352 F.3d 695 (2003), but the appeals court permitted the military to keep Padilla in solitary confinement pending further litigation.

34. *Rumsfeld v. Padilla*, 124 Sup. Ct. 2711 (2004).

35. On the question of jurisdiction, Justice Stevens's opinion for the four dissenters convincingly establishes that the Court could have reached the merits without seriously damaging precedents. *Rumsfeld*, 124 Sup. Ct. at 2730. The majority's decision to delay was optional at best, and indefensible at worst, given the "unique and unprecedented threat to the freedom of every American citizen raised by the case"— certainly Stevens is not exaggerating here. Id. at 2733.

36. *Hamdi v. Rumsfeld*, 124 S.Ct. 2633 (2004).

37. Id. at 2635–36.

38. See Respondent's Brief, *Hamdi v. Rumsfeld*, No. 03-6696, 2004 WL 724020 at 16–17: "The military's authority to detain enemy combatants in wartime is not diminished by a claim, or even a showing, of American citizenship."

39. As Justice O'Connor put the point, the government claimed that "respect for separation of powers" should "eliminate entirely any individual [judicial] process, restricting the courts to investigating only whether legal authorization exists for the broader detention scheme." 126 S. Ct. 2633, 2645.

40. Hamdi was transferred to Norfolk, Virginia, in April 2002. He was "allowed to meet counsel for the first time" in February 2004. Petitioner's Brief, *Hamdi v. Rumsfeld*, No. 03-66906, 2004 WL 378715 at 4; *Hamdi*, 124 S.Ct. at 2636; see note 27.

41. *Hamdi v. Rumsfeld*, 124 S.Ct. 2660–74 (2004) (Justices Scalia and Stevens dissenting). Even these two justices limited their decision to the rights of citizens, leaving in limbo the status of noncitizens subject to the jurisdiction of the United States.

42. U.S. Const. art. 1, §9, cl. 2.

43. *Hamdi*, 124 S.Ct. at 2681, 2680, 2683 (2004).

44. Two others—Justices Souter and Ginsburg—disposed of the case without reaching any constitutional issues, finding that Congress had explicitly barred the detention of citizens, and that it was wrong to interpret the later resolution authorizing force in Afghanistan as containing an exception. *Hamdi*, 124 S.Ct. at 2660.

45. Id. at 2641, 2642.

46. Id. 2643–52.

47. While Justice O'Connor would allow a "properly constituted military tribunal" to conduct the hearing, id. at 2651, she required that it be a "neutral arbiter." id. at 2643. Presumably, this would exclude the handpicked military tribunal in the Quirin case.

48. Id. at 2646–47.

49. Id. at 2647–48. Generally speaking, courts can issue a host of protective orders to safeguard confidentiality, but the defense must get its chance to confront and cross-examine crucial witnesses. See Peter Westen, "Confrontation and Compulsory Process: A Unified Theory of Evidence for Criminal Cases," 91 *Harvard Law Review* 567 (1978).

50. *Hamdi*, 124 S.Ct. at 2669, 2643.

51. The seminal case is *Mathews v. Eldridge*, 424 U.S. 319 (1976).

52. Settlement Agreement between Yaser Hamdi and the United States, September 17, 2004, http://news.findlaw.com/usatoday/docs/hamdi/91704stlagrmnt.html.

53. In detailing its current allegations against Padilla, the government explicitly states that the "atomic bomb plot was too complicated" to be taken seriously by Al Qaeda, though it continues to allege, in conclusory terms, that Padilla was authorized to "revive" a "plan to blow up apartment buildings in the United States." Government's Brief, *Padilla v. Hanft*, U.S. Court of Appeals for the Fourth Circuit 9 (May 6, 2005). For the government's new description of Padilla's activities in Afghanistan, see id. at 8.

54. To state the district court's decision with legal precision, it held that the president's seizure of Padilla was neither "necessary" nor "appropriate" under Congress's Authorization for the Use of Force enacted shortly after September 11. *Padilla v. Hanft*, 2005 WL 465691 (D.S.C. February 28, 2005) at *12.

55. *Padilla v. Hanft*, U.S. Court of Appeals for the Fourth Circuit 7-8 (September 9, 2005).

56. *Padilla v. Hanft*, U.S. Court of Appeals for the Fourth Circuit 12 (December 21, 2005). The new indictment describes a small-scale operation, in

which the alleged conspiracy raised less than $100,000 over nine years, and Padilla never left the country. *United States v. Hassoun et al.,* No. 04-60001-CR-COOKE (S.D. Fla. Nov. 17, 2005), available at http://news.findlaw.com/hdocs/docs/padilla/uspad111705ind.pdf.

57. The Department of Justice initially publicized a running tally of resident noncitizens detained in connection with September 11. The tally reached 1,182 by November 5, 2001, raising public anxiety at the mushrooming total. The government responded by discontinuing all public accounting, on the pretext that it was too hard to keep track, but many more have been detained, and released, since then. See David Cole, *Enemy Aliens* 25–26 (2003).

58. 1 Stat. 596 (1798). Technically speaking, the sunset period was a bit more than two years—the statute was passed on July 14, 1798, and lapsed at the end of the congressional session, March 3, 1801.

59. The first Alien Enemies Act, 1 Stat. 570, was passed on June 25, 1798, and contained a sunset provision of two years, but another permanent provision was enacted the following month. 1 Stat. 577.

60. The Act is presently codified as 50 U.S.C. §§21–24 (2002), and it was upheld by the Supreme Court in *Ludecke v. Watkins,* 335 U.S. 160 (1948). It has been invoked on only three occasions: the War of 1812 and the two world wars. See Gregory Sidak, "War, Liberty, and Enemy Aliens," 67 *N.Y.U. L. Rev.* 1402 (1992).

61. See David Cole, *Enemy Aliens* 25 (2003). While many immigrants have ultimately gained release, they were all under threat of very grave sanctions. If a resident alien has committed a minor violation of immigration laws—something that is very easy to do—he can be deported, and if his home country refuses to admit him, he can be held indefinitely if he is a suspected terrorist. Although indefinite detention has been invalidated by the Supreme Court as a general technique in immigration matters, *Zadvydas v. Davis* 533 U.S. 678 (2001), the justices exempted terrorism from their broad prohibition, and the lower courts have been unwilling to reconsider the Court's dicta. See *Tuan Thai v. Ashcroft,* 336 F.3d 790, 796 n.4 (9th Cir. 2004).

Under the Patriot Act, the attorney general may also hold illegal aliens suspected of terrorism for six-month terms, which are renewable indefinitely. All that is required is that there be "reasonable grounds to believe" that the detainee is a terrorist, though detainees have a right to judicial review of this finding. 8 U.S.C. §1226a (2000). I am not aware of any cases in which the attorney general has invoked this authority.

62. The department has made particularly questionable use of existing statutory provisions for holding material witnesses if they seem likely to flee the jurisdiction. There have been many cases in which the department has abused the witness statute as a pretext for detaining suspects without the need for accusing them of a crime. The administration has kept all information secret, but a recent study has identified at least seventy cases, with one-third involving detentions of more than two months. Some detentions involved aliens; some, citizens. See "Witness to Abuse," 17 *Human Rights Watch* 1 (June 2005).

63. The principle of protection for noncitizens was first announced in *Wong Wing v. United States*, 163 U.S. 228 (1896) and has been reaffirmed many times since. See, e.g., *Matthews v. Diaz*, 426 U.S. 67, 77 (1976); David Cole, *Enemy Aliens* (2003). But see the cautionary theme sounded in note 64.

64. *Zadvydas v. Davis*, 533 U.S. 678 (2001), decided a few months before September 11, provides a suitably Janus-faced answer—on the one hand, announcing a broad rule against the indefinite detention of aliens who cannot be repatriated to their native countries; on the other, suggesting that suspected terrorists might be an exception to this rule.

65. *A and Others v. Secretary of State for the Home Department* [2004] UKHL 56. Great Britain is a signatory to the European Convention on Human Rights, which authorizes a country to derogate from its guarantees "in time of war or other public emergency threatening the life of the nation" so long as this is "strictly required by the exigencies of the situation." Convention for the Protection of Human Rights and Fundamental Freedoms, November 4, 1950, art. 15, 213 U.N.T.S. 221, 232 (entered into force Sept. 3, 1953). By a vote of 8–1, the Lords decided that the detention provisions were not "strictly required."

66. *A and Others* at 97. The Blair government responded by passing new terrorist legislation which applied to citizens and noncitizens alike.

67. Indeed, the Defense Department is now promoting "two senior Army officers who oversaw or advised detention and interrogation operations in Iraq during the height of the Abu Ghraib prisoner-abuse scandal," even though they were singled out for criticism by the special review panel chaired by former Secretary of Defense Schlesinger. Eric Schmitt, "Army Moves to Advance Two Linked to Abu Ghraib," *New York Times*, June 29, 2005.

68. The Supreme Court has given the Guantánamo prisoners the right to contest their confinement in federal court, but its initial decision left undefined the standards by which such lawsuits would be judged. *Rasul v. Bush*, 543 U.S. 466 (2004). It will return to these matters in the near future.

69. In late July 2005, Secretary of Defense Donald Rumsfeld signaled his dissatisfaction with "the war on terror," and suggested "the global struggle against violent extremism" as the overarching description of the administration's enterprise. Eric Schmitt and Thom Shanker, "Washington Recasts Terror War as 'Struggle,'" *International Herald Tribune*, July 27, 2005. It took President Bush precisely one week to reject this sensible proposal: "Make no mistake about it, we are at war." Richard Stevenson, "President Makes It Clear: Phrase is 'War on Terror,'" *New York Times*, August 4, 2005.

Chapter 2: This Is Not a Crime

1. See Neal Kumar Katyal, "Conspiracy Theory," 112 *Yale L.J.* 1307 (2003). For a critical assessment of the current law, see Gerard E. Lynch, "RICO: The Crime of Being a Criminal," 87 *Colum. L. Rev.* 661 (1987).

2. During the Cold War, Communist Party agents in the American government were supervised by the Chief Directorate for Intelligence of the Red Army's General Staff, operating through the Comintern. See Nat'l Sec. Agency and CIA, *Venona: Soviet Espionage and the American Response, 1939–1957,* at viii–ix (Robert Louis Benson and Michael Warner eds., 1996).

3. Presidential restraint is especially noteworthy since statutory authority could have been stretched to support such actions. See Emergency Detention Act of 1950, Pub. L. No. 81–831, §§102–3, 64 Stat. 1019, 1021. This statute was repealed only in 1971 by the Non-Detention Act: "No citizen shall be imprisoned or otherwise detained by the United States except pursuant to an Act of Congress," which serves as the baseline of the present discussion. See 18 U.S.C. §1401(a).

4. For the classic study of the Cuban missile crisis, see Graham Allison, *Essence of Decision* (1971).

5. See John Gaddis, *We Now Know: Rethinking Cold War History* 86 (1997); Paul Pillar, *Terrorism and U.S. Foreign Policy* 22 (2001).

6. For a useful introduction to the social psychological mechanisms generating mass panic, see Cass R. Sunstein, "Terrorism and Probability Neglect," 26 J. *Risk and Uncertainty* 121 (2003).

7. Frank H. Knight, *Risk, Uncertainty, and Profit* 19–21, 197–232 (1921).

8. As leading students of the Mafia have established, the detention of a few key conspirators can disorganize an entire network. See, e.g., Federico Varese, "La mafia russa in Italia," 12 *Limes: Rivista Italiana di Geopolitica* 229–39 (2005).

9. See See note 1.

10. See, e.g., the proposals presented in Philip Heymann and Juliette Kayyem, *Protecting Liberty in an Age of Terror* chap. 2 (2005).

11. Others have been named as unindicted coconspirators, and a very small number are in custody. These include Mustapha Ahmed al-Hawsawi, who allegedly sent funds to Mohammed Atta, one of the hijackers, as well as Ramzi Binalshibh, Atta's Hamburg roommate.

12. See David Cole, *Enemy Aliens* 88–128 (2003).

13. U. S. Dept. Health and Human Services, *Community Containment Measures, Including Non-Hospital Isolation and Quarantine (Supplement D)* 11 (Jan. 4, 2004) This bulletin dealt specifically with the SARS epidemic. In additional to psychological and family support, it also required the provision of more obvious aid in the form of food, household, and medical supplies.

14. See *News Release from the SARS Contingency Committee* (June 9, 2003), at http://sars.doh.gov.tw/news/2003060902.html (last visited August 10, 2005; NT$5,000 compensation for persons quarantined in Taiwan); Colin Perkel, "Sars Patients Compensated," *Hamilton Observer* DI (June 24, 2003) (Ontario paying up to C$6,000 as an "isolation allowance").

15. The leading Supreme Court case upholding quarantines is *Compagnie Française De Navigation A Vapeur v. Louisiana State Bd. of Health,* 186 U.S. 380

(1902), but the great case is *Jacobson v. Massachusetts,* 197 U.S. 11 (1905), involving forced inoculations.

16. For those who are skeptical, perhaps they will be more convinced by more elaborate arguments. See Bruce Ackerman, *Social Justice in the Liberal State,* especially chap. 8 (1980). See also Robert Nozick, *Anarchy, State, and Utopia* 78–84 (1974); George Fletcher, "Fairness and Utility in Tort Theory," 85 *Harv. L. Rev.* 537 (1972). On the morality of quarantines, see Daniel Markovits, "Quarantines and Distributive Justice," 33 *J. Law, Med., Ethics* 323 (2005).

17. Awards have ranged to more than $8.5 million, with average payments in the $1 million range. Overall, $7 billion was disbursed to 5,560 claimants. Kenneth R. Feinberg, Final Report of the Special Master for the September 11th Victim Compensation Fund of 2001 (available at http://www.usdoj.gov/final_report.pdf).

18. In 1988 Congress publicly apologized to Japanese Americans and Aleuts interned during World War II, granting each internee $20,000. 50 U.S.C. app. §§1989–1989d. This amounts to $3.36 per day if the detainee had been confined for two years, and then had allowed the money to accumulate interest at 5 percent until Congress finally acted.

19. See Bruce Ackerman, *Private Property and the Constitution* chap. 4 (1977). A recent essay has come to the same conclusion through a different conceptual route. See Eugene Kantorovich, "Liability Rules for Constitutional Rights," 56 *Stan. L. Rev.* 755 (2004).

20. See Jeremy Waldron, *The Right to Private Property* 137–252 (1988).

21. The Supreme Court has upheld a statute paying material witnesses only $1 a day for every day that they spent in government confinement while waiting to testify at trial, but only because "the Fifth Amendment does not require that the Government pay for the performance of a public duty it is already owed." *Hurtado v. United States,* 410 U.S. 578, 588 (1973). In contrast, innocent detainees have breached no duty whatsoever and should be compensated for their sacrifice to the public good.

22. It is a fair question how much impact these budgetary costs will have on bureaucratic conduct. Skeptics may suggest that agency heads will expect Congress to pay compensation without reducing appropriations to other areas of the agency budget. But even if a partial offset does occur, it would be foolhardy for the agency to expect total financial absolution.

23. The European Convention for the Protection of Human Rights guarantees compensation to anyone who has been unlawfully arrested or detained. See art. 5(5), 213 U.N.T.S. 221, 226 1953). A subsequent protocol authorizes compensation for convicts who have been pardoned, or had their conviction overturned, on the ground of miscarriage of justice. Protocol No. 7, November 22, 1984, Europ. T.S. No. 5, at 60.

24. See generally, the Justice for All Act of 2004, Title IV, Pub. L. No. 108-405, 118 Stat. 2260. The ceiling is $100,000 per year for capital cases and $50,000 per year in noncapital cases. 28 USC §2513. Compensation by states lags far behind the federal government. When I last checked, only four failed to impose very restrictive ceilings on the level of payment. See generally, Adele Bernhard, "When Justice Fails: Indemnification for Unjust Conviction," 6 *U. Chi. L. Sch. Roundtable* 73 (1999).

25. Granting compensation to detainees would make it tougher for the prosecution to obtain plea bargains against those whom they subsequently charge with crimes: by pleading guilty, they would lose their claims to $22,500. Of course, prosecutors will still have lots of tools at their disposal—the prospect of a heavier sentence after a trial is still a very potent bargaining chip. But on the margin, the compensation requirement may well generate more jury trials.

This doesn't seem too high a price to pay for justice. After all, it would also save a lot of process costs if the government merely seized property for highway construction and denied all payment. Presto, and we have saved all the appraisal fees and hearings required for resolving all the heated arguments concerning each parcel's market value. But this hasn't seemed nearly a good enough reason for denying compensation to the people singled out by the highway builders. The same reasoning should apply to those who have been singled out by the emergency authority.

26. See Carl Schmitt, *Political Theology: Four Chapters on the Concept of Sovereignty* 5 (George Schwab trans., 1985) (1922); see also Oren Gross, "The Normless and Exceptionless Exception: Carl Schmitt's Theory of Emergency Powers and the 'Norm-Exception' Dichotomy," 21 *Cardozo L. Rev.* 1825, 1825-30 (2000). For a general overview, see *The Challenge of Carl Schmitt* (Chantal Mouffe ed., 1999).

27. See Michael Ignatieff, *The Lesser Evil* 145–53(2004).

28. This is hardly the place for a mature assessment of the overall operation of emergency powers by the Israeli authorities. For competing views, contrast Claude Klein, "Is There a Case for Constitutional Dictatorship in Israel?" in *Challenges to Democracy: Essays in Honour and Memory of Isaiah Berlin* 157 (Raphael Cohen-Almagor ed., 2000) with Raphael Cohen-Almagor, "Reflections on Administrative Detention in Israel: A Critique," id. at 203.

Chapter 3: This Is an Emergency

Epigraph: http://www.whitehouse.gov/news/releases/2004/01/20040120-7.html

1. U.S. Const. art. 1, §9, cl. 2.

2. For a remarkably complacent view of this cycle, see Mark Tushnet, "Defending *Korematsu*? Reflections on Civil Liberties in Wartime," 2003 *Wis. L. Rev.* 273, 283–98.

3. Approximately 77,000 of the 120,000 were citizens by birth; the rest were legal or illegal resident aliens. See Commission on Wartime Relocation and Internment of Civilians, *Personal Justice Denied* (1982).

4. Exec. Order No. 9066, 7 Fed. Reg. 1407 (February 25, 1942).

5. Act of March 21, 1942, chap. 191, 56 Stat. 173 (1942). Civilian Exclusion Orders 1–99 were ratified by General John L. De Witt's Public Proclamation No. 7 of June 8, 1942 (7 Fed. Reg. 4498) and 100–108 were ratified by Public Proclamation No. 11 of August 18, 1942. 7 Fed. Reg. 6703.

6. As Sidney Osborn, Arizona's governor, delicately put it, "We do not propose to be made a dumping ground for enemy aliens from any other state." Letter to Rep. John H. Tolan, Chairman, House Select Committee (February 28, 1942), quoted in Morton Grodzins, *Americans Betrayed* 248 (1949).

7. Exec. Order No. 9102 (March 18, 1942).

8. As of mid-1942, 92,000 people were already in custody, and there were 106,770 by November. See Commission on Wartime Relocation and Internment of Civilians, *Personal Justice Denied* 135, 149.

9. I don't suggest that these procedures complied with minimum conditions of due process. The fate of each individual was largely determined by his or her answer to questionnaires and ex parte inquiries that sought to determine each person's ongoing contact with Japan, and by his displays of loyalty to the United States. See id. at 191–97; Morton Grodzins, *Americans Betrayed* 256 (1949).

10. Twenty-one thousand detainees were permitted to leave in 1943, and 18,500 more were discharged in 1944. Commission on Wartime Relocation and Internment of Civilians, *Personal Justice Denied* 203.

11. The Court had already upheld the military's authority to impose a nighttime curfew on "all alien Japanese, all alien Germans, all alien Italians, and all persons of Japanese ancestry" residing on the West Coast. *Hirabayashi v. United States,* 320 U.S. 81, 88 (1943). This order was blatantly discriminatory, since it did not impose a curfew upon American citizens of German and Italian ancestry. Nevertheless, *Hirabayshi* did not commit the Court to uphold the more draconian measures involved in exclusion and detention.

12. *Ex parte Mitsuye Endo,* 65 S. Ct. 208, 218 (1944).

13. *Korematsu v. United States,* 323 U.S. 214, 216, 223 (1944).

14. See Peter H. Irons, *Justice at War: The Story of the Japanese American Internment* (1983), for a definitive treatment. Agonizing reappraisal began early, with Dean Eugene Rostow's critique of *Korematsu.* Eugene Rostow, "The Japanese American Cases—A Disaster," 54 *Yale L.J.* 489 (1945). More than forty years later, Rostow claimed that "*Korematsu* has already been overruled in fact, although the Supreme Court has never explicitly overruled it. The case has been overruled in fact because of the criticism it has received." Charles J. Cooper, Orrin Hatch, Eugene V. Rostow, and Michael Tigar, "What the Constitution Means by Executive Power," 43 *U. Miami L. Rev.* 165, 196–97 (1988). So it seemed in 1988, but what will be the view in 2028?

15. See Proclamation No. 4417, 41 Fed. Reg. 7741 (Feb. 20, 1976) (declaring that Proclamation No. 2714, which formally ended World War II, also rescinded President Roosevelt's Executive Order No. 9066). See Roger Daniels, *Prisoners Without Trial: Japanese Americans in World War II* 88–106 (1993); Leslie T. Hatamiya, *Righting a Wrong: Japanese Americans and the Passage of the Civil Liberties Act of* 1988 (1993).

16. *Korematsu* was vacated via a writ of *coram nobis* issued by the original district court. See *Korematsu v. United States,* 584 F. Supp. 1406 (N.D. Cal. 1984). This lower-court decision does not bind the Supreme Court.

17. Chief Justice William Rehnquist leaves the matter in doubt in his book *All the Laws but One: Civil Liberties in Wartime* 209–10 (1998). He agrees that the relocation of the Nisei (American-born children of Japanese immigrants) occurred without sufficient justification. But he defends the military's internment of their noncitizen

parents (the Issei) on the grounds that the Alien Enemies Act of 1798 was still valid law during World War II.

18. Article 16 of the French Constitution authorizes the president to exercise emergency powers (1) "when the institutions of the Republic, the independence of the Nation, the integrity of its territory or the fulfillment of its international commitments are under serious and immediate threat"; and (2) "when the proper functioning of the constitutional public powers is interrupted." Constitution (France) art. 16, translated in 7 *Constitutions of the Countries of the World: France* 6 (Gisbert H. Flanz ed., 2000). The president also decides how long the state of emergency endures. See François Saint-Bonnet, *L'Etat d'Exception* 15 (2001); Michèle Voisset, *L'Article* 16 *de la Constitution du* 4 *octobre* 1958, at 26 (1969). Article 16 has been invoked only once—by President Charles de Gaulle in 1961 in response to an attempted military insurrection in Algeria. This seems to have been an appropriate response, though the president was much criticized for continuing the state of emergency for months after the putsch had been suppressed. See id. at 26. The constitutional text provides abundant potential for this sort of abuse.

19. This rationale for the French approach is explicitly presented by Saint-Bonnet. See id. at 16.

20. See Clinton Rossiter, *Constitutional Dictatorship* 29–73 (Transaction 2002) (1948); Cindy Skatch, *Borrowing Constitutional Designs: Constitutional Law in Weimar Germany and the French Fifth Republic* chaps. 2 and 3 (2005). The German emergency provisions broadly empower the central government to establish public order without regard to the powers normally reserved to the states, but they endorse only very limited incursions on fundamental rights—namely, the detention of individuals for up to four days without judicial hearings and the confiscation of property without compensation or other normal safeguards. See Grundgesetz [GG] art. 115c(2)(1)–(2). As a further safeguard, the Constitution (known as the Basic Law) provides that "neither the constitutional status nor the performance of the constitutional functions of the Federal Constitutional Court or its Judges may be impaired." Id. art. 115g.

21. See Polish Const., art. 23; S. Afr. Const. §37(5)–(6).

22. See Jonathan L. Black-Branch, "Powers of Detention of Suspected International Terrorists Under the United Kingdom Anti-Terrorism, Crime and Security Act 2001: Dismantling the Cornerstones of a Civil Society," 27 *European Law Review,* 19–32 (2002); Adam Tomkins, "Legislating Against Terror: The Anti-Terrorism, Crime and Security Act 2001," *Public Law* 205–20 (2002).

23. Prevention of Terrorism Act, 2005, chap. 2 (Eng.)

24. Orders imposing rigorous restrictions, including house arrest, can be issued only by a judge on application by the secretary of state. Prevention of Terrorism Act 2005, sec. 1(2)(b). The judge must be satisfied, *on the balance of probabilities,* that the controlled person is or has been involved in terrorism-related activity. Id. sec. 4(7)(a). Less severe restrictions require an even lower standard of proof. The secretary of state must merely have *reasonable grounds* for suspecting that the individual is or has been involved in terrorism-related activity. Id. sec. 2(1).

25. The definition of terrorism is also extremely broad, including the threat of serious violence against any person or property that creates a serious risk to the public health or to any electronic system. The limitation, such as it is, comes in the attribution of the actor's purposes. He is a terrorist if he aims to influence the government or to intimidate the public and seeks to advance a political, religious or ideological cause. See the Terrorism Act 2000, chap. 11 (Eng.), incorporated by reference in the Prevention of Terrorism Act 2005, sec. 15(1).

26. The court has broad discretion to place evidence in the confidential file whenever disclosure would be contrary to the public interest. It may require the secretary of state to prepare a summary, but it may not allow even this much if complete confidentiality is in the "public interest." See para. 4(3) of the Schedule to the Prevention of Terrorism Act 2005.

27. Worse yet, the detainee can't talk freely to his special advocate even about nonconfidential issues after the lawyer has seen the confidential file. Instead, he may only communicate about such issues through a legal representative in writing. The special advocate is not allowed to reply except at the direction of the court. See Civil Procedure Rules, Part 76, Proceedings under the Prevention of Terrorism Act 2005, Rule 76.25. These extraordinary limitations have been justly criticized by the Constitutional Affairs Committee of the House of Commons, *The Operation of the Special Immigration Appeals Commission and the Use of Special Advocates* 27–40 (2005).

28. See "Terror Defence Lawyer to Quit," *Sunday Times,* December 19, 2004; "Second Terror Lawyer Quits," *Independent,* January 17, 2005. Technically, these resignations occurred when terrorism was regulated by a predecessor statute, but the procedures remain much the same.

29. The Blair government has not yet chosen to impose house arrest (see "This Is a Bad Law and a Dangerous Precedent," *Independent on Sunday,* March 13, 2005), but suspects have been forced to stay at home at night; see "Freed Terror Suspects Face Rigid Regime," *Guardian,* March 12, 2005. See the Prevention of Terrorism Act 2005, Section 1(4) for authorization of a host of measures falling short of house arrest.

30. Franz Kafka, "Before the Law," in *The Complete Short Stories* 3 (Nahum Glatzer ed., 1971).

31. Draft Bill, part 1, clause 2 (Glorification of terrorism, etc.), submitted by Home Secretary Clarke to the leaders of the opposition parties on September 15, 2005, available at www.homeoffice.gov.uk/docs4/Print-02C.pdf.

32. Id. at clause 3 (Dissemination of terrorist publications).

33. Blair was defied by forty-nine Labour Party rebels, who agreed to the compromise of twenty-eight days. It was Blair's first parliamentary defeat. See Sarah Lyall, "House of Commons Rebuffs Blair on Antiterror Provision," *New York Times,* November 10, 2005. The bill provides a judicial check on abuse by requiring a weekly review of each case. But this protection is chimerical, since the bill specifically authorizes the police to continue detention for the purpose of developing and analyzing the

evidence relevant to their investigation. See Draft Bill, part 2, clause 24 (grounds for extending detention).

34. The basic rights of suspects are set out in section 5 of the European Convention, and the terms for derogation are provided by section 15. The authoritative text is provided by the Council of Europe at its website: http://www.hri.org/docs/ECHR50.html.

35. See, for example, the efforts by Britain's attorney general to portray his government's derogations from the Convention as a reasonable compromise with fundamental rights, even in cases where the House of Lords subsequently declared that they represented an illegitimate exercise of power. See Peter Goldsmith, "Ramo Lecture: Terrorism and the Rule of Law," 35 *N.M. L. Rev.* 215, 225 (2005).

36. For example, the current version of the Prevention of Terrorism Act is not yet a permanent fixture in the statute books. Though the Blair government resisted a sunset clause, the opposition forced one on it, and the statute will require explicit renewal within two years. See sec. 13(a)–(d). For a report on the debate, see The Longest Day, Guardian 1 (March 12, 2005)). Given the July 2005 terrorist bombings, it is unlikely that parliament will take advantage of the sunset law to repeal the worst parts of this ill-conceived legislation.

Chapter 4: The Political Constitution

1. For a concise description of the Roman dictatorship, see Clinton Rossiter, *Constitutional Dictatorship* 15–28 (Transaction Publishers 2002) (1948).

2. Id. at 24. During the later history of the office, the dictatorship was occasionally employed for ceremonial purposes or other lesser functions. Id. at 22.

3. Rossiter provides an illuminating review of the use of emergency powers in Germany, France, and England during the nineteenth century, continuing through the 1930s. See id. at 31–205.

4. For the special problems that arise if the terrorist attack destroys the central institutions of government, see Chapter 7.

5. But will there be enough contrarian legislators to serve as an effective check? The American Civil Liberties Union compiled a scorecard on each member of the House that passed the Patriot Act based on his or her vote on fifteen civil liberties issues. One hundred ninety-eight representatives voted the ACLU way on at least 50 percent of the issues, 176 on 60 percent, 150 on 70 percent, and 115 on 80 percent or more. See ACLU, National Freedom Scorecard, at http://scorecard.aclu.org (providing an interface that lets visitors look up how their representatives scored). On the Senate side, 44 senators voted with the ACLU on at least three of the five issues included in its scorecard. See id. This didn't prevent the House and Senate from succumbing to panic when passing the Patriot Act, but it does suggest substantial support for civil liberties over the longer run.

In parliamentary systems in Europe, individual deputies generally have much less freedom of action than in the United States, but this is typically offset by a greater number of parties in parliament due to the prevalence of proportional representation.

The crucial decision in these cases will be made by the leaders of each parliamentary party, not by individual members.

6. Once an emergency expires, the supermajoritarian vote needed to declare another one should deescalate on the same schedule with which it escalated previously. If 80 percent support is required, the percentage drops to 70 percent after two months, then to 60, then to a simple majority, as time marches on.

7. Or almost all. Congress does make an exception for the committee that investigates the ethics of individual members, giving each party equal representation. The House committee has five members from each party, the Senate three. Parity is established by House Rule V(a)(3)(A); the Senate regulates this practice by convention.

8. See German Bundestag, "The Organization: Committees," at http://www.bundestag.de/htdocs_e/orga/03organs/04commit/01comminf.html. Though the British House of Commons grants broad control to the majority party, the government generally grants ten or so chairs to the minority. See Comm. Office of the House of Commons, "The Committee System of the House of Commons" 13 (2003), http://www.parliament.uk/commons/selcom/ctteesystemmay2003.pdf (last visited June 2004).

9. In a parliamentary system, the identity of political minorities is straightforward— these are the parties that remain outside the governing coalition. But in a presidential regime, like that of the United States, identifying "the opposition" can be tricky when different parties control the presidency and Congress. In these cases, legislative oversight should go to the party that does not control the presidency, even if it does hold the majority in Congress. Since the emergency constitution aims to challenge the executive's informational monopoly, the watchdog role should not be turned over to the president's party, even if it happens to have "minority" status in the House or Senate.

10. The requirement of parliamentary approval applies only to those emergencies generated by external threats. GG art. 80a. The Basic Law also envisions a heightened state of emergency that it calls a "state of defense" for cases where armed attack is imminent. A two-thirds majority of the Bundestag is required to move into this condition, and the consent of the Bundesrat is also required. Id. art. 115a(1). If it is impossible for Parliament to convene, this decision can also be made by a special joint committee created for interim decision making. See id. arts. 53a, 115e(1).

11. Id. art. 115l(2). This provision applies to the heightened "state of defense." Through a technical oversight, no similar article regulates the basic state of emergency established by article 80a.

12. Konst. RF (1993) arts. 87–88, 102.

13. A. A Magyar Köztársaság Alkotmánya [Constitution] art. 19(4). For a useful (but occasionally obsolete) overview, see Venelin I. Ganev, "Emergency Powers and the New Eastern European Constitutions," 45 A. J. Comp. L. 590 (1997).

14. See, e.g., Constitución Política de la República de Chile art. 40(2), (6), translated into English in 4 *Constitutions of the Countries of the World* (Gisbert H. Flanz ed. 2004); Constituição da República Portuguesa art. 19(5) translated in 15 id.; Türkïyeᴇ Cumhurïyetï Anayasasi arts. 120–21, translated in 18 id.

15. Konstytucja Rzeczypospolitej Polskiej [Constitution] arts. 230(1), (2), translated in 15 *id.*

16. See M. B. Biskupski, *The History of Poland* 164–68 (2000).

17. See Oren Gross, "Chaos and Rules: Should Responses to Violent Crises Always Be Constitutional?" 112 *Yale L.J.* 1011 (2003); Mark Tushnet, "Defending Korematsu? Reflections on Civil Liberties in Wartime," 2003 *Wis. L. Rev.* 273, 299.

18. See Gross, "Chaos and Rules," at 1111–15.

19. The Indian experience with emergency powers provides a cautionary tale. Prime Minister Indira Gandhi egregiously abused these powers, but not in response to some catastrophic event, like a terrorist strike. Her decision was provoked by a judgment of the Allahabad High Court finding her guilty of two counts of electoral wrongdoing. Gandhi appealed to the Indian Supreme Court, which gave her a conditional stay but also limited her participatory powers as a member of the Indian parliament. She responded to this threat to her political position with the declaration of emergency. See Venkat Iyer, *States of Emergency: The Indian Experience* 152–155 (2000); Granville Austin, *Working a Democratic Constitution* 296 (1999).

20. For some important recent reflections, see José Antonio Aguilar Rivera, *En pos de la quimera: Reflexiones sobre el experimento constitucional atlántico* 57–94 (2000).

21. For the best legal account of the South African state of emergency, see Stephen Ellmann, *In a Time of Trouble* (1992).

22. See S. Afr. Const. §37. The structure of the constitutional provisions is slightly more complex than the text suggests. Under Section 37, a simple majority of Parliament first approves a state of emergency that endures for twenty-one days at most. During this time, Parliament can approve an extension of no more than three months through a simple majority. It is only at this point that the 60 percent escalator operates for all further extensions. See G. E. Devenish, "The Demise of Salus Republicae Suprema Lex in South Africa: Emergency Rule in Terms of the 1996 Constitution," 31 *Comp. and Int'l L.J. S. Afr.* 142 (1998).

23. S. Afr. Const. §37(2)(b).

24. During the 1999 general election, the African National Congress won 266 of 400 seats in parliament—barely less than two-thirds of the total. S. Afr. Gov't, Election Results 1999, at http://www.gov.za/elections/results99.htm (last visited October 4, 2003; inactive on August 31, 2005).

25. S. Afr. Const §37(1)(a).

26. See Emergencies Act R.S.C., chap. 22, §18(2) (setting a 30-day limit for public order emergencies); id. §39(2) (war emergencies must be renewed every 120 days); cf. id. §7(2) (public welfare emergencies have 90-day renewal periods); id. §29(2) (international emergencies require renewal every 60 days).

27. Civil Contingencies Act, 2004, c. 36 (Eng.), sec. 19(1)). As another example of ill-considered draftsmanship, the British statute authorizes the declaration of an emergency on the mere basis of a "threat" to national security—not even demanding that there be a "clear and present" danger.

28. Id. sec. 22(3)(f).

29. For a classic treatment, see Thomas Emerson, *Toward A General Theory of the First Amendment* (1966).

30. Even the relatively uncontroversial matter of defining emergency power for public health crises has proved extremely contentious. See John M. Colmers and Daniel M. Fox, "The Politics of Emergency Health Powers and the Isolation of Public Health," 93 *Am. J. Pub. Health* 397 (2003).

31. Although the judiciary has a valuable role to play in assuring operational primacy, only the legislature can plausibly make the policy decisions required by the "demotion option."

32. Bradley Graham, "War Plans Drafted to Counter Terror Attacks in U.S.: Domestic Effort Is Big Shift for Military," *Washington Post,* August 8, 2005. Current law is based on an antique statute enacted to rein in the Union army at the end of Reconstruction. The Posse Comitatus Act of 1878 reads: "Whoever, except in cases and under circumstances expressly authorized by the Constitution or Act of Congress, willfully uses any part of the Army or the Air Force as a posse comitatus or otherwise to execute the laws shall be fined under this title or imprisoned not more than two years, or both." 18 U.S.C. §1385. This statute has been construed to impose stringent limits on military assistance to civilian police during normal times.

But matters would get more complicated in the event of a terrorist attack. The Posse Comitatus Act expressly exempts the Insurrection Act of 1807 from its ban. This early statute authorizes the use of the regular army in "cases of insurrection or obstruction to the laws." See Robert Coakley, *The Role of Federal Military Forces in Domestic Disorders, 1789–1878* 345 (1988). Whether an attack amounted to an "insurrection" or "obstruction" would depend on the facts of the case.

The Posse Comitatus Act also exempts "cases . . . expressly authorized by the Constitution," leaving it open for the president to assert sweeping authority as commander in chief. Courts weighing these claims would have to confront compelling evidence of the Founders' deep opposition to the president's unilateral exercise of military power. See generally, Stephen Vladeck, "Emergency Power and the Militia Acts," 114 *Yale L. J.* 149, and esp. 156–159 (2004).

Chapter 5: The Role of Judges

1. On the "passive virtues" see Alexander Bickel, *The Least Dangerous Branch: The Supreme Court at the Bar of Politics* (1962)

2. The attentive reader will recognize that we have already reached this conclusion through a different conceptual route. See the discussion in Chapter 4 of the "minimalist" case for judicial review to assure the operational primacy of the emergency regime.

3. In America the forty-five-day delay would require Congress to enact a limited suspension of the writ of habeas corpus, and Chapter 6 deals with the constitutional problems that arise. In Europe the delay would require governments to derogate from the right to the "prompt" judicial hearing guaranteed by the European

Convention on Human Rights. Convention for the Protection of Human Rights and Fundamental Freedoms, art. 5(3), 213 U.N.T.S. at 226.

4. See Alan Dershowitz, *Why Terrorism Works: Understanding the Threat, Responding to the Challenge* 142–63 (2002). For another provocative essay, see Sanford Levinson, "'Precommitment' and 'Postcommitment': The Ban on Torture in the Wake of September 11," 81 *Tex. L. Rev.* 2013 (2003).

5. See Dershowitz, *Why Terrorism Works,* at 158–61.

6. See id. at 145.

7. For some thoughtful discussions, see Sanford Levinson ed., *Torture: A Collection* (2004); Michael Ignatieff, *The Lesser Evil* 141–44 (2004).

8. Although the "torture memos" scandal provides a useful cautionary tale, I should note an important caveat. The memos dealt with the treatment of detainees held abroad, but this book deals with states-of-emergency detainees held domestically. Within the United States, all officials are bound by the Eighth Amendment's ban on "cruel and unusual punishment," and by the Fifth and Fourteenth Amendments' guarantees of due process, which forbid torture in preconviction settings. *Bell v. Wolfish,* 441 U.S. 520, 535–37 (1979). However, since the "torture memos" dealt with acts outside the country, analysis begins with the United Nations Convention defining torture as "any act by which severe pain or suffering, whether physical or mental, is intentionally inflicted on a person for such purposes as obtaining . . . information," and which is unconditionally binding. Convention Against Torture (CAT), arts. 1 and 2(2), G.A. Res. 39/46, Annex, 39 U.N. GAOR Supp. No. 51, U.N. Doc. A/39/51(1984). The United States ratified the Convention in 1994, and Congress passed implementing legislation defining "torture" as "an act committed by a person acting under the color of law specifically intended to inflict severe physical or mental pain or suffering (other than pain or suffering incidental to lawful sanctions) upon another person within his custody or physical control." 18 U.S.C. §2340(1). In contrast, the Justice Department memo of August 1, 2002, limited torture to the infliction of "*physical pain . . . equivalent in intensity to the pain accompanying serious physical injury, such as organ failure, impairment of bodily function or even death.*" Memorandum of August 1, 2002, from Jay S. Bybee, Assistant Attorney General, Office of Legal Counsel, for Alberto R. Gonzales, Counsel to the President, re Standards of Conduct for Interrogation Under 18 U.S.C. §§2340–2340A at 1, available at http://news.findlaw.com/nytimes/docs/doj/bybee80102mem.pdf (emphasis provided). The narrowing construction is especially egregious since the Supreme Court may well decide that the Constitution's prohibitions on torture provide a source of law that is superior to the statute in foreign as well as domestic contexts. See John T. Parry, "Escalation and Necessity," in *Torture* 143, 148 (Sanford Levinson ed.)

9. As Harold Koh has rightly emphasized, the narrow definition of torture elaborated by the Justice Department is incompatible with the Bush administration's assessment of Saddam's inhumane actions. See Statement of Harold Hongju Koh, Nomination of Alberto R. Gonzales as Attorney General to the United States:

Hearing Before the Senate Comm. on Judiciary, 109th Cong. (Jan. 7, 2005), citing White House statement, "Saddam Hussein's Repression of the Iraqi People": "Iraqi security services routinely and systematically torture detainees. According to former prisoners, torture techniques included branding, electric shocks administered to the genitals and other areas, beating, pulling out of fingernails, burning with hot irons and blowtorches, suspension from rotating ceiling fans, dripping acid on the skin, rape, breaking of limbs, denial of food and water, extended solitary confinement in dark and extremely small compartments, and threats to rape or otherwise harm family members and relatives. Evidence of such *torture* often was apparent when security forces returned the mutilated bodies of torture victims to their families." Available at http://www.whitehouse.gov/infocus/iraq/decade/sect4.html (emphasis added). Many of these acts would be permissible under the Justice Department's "torture memos."

10. The August 1 memorandum asserts that torturers may escape prosecution on the ground that "they were carrying out the President's Commander-in-Chief powers," and that this executive privilege precludes the application of a valid federal criminal statute "to punish officials for aiding the President in exercising his exclusive constitutional authorities." See August 1, 2002, Bybee Memorandum at 35. It goes on to deny that Congress can constitutionally limit the president's discretion to abuse detainees, asserting that "any effort by Congress to regulate the interrogation of battlefield combatants would violate the Constitution's sole vesting of the Commander-in-Chief authority in the President. . . . Congress can no more interfere with the President's conduct of interrogation of enemy combatants than it can dictate strategic or tactical decisions on the battlefield." Id. at 39.

11. The leaks began in May 2004 (see, Neil Lewis, "Justice Memos Explained How to Skip Prisoner Rights," *New York Times,* May 21, 2004), but it was only on June 8, 2004, that the *Washington Post* reported the contents of the crucial memorandum of August 1, 2002. Dana Priest and R. Jeffrey Smith, "Memo Offered Justification for Use of Torture; Justice Dept. Gave Advice in 2002," *Washington Post,* June 8, 2004.

12. In a June press conference, Attorney General Alberto Gonzales did not explicitly repudiate the memorandum, offering instead some bureaucratese worthy of memorialization. He blandly assured the assembled reporters that "unnecessary, over-broad discussions in some of these memos that address abstract legal theories, or discussions subject to misinterpretation, but not relied upon by policymakers *are* under review, and may be replaced, if appropriate, with more concrete guidance addressing only those issues necessary for legal analysis of actual practice." Press Briefing by White House Counsel Judge Alberto Gonzales et al., June 22, 2004, available at http://www.whitehouse.gov/news/releases/2004/06/20040622–14.html (italics in original). The August 1 memorandum was rescinded officially only six months later by a memorandum of December 30, 2004: from Daniel Levin, Acting Assistant Attorney General, Office of Legal Counsel, for James B. Comey, Deputy Attorney General, Regarding Legal Standards Applicable Under 18 U.S.C. §§2340–2340A, available at http://www.justice.gov/olc/dagmemo.pdf.

13. Although the Justice Department's memorandum of December 30, 2004, "supercede[d] the August 2002 Memorandum in its entirety," it did not specifically replace or renounce the memo's extreme claims about the president's power to define interrogation techniques in disregard of the commands of Congress. Id. at 1. It merely stated that legal analysis of the question was "unnecessary" since "it is the President's unequivocal directive that United States personnel not engage in torture." Id. This falls far short of conceding that the president is bound by acts of Congress on the subject of torture. It merely says that the president currently does not intend to flout congressional will.

14. The memo bearing Bybee's signature was dated August 1, 2002; Bybee was nominated by President Bush on May 22, 2002. See Henry Weinstein, "Federal Official Nominated for Judgeship," *Los Angeles Times,* May 23, 2002.

15. 139 *Cong. Rec.* at S3693 (quoted by Sen. Richard Durbin). Bybee's oral hearing was cursory, since it occurred at the same time that Colin Powell was presenting the administration's case for invading Iraq to the United Nations. The nominee's stonewalling occurred in his written responses to written queries by Senator Edwards, Feingold, and others. See 149 *Cong. Rec.* S3692-93 (2003) (statement of Sen. Russ Feingold). Id. at S3693. Statement of Sen. Richard Durbin, id. at S3964. Senate Roll Call Vote 54, 108th Cong., Mar. 13, 2003.

16. Dana Priest and Jeffrey R. Smith, "Memo Offered Justification for Use of Torture," *Washington Post,* June 8, 2004, available at http://www.washingtonpost. com/wp-dyn/articles/A23373-2004Jun7.html.

17. At his confirmation hearings in 2005 for the position of deputy attorney general, Timothy Flanagan said "he found the Justice Department's conclusion that the president had the power to override Congressional mandates on prisoner treatment to be 'sort of sophomoric' and inappropriate." Flanagan himself was involved in the deliberations on the memo, but this did not sink his candidacy. Only a looming corruption scandal led to his withdrawal from consideration. Eric Lichtblau, "Justice Nominee Is Questioned on Department Torture Policy," *New York Times,* July 27, 2005.

18. The Supreme Court upheld this arrangement in *Mistretta v. United States,* 488 U.S. 361 (1989). Commissioners serve for a six-year term, which can be renewed once. No more than four can be members of the same political party. See id. at 368–69; 28 U.S.C. §§992(a) and (b).

19. As time marches on, the litigated cases will slowly reach the Supreme Court, probably at a time when the emergency has been terminated. By this point, the Court will have had a chance to test the initial guidelines formulated by the Decency Commission against recent experience and to determine how they fare under the Eighth Amendment's prohibition against "cruel and unusual punishment," applied to the context of detention through the Due Process Clauses. *Bell v. Wolfish,* 441 U.S. 520, 535–37 (1979). This initial round of cases may well provoke an ongoing dialogue with the commission, requiring it to revise its operational standards in line with the Court's decisions.

20. See, e.g., Nickolas A. Kacprowski, Note, "Stacking the Deck Against Suspected Terrorists: The Dwindling Procedural Limits on the Government's Power to Indefinitely Detain United States Citizens as Enemy Combatants," 26 *Seattle U. L. Rev.* 651, 666 (2003).

21. As a further safeguard, judicial hearings on torture complaints should be expedited, and security officers found to be complicit should be subjected to immediate administrative discharge and timely criminal prosecution.

22. For some profound reflections on this subject, see Avishai Margalit, *The Decent Society* (1996).

23. International Covenant on Civil and Political Rights, art. 4, S. Exec. Doc. E, 95–2, at 24, 999 U.N.T.S. at 174 (emphasis added).

24. S. Exec. Rep. No. 102-23, at 22 (1992).

25. Sara Kehaulani Goo, "Faulty 'No-Fly' System Detailed," *Washington Post*, October 9, 2004 (reporting number of names on "no-fly" list).

26. For a plausible proposal, see Justin Florence, "Making the No Fly List Fly: A Due Process Model for Terrorist Watchlists," forthcoming, *Yale L. J.*

Chapter 6: American Exceptionalism

1. The last controversial amendments were the product of the agitations of the Progressive era—involving the income tax, women's suffrage, and the prohibition of alcohol (which was repealed in 1933). Since then, uncontroversial amendments involving the organization of government, especially the presidency, have dominated the agenda. Perhaps the imposition on the president of a two-term limit was the most controversial to succeed. Even a measure granting equal status to women proved too hot to handle, despite its sustained support by a broad national majority. See Jane Mansbridge, *Why We Lost the ERA* (1986).

2. Pub. L. No. 79–404, 60 Stat. 237 (1946) (codified as amended in scattered sections of 5 U.S.C.).

3. See the great treatises codifying these principles by Kenneth Davis & Richard Pierce, *Administrative Law Treatise* (3d. ed. 1994), and Louis Jaffe, *Judicial Control of Administrative Action* (1965).

4. See Special Commission on National Emergencies and Delegated Powers, *A Recommended National Emergencies Act,* S. Rep. No. 93–1170, at 2 (1974), reprinted in Senate Committee on Government Operations and the Special Commission on National Emergencies and Delegated Emergency Powers, *The National Emergencies Act (Public Law 94–412), Source Book: Legislative History, Texts, and Other Documents* 20 (1976); Special Commission on the Termination of the National Emergency, *Emergency Powers Statutes: Provisions of Federal Law Now in Effect Delegating to the Executive Extraordinary Authority in Time of National Emergency,* S. Rep. No. 93–549, at iv (1973).

5. Pub. L. No. 94-412, 90 Stat. 1255 (codified as amended at 50 U.S.C. §§1601–51 (2000)). For example, the National Emergencies Act requires that all future declara-

tions of national emergency be published in the *Federal Register,* id. §1621, that the president specify the statutory powers to be exercised during the emergency, id. §1631, and that the president report to Congress on emergency orders and expenditures, id. §1641.

6. See Abraham Ribicoff, Commission on Government Operations, *National Emergencies Act,* S. Rep. No. 94–1168, at 3 (1976), 1976 U.S.C.C.A.N. 2288, at 2289, reprinted in *The National Emergencies Act Source Book,* at 290, 292.

7. One year after passage of the NEA, Congress passed the International Emergency Economic Powers Act (IEEPA), Pub. L. No. 95–223, §§201–8, 91 Stat. 1625 (1977) (codified as amended at 50 U.S.C. §§1701–7). The IEEPA authorizes the president to exercise wide-ranging emergency economic powers in response to "any unusual and extraordinary threat, which has its source in whole or substantial part outside the United States, to the national security, foreign policy, or economy of the United States." Id. §§1701–2. These powers are regulated by the NEA framework, but the IEEPA also imposes additional procedures. For example, the president must consult with Congress "in every possible instance" prior to invoking the statute, id. §1703(a), and he must specify the circumstances constituting the emergency, id. §1703(b), and report back to Congress every six months §1703(c).

8. During the 1990s, the IEEPA was used increasingly against terrorist groups, but never to arrest or detain suspects. See James J. Savage, "Executive Use of the International Emergency Economic Powers Act—Evolution Through the Terrorist and Taliban Sanctions," *Currents: Int'l Trade L.J.* 28, 32–37 (2001).

9. Lobel, "Emergency Power," provides the best essay on the real-world operation of the NEA and the IEEPA.

10. 50 U.S.C. §1622. The IEEPA imposes additional procedural requirements to those demanded by the NEA, but these safeguards have fared no better in real life. See Lobel, "Emergency Power," at 1415–16; Note, "The International Emergency Economic Powers Act: A Congressional Attempt to Control Presidential Emergency Power," 96 *Harv. L. Rev.* 1102, 1118–19 (1983).

11. Lobel, "Emergency Power," at 1417. When he was a circuit court judge, Justice Stephen G. Breyer interpreted the provision as granting Congress a discretionary "chance to force a vote on the issue." *Beacon Prods. Corp. v. Reagan,* 814 F.2d 1, 4–5 (1st Cir. 1987).

In its major decision in the area, the Supreme Court also took a very deferential posture toward the exercise of executive emergency power under the IEEPA. See *Dames & Moore v. Regan,* 453 U.S. 654 (1981). See Harold Koh, "Why the President (Almost) Always Wins in Foreign Affairs: Lessons of the Iran-Contra Affair," 97 *Yale L.J.* 1255, 1311 (1988).

12. 50 U.S.C. §1622(d). To renew an emergency declaration, the president need only publish a statement in the *Federal Register* and provide notice to Congress that the emergency continues in effect. See id. Looking only at the years 2001 and 2002, I have found eight presidential renewals in the *Federal Register,* ranging from the annual ritual on Iran (Notice of President, 66 *Fed. Reg.* 56,966 [November 9, 2001])

to such arcana as the "Emergency with Respect to Significant Narcotics Traffickers Centered in Colombia" (Notice of President, 66 *Fed. Reg.* 53,073 [October 16, 2001]).

13. National Emergencies Act, Pub. L. No. 94-412, §202, 90 Stat. 1255, 1255–57 (1976) (current version at 50 U.S.C. §1622).

14. See Foreign Relations Authorization Act, Fiscal Years 1986 and 1987, Pub. L. No. 99–93, §801, 99 Stat. 406, 448 (1985) (codified at 50 U.S.C. §1622). On unconstitutionality of legislative vetoes, see *INS v. Chadha,* 462 U.S. 919 (1983).

15. See David Cole, "The Priority of Morality: The Emergency Constitution's Blind Spot," 113 *Yale L.J.* 1753, 1765–66 (2004).

16. For quantitative data supporting this claim, see Chapter 4, note 5.

17. Other constitutional questions may well arise, depending on the particular way in which the basic ideas are elaborated into a framework statute. But for now, it is enough to focus on the fundamental problems.

18. U.S. Const. art. 1, §9, cl. 2.

19. This is how the provision read when it came to the floor for debate on August 28, 1787. See James Madison, *Journal,* August 28, 1787, reprinted in 2 *The Records of the Federal Convention of* 1787, at 437, 438 (Max Farrand ed., rev. ed. 1966). Pinckney had first introduced a significantly different proposal on August 20, providing that "the privileges and benefit of the Writ of Habeas corpus . . . shall not be suspended by the Legislature except upon the most urgent and pressing occasions, and for a limited time not exceeding [ ] months." Madison, *Journal,* August 20, 1787, reprinted in 2 *Convention Records,* at 340, 341. On August 28, however, he deleted the phrases "by the Legislature" and "and pressing" and specified a 12-month sunset clause.

20. Madison, *Journal,* August 28, 1787, reprinted in 2 *Convention Records,* at 438–39.

21. See Francis Paschal, "The Constitution and Habeas Corpus," 1970 *Duke L.J.* 605, 610.

22. Each of the individual states established the writ of habeas corpus before the Constitutional Convention (see William F. Duker, *A Constitutional History of Habeas Corpus* 115 [1980]), and there were already precedents for the states to suspend the writ in times of emergency, id. at 142. At the Convention, John Rutledge argued that this made a federal suspension power unnecessary. He did not "conceive that a suspension could ever be necessary at the same time through all the States." Madison, *Journal,* reprinted in 2 *Convention Records,* at 438. Anti-Federalists continued to make this argument during the ratification debates. Luther Martin, *The Genuine Information Delivered to the Legislature of the State of Maryland Relative to the Proceedings of the General Convention Lately Held at Philadelphia* (1787), reprinted in 3 *Convention Records,* at 172, 213.

23. "That the privilege of Habeas Corpus shall not by any law, be suspended for a longer term than six months, or until twenty days after the meeting of the Congress, next following the passing of the act for such suspension." *Recommendatory*

Amendments, Poughkeepsie County Journal, August 12, 1788, reprinted in 18 *Documentary History,* at 301, 302. This proposed amendment was part of New York State's ratifying submission to the Continental Congress. See id. at 294–97.

24. Act of April 20, 1871, chap. 22, §4, 17 Stat. 13, 14 (emphasis added). The act also contained a sunset clause, specifically that "the provisions of this section shall not be in force after the end of the next regular session of Congress." Id., 17 Stat. at 15. The Ku Klux Klan can be seen as a prototype for modern terrorist groups; although it challenged state power, it never claimed to be the legitimate political authority of the South.

Beginning in 1870, President Grant used these powers to put more than forty counties under martial law. See William L. Richter, *The ABC-CLIO Companion to American Reconstruction, 1862–1877,* at 198 (1996). In suspending habeas corpus, President Grant did not claim that the Klan was going to overthrow Southern governments, but explicitly availed himself of the expanded definition of "rebellion" created by the authorizing statute. Ulysses S. Grant, A Proclamation, October 17, 1871, reprinted in 7 *A Compilation of the Messages and Papers of the Presidents, 1789–1897,* at 136–37 (James D. Richardson ed., 1896–99).

25. Jed Rubenfeld has many useful things to say about the use of paradigm cases in constitutional interpretation. See his *Freedom and Time* (2001) and *Revolution by Judiciary* (2005).

26. *Duncan v. Kahanamoku,* 327 U.S. 304 (1946).

27. Id. at 329–30 (Stone, C.J., concurring, emphasizing this point). In the District Court, Judge Metzger found that "while the Island of Oahu may have been on March 2, 1944, and thereafter to this day, subject to possible attack by enemies at war, that it was not then, nor is it now, in imminent danger of invasion by hostile forces, neither was or is it in rebellion." *Ex parte Duncan,* 66 F.Supp. 976, 981 (1944).

28. See id. at 313–14, 324.

29. Id. at 319.

30. James Madison, *Federalist No. 48* 332, 333 (Jacob E. Cooke ed. 1961).

31. See §224, 115 Stat. 272, 295.

32. The text of the original Constitution contains seven supermajoritarian provisions. See U.S. Const. art. 1, §3, cl. 6 (Senate impeachment trials); §5, cl. 2 (expulsion of a member of either house); §7, cl. 2 (override of a presidential veto); art. II, §1, cl. 3, amended by U.S. Const. amend. 12 (two-thirds quorum of state delegations in the House for election of the president upon deadlock in the electoral college); §2, cl. 2 (Senate ratification of a treaty); art. 5 (proposal and ratification of a constitutional amendment); art. 7 (ratification of the original Constitution by the states). Two more supermajority provisions have been added by amendment. See id. amend. 14, §3 (amnesty for rebels); amend. 25, §4 (presidential disability).

33. The leading case is *INS v. Chadha,* 462 U.S. 919 (1983), in which the Court struck down a "legislative veto" as inconsistent with the Presentment Clause.

34. Recently, Eric Posner and Adrian Vermeule have suggested that Congress not only has a broad power to create supermajority rules, but that the Constitution also

gives each Congress a general power to entrench these supermajoritarian rules against repeal by future Congresses through simple majority votes. See Eric A. Posner and Adrian Vermeule, "Legislative Entrenchment: A Reappraisal," 111 *Yale L.J.* 1665 (2002). Adopting their position would permit a clean-cut solution to the puzzles presented in the following paragraphs. Unfortunately, I do not find their claims plausible, partly for reasons elaborated in Stewart E. Sterk, "Retrenchment on Entrenchment," 71 *Geo. Wash. L. Rev.* 231 (2003) and John O. McGinnis and Michael B. Rappaport, "Symmetric Entrenchment: A Constitutional and Normative Theory," 89 *Va. L. Rev.* 385 (2003), and partly for reasons suggested in 1 Bruce Ackerman, *We the People: Foundations* (1991) and 2 *We the People: Transformations* (1998).

35. The Constitution does contain special rules that make it practically impossible to impose "direct" taxes. See Bruce Ackerman, "Taxation and the Constitution," 99 *Colum. L. Rev.* 1 (1999). But this is merely a detail, which does not undermine the main point made in the text.

I use taxation as my example because, during the mid-1990s I played a role in a campaign against an effort by House Speaker Newt Gingrich to require a supermajority vote of 60 percent for tax increases. See Bruce Ackerman et al., "An Open Letter to Congressman Gingrich," 104 *Yale L.J.* 1539 (1995) (presenting a letter endorsed by sixteen other law professors). I also participated as counsel in subsequent litigation initiated by members of the House of Representatives. See *Skaggs v. Carle,* 110 F.3d 831 (D.C. Cir. 1997). The majority of the *Skaggs* panel denied standing to the representatives, but a strong dissenting opinion reached the merits and rejected the constitutionality of the new supermajority rule enacted by the House. See id. at 841 (Edwards, C.J., dissenting).

Since I continue to believe that a majoritarian baseline should generally be enforced, my argument in the text carves out a limited exception in the case of the Suspension Clause.

36. For the classic exploration of Congress's role as a constitutional interpreter, see Paul Brest, "The Conscientious Legislator's Guide to Constitutional Interpretation," 27 *Stan. L. Rev.* 585 (1975).

37. See generally Paul Pierson, *Politics in Time: History, Institutions and Social Analysis* (2004).

38. Chief Justice Roger Taney famously denied that Lincoln had the power to suspend habeas unilaterally and ordered the release of a detainee in *Ex parte Merryman,* 17 Fed. Cases 144 (1861). Lincoln ignored Taney's order, but in a month or so, his military commander procured an indictment for treason before a grand jury. Merryman was then released on bail and never tried. See Carl Swisher, 5 *History of the Supreme Court of the United States: The Taney Period* 844–854 (1974).

When Congress met in special session on July 4, it took only a month before it retrospectively ratified "all the acts, proclamations, and orders of the President of the United States after the fourth of March, eighteen hundred and sixty-one, respecting the army and navy of the United States, and calling out or relating to the militia or volunteers from the States," giving them the "same effect as if they had been issued and done under the previous express authority and direction of the Congress of the United States." 12 Stat. 326 (August 6, 1861). It is possible to deny that this text authorizes Lincoln's suspension of habeas corpus, since the Great Writ is a remedy for civilians, not soldiers. But this restrictive reading does not do justice to Congress's intentions at this moment of grave crisis.

39. Act of March 3, 1863, 12 Stat. 755.

40. *Ex parte Milligan*, 71 U.S. 2, 127, 140 (1866).

41. *Youngstown Sheet & Tube Co. v. Sawyer*, 343 U.S. 579 (1952).

42. Id. at 637–38.

Chapter 7: If Washington Blows Up?

1. This is a good time to note that Professors Akhil and Vikram Amar challenge the constitutionality of Congress's decision to place members of that body in line for the presidency. Amar and Amar, "Is the Presidential Succession Law Constitutional?" 48 *Stan. L. Rev.* 113 (1995). The Amar brothers' objection has a very long lineage (see Bruce Ackerman, *The Failure of the Founding Fathers* 41–45, 269–75 [2005]), but so do the constitutional arguments in support of the existing statute. And since a long line of Congresses has read the Constitution to authorize the succession of Representatives and Senators, it's a bit late in the day to launch a serious constitutional challenge to the current statute. Surely it would be a big mistake to use this objection to unsettle the line of succession during a crisis.

2. U.S. Const., art. 1, §5.

3. Since senators have six-year terms, and one-third will be in their last two years in office, more recently elected governors may choose replacements that shift Senate control from one party to the other, especially if there had been a close division previously. But this won't seem like such a terrible thing, since the incumbents might have had trouble winning another term in their state's shifting political environment.

4. When Senator Frank Murkowski won the Alaska governorship, he appointed his own daughter, Lisa, as his senatorial replacement. Alaska rewarded Murkowski's chutzpah by awarding his daughter a narrow victory at the next election. See Robin Toner and Katharine Seelye, "The 2004 Elections: The Senate," *New York Times*, November 3, 2004. The power of incumbency revealed by this episode is troubling, but it is a relatively minor problem compared to those we will be encountering in our tour of existing arrangements.

5. The Senate Rules call for "a majority of the Senators duly chosen and sworn," making no mention of whether they are alive or capable of casting a ballot. See Senate Rule VI. If a blast killed or incapacitated fifty-one members, the Senate could not function until gubernatorial replacements arrived.

6. Currently, the only official word on "vacancies" comes from 2 U.S.C. §8, which states that "the time for holding elections in any State . . . for a Representative or Delegate to fill a vacancy, whether such vacancy is caused by a failure to elect at the time prescribed by law, or by the death, resignation, or *incapacity* of a person

elected, may be prescribed by the laws of the several States" (emphasis added). The text requires a good deal of elaboration before it could become useful to senators rendered insensible by an attack.

7. House Rule XX(5)(c)(7)(B).

8. The House began to fiddle with quorum requirements in 1861, when Speaker Galusha Grow refused to allow the absence of seceding southern representatives to count in quorum calls. See generally, Bruce Ackerman, 2 *We the People: Transformations* chapters 4–8 (1998). But the end of Reconstruction led to a return to the traditional practice, and it was only in 1891 that Speaker Thomas B. Reed ruled that only living members would be counted. This enabled him to move immediately to a final vote on an issue of minor importance. For a useful historical summary, see Continuity of Government Commission, *Preserving Our Institutions* 8–10 (2003).

9. Under the procedures set out by the new House Rule XX(5)(c)(7)(A), the twenty members who responded to the quorum call within seventy-two hours would constitute the "provisional number of the House," which would then serve as the number "upon which a quorum shall be *computed*" (emphasis added).

10. See 151 *Cong. Rec.* H9–H10.

11. Only Congressman John Larson of Connecticut presented a constitutional critique on the floor, but his compelling statement failed to provoke any response. See 151 *Cong. Rec.* H28–H29. This arrogant refusal to engage in reasoned debate will not help the rule's defenders if they seek to invoke it during a moment of crisis.

12. U.S. Const., art I, §2.

13. I would define the notion of a "decapitating strike" to include any attack that killed or incapacitated a significant number of representatives, setting the threshold at forty or fifty. Policy continuity could be disturbed dramatically if "only" forty or fifty members were eliminated, since they might largely be members of the same political party.

14. See *Constitucion Politica de los Estados Unidos Mexicanos,* arts. 84–85, translated in 12 *Constitutions of the Countries of the World* 52 (Albert P. Blaustein and Gilbert H. Flanz eds. 2004). On the other hand, concerns about assassination may make it plausible to provide for a second vice president, as does Panama. See *Constitucion Politica de la Republica de Panama de 1972,* art. 184, translated in 14 *Constitutions of the Countries of the World* 149.

15. See 1 Stat. 239 (1792). See Bruce Ackerman, *The Failure of the Founding Fathers* 38–39 (2005).

16. The present interpretive problem resembles others in which the Founding understanding was constrained by implicit technological premises. For example, the Constitution explicitly grants power to Congress to maintain "armies" and a "navy," but the Founders lived before the airplane, and so didn't grant Congress the power to establish an "air force." Nevertheless, it's plain enough that the Framers would never have blocked such a move had they known that it was possible to fly.

I am offering the same kind of argument here. While the Framers provided for a vice president, they thought it was technologically impossible to decapitate the entire House of Representatives, and so they were silent about the possibility of creating vice representatives. Now that such a thing is possible, there is no reason to read the Founding silence to suggest Founding opposition to the idea. See generally, Lawrence Lessig, "Fidelity in Translation," 71 *Tex. L. Rev.* 1165 (1993).

17. The Constitution does not explicitly grant Congress power to assure the continuity of constitutional government, but this is an obvious presupposition of the entire framework. For those who desire a more explicit textual authorization, the statute should be read as necessary for Congress to discharge its power to "suppress Insurrections and repeal Invasions" posed by a terrorist attack.

18. During the 1990s, the reelection rate of House incumbents ranged from 88 to 98 percent. See Norman Ornstein, Thomas Mann, and Michael Malbin, *Vital Statistics on Congress* 57–58 (2000).

19. See H.J. Res 83; see also 150 Cong. Rec. H3665.

20. The amendment required the victor only to prepare his list before he took the oath of office, and gave him the right to revise his list "at any time" during his term in Congress. Congressman Dana Rohrbacher proposed an amendment that required congressmen to prepare their lists before the election, H.J. Res. 92, but this proposal was not put up to a vote.

21. The vote was 63–353. See 150 *Cong. Rec.* H3665–H3681 (June 2, 2004).

22. The original bill, H.R. 2244, passed the House, 306–97, on April 22, 2004. It contemplated a forty-five-day expedited election schedule. See 150 *Cong. Rec.* H2297. This was changed to forty-nine days when the bill was tacked onto the appropriations bill during the 109th Congress.

23. See H.R. 2985, 109th Cong. §301 (2005), enacted as part of the Legislative Branch Appropriations Act of 2006, Pub. L. No. 109-55, 119 Stat. 565.

24. The Continuity of Government Commission, organized by AEI and Brookings, found that special elections took about four months on average, and that under ideal conditions, this period might be cut to two months. But it cautioned that in the aftermath of a terrorist strike "it would be difficult for even the most expedited elections to take place within three months." Continuity of Government Commission, *Preserving Our Institutions,* at 7.

25. I entirely disagree with an otherwise thoughtful report of the AEI-Brookings Commission, which concludes that "there is simply no effective way, short of a constitutional amendment, to replace members of the House" who die or are incapacitated by a devastating terrorist attack. See id. at 14. Nothing in the commission's report adequately defends this conclusion.

I also have problems with the commission's proposed constitutional amendment, which would authorize Congress to designate one or another appointing authority to fill seats on a temporary basis, pending special elections. While preserving congressional flexibility, the commission seems to favor proposals, like Baird's, which gives the power to congressmen or proposals that would vest the power in governors. Since governors already have the power to replace senators, I think it would be unwise to give them a similar power in the House. If forced to go down this route, I would prefer each state's legislature to make the House selections.

But more important, I am puzzled by the commission's failure to consider statutory approaches. Its discussion of nonamendment options focuses exclusively on the possibility that the House might change its internal rules to facilitate continuity of government. I agree that this would be an inappropriate, and perhaps an unconstitutional, way to proceed. See id. at 21–22. But this hardly suggests that Congress and the president can't solve the problem by enacting statutory solutions of the kind I have proposed, and the commission simply fails to consider this approach.

26. See U.S. Const. amend. 25, §2. Under this provision, it is conceivable that the new acting president might press forward immediately with a nomination and seek to obtain confirmation by a majority vote of a rump House and a Senate composed principally of gubernatorial appointees—provided, of course, that the rump could withstand the blistering critique of its status that is sure to arise. In any event, one might hope that the acting president would show more restraint and await the convocation of a more appropriate Congress before forwarding a nomination.

27. See 3 U.S.C. §19.

28. Here is the order of succession of cabinet officers: secretaries of state, the treasury, and defense; attorney general; and secretaries of the interior, agriculture, commerce, labor, health and human services, housing and urban development, transportation, energy, education, veterans affairs, and homeland security. 3 U.S.C. § 19(d)(1).

29. See Americo Cinquegrana, "Presidential Succession Under 3 U.S.C. 19 and the Separation of Powers: 'If at First You Don't Succeed, Try, Try Again,'" 20 *Hastings Con. Law. Q.* 105, 110–11 (1992).

30. Id. at 115–16.

31. I owe this proposal to Congressman Brad Sherman, who made it shortly after September 11. See H.R. 3816 (February 22, 2002). Sherman's proposal was referred to the judiciary committee, but it does not seem to have been seriously considered.

32. S. 442, 109th Cong. (2005); see 151 Cong. Rec. S9057.

33. Amar doesn't use the title minister without portfolio in the public presentation of his idea, but suggested it during a provocative lunchtime conversation. Otherwise, the substance of his proposal is found at Presidential Succession Act: Hearing Before the Subcommittee on the Constitution of the House Committee on the Judiciary, 108th Cong. 38 (2004) (statement of Akhil Reed Amar, Southmayd Professor of Law and Political Science, Yale Law School).

34. I would oppose the selection of a retired president, if he has already served two terms, to serve as the minister without portfolio. The principle announced by the Twenty-second Amendment, limiting the president to two elected terms, represents a considered judgment by the American people, after Franklin Roosevelt's lengthy stay in the White House, which deserves continuing respect. It should not be eroded by ingenious constructions which limits its application to election, and opens up the prospect of a third term through the manipulation of the appointment power, as suggested by Scott Peabody and Bruce Gant, "The Twice and Future President:

Constitutional Interstices and the Twenty-Second Amendment," 83 *Minn. L. Rev.* 565 (1999).

35. U.S. Const., Art. 2, § 2, para. 3.

36. Six justices make a quorum on the Supreme Court. See 28 U.S.C. §1; S. Ct. R. 4.

37. If we begin with the justices sitting on the Court in *Brown,* the average tenure during the modern period is about twenty years.

38. I would fill all vacant positions with circuit judges, not just the number necessary to regain a bare quorum. One reason is policy continuity. If five justices are killed, and they were previously members of a stable majority coalition, the four dissenters would be the new majority of six justices. Even if some replacements were sympathetic to the jurisprudential views of the four remaining justices, they would be painfully aware of their anomalous status on the Court, and therefore give a very heavy weight to stare decisis, stabilizing constitutional doctrine.

Reconstituting a nine-member Court also permits the acting president and the Senate to avoid time-consuming confirmation battles, and to focus on the pressing business of emergency management.

39. I exclude the United States Court of Appeals for the Federal Circuit since it is not a court of general jurisdiction, and its judges lack the requisite breadth of legal experience.

40. According to 28 U.S.C. §45, the most senior judge under sixty-four fills his circuit's vacant chief judgeship, provided he has served at least one year and has not been the chief already. He may serve up to seven years, or up to the age of seventy, whichever comes first.

41. If the presidency and the Senate have been generally dominated by one party during the preceding generation, this fact will be expressed by the general constitutional orientation of the chief judges. But this is as it should be.

42. In 2005 chief judges were, on average, sixty-four years of age. All of them were nominated by George H. W. Bush (three), Ronald Reagan (seven) or Jimmy Carter (two). A random draw of nine would yield a panel roughly similar in character to the present court, which has seven Republican and two Democratic appointees.

43. The best scholarly essay is by Randolph Moss and Edward Siskell, "The Least Vulnerable Branch: Ensuring the Continuity of the Supreme Court," 53 *Cath. U. L. Rev.* 1015 (2004), which contains a good review of the basic options, and an interesting proposal. They would create a special Emergency Appellate Court in case the Supreme Court loses its quorum. Its members would consist of all surviving Supreme Court justices and selected chief judges of the court of appeals. It would resolve pressing appellate controversies until the Supreme Court regained a quorum.

In looking to chief judges, my own proposal draws on theirs, but I don't think that their ingenious suggestion solves the basic problems. On the one hand, it does not stop the acting president from making recess appointments to the Court, and thereby extinguishing the emergency court. On the other hand, it doesn't prevent the president and the Senate from packing the Supreme Court with lots of new justices, thereby freezing the momentary orthodoxy into the law for thirty or forty years. While Moss and Siskell glimpse these problems in their discussion, they don't confront them squarely.

44. The Court originally had six members, but the Federalist judiciary act of 1801 reduced it to five. See Ackerman, *Failure of the Founding Fathers,* chaps. 6 and 7. Repeal of the act in 1803 returned the number to six; it gradually went up to ten during the Civil War and afterward was reduced to seven, until the number was stabilized at nine during the Grant administration. See Ackerman, 2 *We the People,* at 239–40.

45. I discuss the case, *Stuart v. Laird,* in *Failure of the Founding Fathers,* chap. 8.

46. With the exception of the short-lived Federalist judiciary act of 1801, it was not until 1891 that the United States had a system of courts of appeals staffed by a special cadre of permanent judges. See 26 Stat. 826. chap. 517. Throughout the nineteenth century, Supreme Court justices were assigned to circuit riding duty and formed appellate panels with local district judges to review decisions made by the district judge when sitting alone. Under this system, district judges regularly heard appeals from their own cases while serving on the circuit courts. While the Evarts Act of 1891 banned that practice, it specifically authorized district judges to sit on the courts of appeals for cases of other district judges. See 13 Charles A. Wright et al., *Federal Practice and Procedure* §3504 (2d ed. 1984). Thus the practice (or at least the idea) of district court judges sitting by designation on higher courts goes all the way back to the Founding period. Congress's current authorization of the practice is to be found at 28 U.S.C. §292.

47. Some far-sighted critics of the statute might want to litigate before a decapitating attack and challenge the statute before the current Supreme Court. But it is up to the justices to decide whether they want to hear such a case, and a wise Court would refuse rather than engage in a speculative exercise distinguishing between those cases, involving political retaliation, in which reassignment would be unconstitutional, and those cases, involving emergencies, where it would be desirable. But if the Court wants to resolve the matter authoritatively, it wouldn't be hard to write the opinion.

48. The Supreme Court could, of course, try to declare a statute reassigning the emergency justices as an unconstitutional assault on the fundamental principles of judicial independence. Except for very special facts, this would be an extreme response, and it is very likely that the judges would—and should—defer to congressional power. For an analogous episode in constitutional history, see Bruce Ackerman, *Failure of the Founding Fathers,* chap. 8.

49. I discuss this episode in 1 *We the People,* chaps. 9–12.

50. See 1 Stat. 239 (1792). These provisions were changed in 1886, when a new statute authorized Congress to decide whether to call a special election to pick a new president. Chap. 4, §1, 24 Stat. 1 (1886).

51. Should the president who wins the special election serve out the remaining two years of the original presidential term, or should he be granted a full four years? The 1792 statute from the Founding era explicitly authorized the specially elected presi-

dent to serve four years; see sec. 12, 1 Stat. 239, 241. For further discussion of the historical context, see Bruce Ackerman, *Failure of the Founding Fathers,* chap. 2. Since the 1792 statute endured for almost a century, the commonsense solution—give the winner a full four years—has a very substantial historical pedigree.

Some may believe that Article 2 of the Constitution requires a different result, limiting the winner to the two years remaining from the prior president's term. This view, however, is based on an exaggerated reading of the bit of text which vests the executive power "in a President of the United States of America. He shall hold his office during the term of four years, and together with the Vice President, chosen for the same term, be elected as follows."

This provision explicitly guarantees a four-year term only to the persons elected to the presidency and vice presidency, and does not say how long a successor should serve if both elected officials have vacated the office. The Congress of the Founding era acted appropriately, then, in filling this gap by deciding that a special election should entitle the winner to a full four-year term. We should follow their commonsense choice: since the special election will expose the candidates to precisely the same democratic test as an ordinary presidential election, only at an earlier time, there is no good reason for denying the victor the normal fruits of his success: four years of power.

52. See *U.S. Term Limits v. Bryant,* 514 U.S. 779 (1995).

Chapter 8: The Morning After

1. To emphasize the obvious, this book *isn't* about the conditions under which it is appropriate or legal to engage in foreign military interventions in response to terrorism. While I have made ad hoc journalistic interventions on this subject (see Chapter 1, note 13), I have not (yet) attempted a systematic exploration of the problem.

2. The White House had tried very hard to push Congress into meeting the original deadline of December 31, 2005, lobbying for a House-Senate "compromise" that would have rendered permanent fourteen of the sixteen provisions that had previously been subject to the sunset system. But a successful Senate filibuster blocked passage of the compromise, deferring a satisfactory solution to the next session. The new deadline for legislative action became February 3, 2006—but obviously, this date wasn't set in stone. See Sheryl Gay Stolberg, "Postponing Debate, Congress Extends Terror Law by Five Weeks," *New York Times,* December 23, 2005.

3. It is a shame that Congress did not impose a sunset on the entire act, as some of us urged at the time; see Bruce Ackerman, "Sunset Can Put a Halt to Twilight of Liberty," *Los Angeles Times,* September 20, 2001. But at least it did create a precedent, and that is even more important. The need for sunset provisions is also a recurring theme in the British debate.

ACKNOWLEDGMENTS

September 11 was a shock to us all—but how to respond?

From early on, I had a sinking feeling that we were plunging down the wrong path. Within a week of the tragedy, I was scribbling about the need to impose a strict sunset provision on the Patriot Act then barreling its way through Congress. My essay in the *Los Angeles Times* helped get this issue onto the public agenda, and when Congress adopted an (inadequate) sunset provision in its new antiterrorism statute, I was encouraged to think more generally about the distinctive character of emergency legislation.[1]

The *London Review of Books* kindly offered me the chance to write up some further reflections in a fair-sized essay, which then provoked an invitation to a June 2002 conference on Terror and the Liberal Conscience convened under the auspices of the All Souls Foreign Policy Studies Programme at All Souls College, Oxford.[2] Many thanks to Jan-Werner Mueller for organizing the event, and to Michael Byers, Steven Lukes, and Adam Tomkins, for particularly perceptive comments.

I was now convinced that the project merited sustained attention, and I plunged into a yearlong investigation of its different angles, with the

1. Bruce Ackerman, "Sunset Can Put a Halt to Twilight of Liberty," *Los Angeles Times*, September 20, 2001.

2. Bruce Ackerman, "Don't Panic," *London Review of Books*, February 7, 2002, 15–16.

assistance of a resourceful band of students drawn from Yale's law school and political science department: Lindsay Barenz, Ivana Cingel, Inayat Delawala, David Gamage, Markus Gehring, Marcio Grandchamp, Anand Kandaswamy, Thomas Pulham, and Amy Sepinwall, who later gave way to another outstanding group as the work proceeded through 2005: Roy Altman, Sonu Bedi, Eric Citron, Andrew DeFilippis, Justin Florence, Dan Margolis, Laura Moranchek, Jennifer Nou, and Daniela Thurnherr. As always, Gene P. Coakley and Jill Tobey helped make my task manageable. All this effort gave me the scholarly momentum to prepare an initial essay that appeared in the March 2004 issue of the *Yale Law Journal*.[3] In the run-up to publication, I tested out my ideas at three stimulating conferences—the first at Yale's annual World Constitutionalism Seminar, where my draft provoked a lively discussion from some of the world's leading constitutional court justices; the second, a conference on contemporary constitutionalism at the Harvard Law School, where it received searching criticisms from an outstanding group of scholars, initiated by the probing commentary of Dean Elena Kagan; the third, a conference on states of emergency at Cardozo School of Law, organized by Professor Michel Rosenfeld. I am much indebted to his perceptive observations, and the trenchant remarks of Stephen Holmes and Carlos Rosenkrantz.

Once it was published, the Yale essay quickly provoked two broad-ranging critiques by Professors David Cole and the formidable scholarly team of Professors Laurence Tribe and Patrick Gudridge. Both essays sought to expose and refute my work's basic premises. The *Yale Law Journal* was good enough to devote most of its June 2004 issue to the two critiques and my response.[4] Those interested in the point-by-point exchange should turn to this issue. It didn't seem profitable to continue the parry-and-thrust in this book—far better to reflect on the trialogue and try to clarify my arguments, and rethink my conclusions, in its light. I'm sure that Professors Cole, Gudridge, and Tribe, won't find my pres-

3. Bruce Ackerman, "The Emergency Constitution," 113 *Yale L.J.* 1029 (2004).

4. See David Cole, "The Priority of Morality: The Emergency Constitution's Blind Spot," 113 *Yale L.J.* 1753 (2004); Laurence H. Tribe and Patrick O. Gudridge, "The Anti-Emergency Constitution," 113 *Yale. L.J.* 1801 (2004); Bruce Ackerman, "This Is Not a War," 113 *Yale L.J.* 1871 (2004).

ent position at all satisfactory. Nevertheless, their astringent commentaries have greatly clarified my own thinking, and they have helped me write a better book. Thank you.

As the manuscript was reaching completion, I presented its principal arguments to a seminar, organized by Julien Cantegreil, at the École Normale Supérieure in Paris, where Professor Bernard Manin's commentary provoked some significant refinements. And I received another round of comments from John Ferejohn, Eugene Fidell, George Fletcher, Philip Heymann, Stephen Holmes, Michael Ignatieff, Paul Kahn, Neal Katyal, Norman Ornstein, and Pasquale Pasquino. Our conversations were a lot of fun, and the resulting insights have made a very real difference. As I made my sprint to the finish line, Michael O'Malley, my editor at Yale University Press, provided a thorough line-edit, aiming to make the book more transparent to a broader audience. His consistently intelligent suggestions accomplished more than this, provoking me to rethink important issues as I labored to make my meanings clear.

Through it all, I have had the ongoing support of my wife, Susan Rose-Ackerman, who has been obliged to correct countless mistakes over the breakfast table, and my colleagues at the Yale Law School, who have carried on my wife's critical mission to lunchtime at countless New Haven restaurants. My two friends who served as dean of the Yale Law School during the gestation period, Tony Kronman and Harold Koh, have been unstinting in their support.

Looking back over the last four years, I am touched by the enormous amount of time and energy that others have contributed to my enterprise, and how much I have profited from their efforts. Upon further reflection, the roots of this project go farther back in time, to my initial encounters with the scholar who introduced me to political and legal philosophy as my tutor at Harvard College. Some forty years ago, Judith Shklar opened the path that I have since traveled, and over later decades, she engaged me in some fascinating conversations about the liberalism of fear. I was skeptical then, and remain skeptical now, but her forceful arguments seem to have penetrated my thick skull nevertheless.[5]

5. See my contribution to Judith Shklar's Festschrift, Bruce Ackerman, "The Political Case for Constitutional Courts," in Bernard Yack, ed., *Liberalism Without Illusions* 205, 217–18 (1995).

INDEX

Abu Ghraib prison abuses, 38, 182n67
Administrative Procedure Act, 124
Afghanistan, 16, 24, 32, 180n44
Afghanistan war, 27, 28, 29, 30, 38
aftermath of terrorist attack: behavior of judges during, 114–15; bureaucratic chaos, 15, 46, 51, 83–84, 86, 106, 120, 154, 156, 166, 167; Congressional role in, 78; continuity of government issues, 78; emergency measures needed in, 86; framework for response to, 40; future of the Supreme Court, 78; need for reassurance of the public, 60, 84, 123; options and choices, 86–87; partisan power plays, 142; public panic, 19, 47; recovery, 21; right to counsel issues during, 112, 113; risk analysis during, 86–87; role of judicial, 115–16; role of judiciary, 119; role of supermajoritarian escalator in, 131; secret decision making during, 86–87; security services and, 46; speed of response, 109; uncertainty, 45, 50, 128. *See also* reconstruction of government after a terrorist attack
Ahmed al-Hawsawi, Mustapha, 183n11
Algeria, 187n18
Alien Enemies Act, 36, 181nn59,60
aliens. *See* enemy aliens; resident alien(s)

Al Qaeda, 21, 25, 32, 41, 50, 108, 178n26, 179n31; combat operations against, 180n54; criminal law applied to, 40; effect on public confidence, 42; Padilla and, 180n52; as threat to the sovereignty of the state, 43
Amar, Akhil, 159, 204n32
American Civil Liberties Union, 189n5
American Enterprise Institute (AEI), 153, 168, 203nn24,25
American Revolution, 169
anarchists, 50
anti-Communism, 41
antinormalization principle, 138
appellate courts, 32–33, 111, 162, 163, 164, 166, 167, 180n54, 205n43; detention lawsuits and, 116; reassignment of judges to Supreme Court, 161
Arab Americans, 81–82
Arab world, 81, 82, 117
arrests, 26. *See also* detention; seizure
articles of war, 23
Ashcroft, John, 49–50, 53, 178n26; extreme politics of, 176n6; Padilla case and, 24–25, 31–32, 32, 33; proposal for Patriot Act, 175n1
assassinations, 202n14
Atta, Mohammed, 183n11
attorney general, 158, 159, 165

demonization of terrorists, 81–82
demotion strategy, 97, 192n31
deportation of aliens, 181n61
Dershowitz, Alan, 108–12, 109
detainees: abuse of, 120; basic rights
of, 189n34; confidential information
regarding, 188n27; court decisions
regarding, 101; designated as enemy
combatants, 24–25, 29, 31, 32–34; double jeopardy principle and, 113–14; held
abroad, 193n8; lawsuits brought by,
116, 117; release of, 108, 136, 186n10;
seizure of, upon release, 113–14
detention, 20, 47, 62, 64, 137; arbitrary, 26,
36–37; on the basis of reasonable suspicion, 71; in cases of rebellion or invasion,
27, 28; civil liberties endangered by, 29;
criminal law regarding, 106; deprivation
of rights and, 29; emergency, 47, 53,
54–56, 57, 107, 126, 127, 137; under the
emergency constitution, 45–46; emergency constitution framework and, 106;
habeas corpus as protection from, 26;
hearings, 118; indefinite, 28, 34, 137,
181n61, 182n64; of innocent people, 47,
49, 51, 54, 82, 84, 106–8, 119, 184n21;
of Japanese Americans during Second
World War, 20, 36, 50, 54, 61–63, 184n18,
186n17; limitations on, 128; limited
to forty-five days, 48–49, 55, 56, 106,
107, 108, 113, 114, 116, 126, 127, 192n3;
long-term or indefinite, 55, 137, 188n3; on
military authority, 179n39; of noncitizens, 181n57; normalization of, 137; preventive, 188n3; probable cause for, 48;
public safety as excuse for, 28; referral to
the criminal justice system and, 55, 56;
role of judges in cases of, 108; secret, 37;
short-term, 51, 57; of suspected terrorists,
182n64; through presidential authority,
23–24; until the end of the war on terrorism, 25, 26, 27, 34; during the war on
terrorism, 34; without accusation of
crime, 181n62; without due process, 7,
24, 126, 127; without evidence of guilt,
71, 80; without habeas corpus writ,
178n27; without probable cause, 49–50.

See also compensation; Padilla,
José / *Padilla* ruling; seizure; torture
detention of enemy aliens, 36–37, 182n64;
in cases of formal declaration of war,
36; in cases of imminent invasion, 36;
lack of grounds for, 36; without due
process, 37–38
dictatorship, 79, 104
dirty bombs, 179n31
district courts, 162, 206n46
DNA testing, 55
doomsday scenario. *See* reconstruction of
government after a terrorist attack
double jeopardy principle, 113–14
double veto, 17
Douglas, William O., 62, 176n2, 178n23
dragnets, 47, 49–50, 80, 82, 84, 109, 118,
119, 128–29
Dreir, David, 154
drug trade, 14, 40, 59
due process, 39, 41, 71; applicable to all
persons, 36; detention without, 37–38,
96, 126, 127, 195n19; emergency, 112–14;
emergency constitution and, 39; guarantee of, 65; ignored in cases of detention
of citizens, 26–27, 29; minimum conditions for, 186n9; no-fly lists and, 118–19;
Supreme Court definition of, 30–31; in
torture cases, 112–14
Duncan v. Kahahamoku, 130–31
Durbin, Richard, 111

eastern Europe, 88
Edwards, John, 111
Eighth Amendment, 193n8, 195n19
elections, 143. *See also* special elections
emergency, 167–68, 170; management, 65;
measures, 81; rhetoric of, 59, 72, 73
emergency constitution, 15, 19, 57, 72, 99,
121, 122, 163, 167, 168, 174; activated by
actual attack, 101; applicability to all
residents, 38; challenge to presidential
monopoly, 190n6; checks and
balances in, 77, 94, 95, 96, 123;
compensation requirement, 54–55, 106;
courts as guardians of, 104–5; criminal
law and, 39, 40; dangers inherent in,

Northern Ireland, 171, 172
nuclear weapons, 41, 42

O'Connor, Sandra Day, 28–29, 31, 32, 33,
    34, 179n39, 180n47
Oklahoma City bombing, 14, 172
operational primacy of emergency
    regime, 97, 190n5, 9, 10, 192nn2,31
opposition party, 85, 86, 190n9
"orange" alerts, 91
Osborn, Sidney, 185n6
oversight committees, 85, 103, 120, 125,
    156, 190n6

Padilla, José/Padilla ruling, 24–27,
    30, 31–32, 34–35, 38, 64, 126, 180nn52,55;
    designation as enemy combatant,
    32–34, 178n27; detention of, without
    habeas corpus writ, 179n33; evidence
    against, 178n26, 179n30; presidential
    unilateralism in, 65
Padilla v. Hanft. See Padilla,
    José/Padilla ruling
Padilla v. Rumsfeld, 178n24, 179n31
Pakistan, 179n31, 180n54
Palmer, Alexander, 20, 50
panic reaction, 13, 14, 47, 92, 133; as base for
    authoritarian rule and repression, 68;
    cycles of, 56, 57, 72; laws passed during
    times of, 105; management, 51; mass,
    183n6; presidential exploitation of, 90; as
    threat to liberal democracy, 134
parliamentary systems, 77, 88, 90, 189n5,
    190n9
Patriot Act, 57, 69, 98, 132, 174, 175n1,
    181n61, 189n5, 207n2
Pearl Harbor, 14, 22, 36, 45, 61, 130, 131
Persian Gulf, 17
Pinckney, Charles Coatesworth, 128, 130,
    198n19
plea bargaining, 185n25
pluralist societies, 81
Poland, 68, 88, 89
police, 192n32
police actions, 171, 173
police state, 72, 109
political liberties, 67–68, 93–96

political morality, 56, 57
political organizations, 95
Portugal, 88
Posse Comitatus Act, 192n32
Powell, Colin, 159, 195n15
precedents of presidential powers: civil
    liberties and, 32; contradictory, 60;
    extended to war on terrorism, 63;
    future use of, 44; judicial authority
    and, 102; limited, 32; repressive, 20;
    from Second World War, 30; in the
    United Kingdom, 71; wartime, 20, 21
presidency, 124; problem of entrench-
    ment in, 165–66; reconstruction of,
    after a terrorist attack, 142, 143, 146,
    149; relationship to the legislature,
    138–39; term limits, 196n1, 207n51
president, 64; abuse of war powers, 59;
    acting, 165–66, 204n26, 205n43;
    arbitrary action by, 35; authority as
    commander-in-chief, 16–17, 24, 99,
    120, 136, 138, 140, 192n32, 194n10;
    authority to declare war, 16, 18, 31, 35,
    38, 72, 138; authority to detain enemy
    aliens, 35–37; authority to detain
    persons suspected of terrorism
    indefinitely, 25, 27–29, 31, 32, 34, 35;
    authority to suspend habeas corpus,
    129, 139; authorization of torture by,
    110, 111, 194n10, 195n13, 17; breach of
    the rule of law by, 104; checks and bal-
    ances on, 81; checks and balances on
    emergency powers of, 81, 156; consent
    required from Congress and the UN
    to declare war, 17–18; constitutional
    authority, 16; disregard for civil liber-
    ties, 20, 43; extraordinary powers used
    by, 25, 31, 38, 59, 65; judicial appoint-
    ments by, 164; lame-duck, 165;
    operational authority of, 87, 120;
    overreaching of power by, 32, 33–34,
    59, 125; political resistance to authority
    of, 16; power to act without consent of
    Congress, 17, 20; recess appointments
    to the Supreme Court by, 161, 163;
    refusal to accept termination of the
    state of emergency, 140, 197n12; refusal

president (continued) to give up emergency powers, 102; rule by emergency
decree, 143; sources of authority,
96–97; Supreme Court and, 16;
Supreme Court appointments by, 64;
unilateral action by, 4, 5, 6, 8, 16, 20,
24–25, 28, 63, 64–65, 67, 80, 87, 88,
96–97, 102, 125, 137, 140, 176n7; veto
authority, 125, 132
presidential regimes, 190n6
presidential succession, 144–45, 155–59,
204n28; bumping mechanism in,
155–57; order of, 163, 166, 201n1
presidential tyranny, 26, 28, 34
press, 84
presumption of innocence, 26, 29, 53
Prevention of Terrorism Act (UK),
69–70, 187n24, 188n25, 189n36
probable cause, 48, 106
Progressive era, 196n1
property seizure, 54, 185n25
public: confidence shaken by September
11, 2001 terrorist attack, 42, 128; declaration of war and, 16; early support of
George W. Bush, 18; emergency constitution and, 98; emergency powers and,
90; impact of torture issues on, 109,
110–11; information provided to, during state of emergency, 86; informed
consent by, 86; justification for war
and, 14; reaction to terrorist attack, 15,
84; uncertainty following terrorist
attack, 50, 128; understanding of the
nature of war, 16. See also reassurance
of the public
public health crises, 192n30
public opinion: changes in, 63; of foreign
policy, 176n5; polls, 177n12
public safety: as excuse to detain
citizens, 28

quarantines, 51–53, 183n15
Quirin case/Ex parte Quirin, 23, 24, 25,
30, 177n18, 178n24, 180n47
quorum requirements in the
Constitution, 146, 148, 153, 154, 156,
157, 202nn8,9

reasonable doubt, 25, 27, 32, 71
reassurance of the public, 44–47, 57, 60,
72, 82, 129, 142; aftermath of terrorist
attack and, 60, 84, 123; civil liberties
and, 57, 89; criminal law and, 48; in
emergency constitution, 45–47, 49;
emergency powers and, 68; during
reconstruction of government after a
terrorist attack, 145
rebellion: emergency powers evoked in
cases of, 60; as justification for detention, 27, 28; as justification for suspension of habeas corpus, 127–31, 132, 133,
135, 139, 141, 199nn24,27
Reconstruction, 129
reconstruction of government after a
terrorist attack: checks and balances,
143; confirmation struggles, 160; constitutional problems of, 163; election
rescheduling, 143; emergency powers,
158; entrenchment problem, 143–44,
145, 151–52, 160, 164–67; incapacity of
politicians, 145–46, 163, 201n6; judicial
independence issues, 160; policy continuity concerns, 78, 144–45, 146, 151, 154,
157, 166, 203nn17,25, 205n38; proposal
for filling vacancies in advance, 149–55;
reassurance of the public during, 145;
special elections for, 146, 150, 153, 154,
166, 203n24, 206n51; speed of, 142, 144,
163; statesmanship issues, 144–45, 151–52,
157, 159; supermajoritarian escalator and,
143, 156
Rehnquist, William, 186n17
repression: cycles of, 173; in legislation,
70, 172; in precedents of presidential
powers, 70; as response to terrorism,
70–71, 72, 172–73
resident alien(s), 36–37, 38, 97; protection
of, 37; status, 181n61, 185n3
right to counsel, 112, 113
risk management, 44–45
Roman Republic, 78–79
Roosevelt, Franklin D., 186n15, 204n34;
authority as commander in chief,
178n19; authorization of wartime
detentions, 63; court-packing by,

war on crime, 40
war on terrorism, 38, 174; corrosive
    influence of, 17; definition of torture
    and, 110; extension of precedents of
    presidential powers to, 63; as extension
    of the war against the Taliban, 30; foot
    soldiers in, 26; legal definition of, 111;
    long-term or indefinite, 115, 170;
    never-ending and boundaryless, 15, 19,
    28; pathological consequences of, 59,
    77, 105, 156, 176n2; presidential author-
    ity and, 35; presidential detentions
    and, 32; public support of, 18; rhetoric
    of, 16–17, 20, 39, 40, 72, 73; separate
    from conventional war, 28; against a
    sovereign rogue state, 16–17, 19. *See
    also* aftermath of terrorist attack
War Relocation Authority, 61–62
war talk, 13; aggressive, 59; critique of,
    49; dangers of, 14–15, 44; effect on

criminal law, 43; impact of, on exist-
    ing practices, 15; as justification for
    use of emergency powers, 41; mind-
    less and unthinking repetition of,
    17, 21, 22; obscurity/fog of, 14, 60,
    63, 64, 90; public preference for, 44
Washington, D.C., as target for terrorist
    attack, 142, 151, 159, 168
Washington, George, 158
Washington Post, 111
weapons, 157
weapons of mass destruction, 61, 151
Western constitutions, 60; emergency
    powers as element of, 66

Yoo, John, 17
Youngstown Sheet & Tube v. Sawyer, 138,
    140, 141

Zubaydah, Abu, 179n31